Accession no.
36170260

KU-475-805

Case Study Research
Principles and Practices

Case Study Research: Principles and Practices aims to provide a general understanding of the case study method as well as specific tools for its successful implementation. These tools can be utilized in all fields where the case study method is prominent, including anthropology, business, communications, economics, education, medicine, political science, social work, and sociology. Topics covered include the definition of a case study, the strengths and weaknesses of this distinctive method, strategies for choosing cases, an experimental template for understanding research design, and the role of singular observations in case study research. It is argued that a diversity of approaches – experimental, observational, qualitative, quantitative, ethnographic – may be successfully integrated into case study research. This book breaks down traditional boundaries between qualitative and quantitative, experimental and nonexperimental, positivist and interpretivist.

John Gerring is currently associate professor of political science at Boston University. His books include *Party Ideologies in America, 1828–1996* (1998) and *Social Science Methodology: A Criterial Framework* (2001).

Case Study Research

Principles and Practices

JOHN GERRING
Boston University

LIS - LIBRARY

Date	Fund
22/08/12	bs-che

Order No.
232442282

University of Chester

CAMBRIDGE
UNIVERSITY PRESS

CAMBRIDGE UNIVERSITY PRESS
Cambridge, New York, Melbourne, Madrid, Cape Town, Singapore, São Paulo, Delhi

Cambridge University Press
32 Avenue of the Americas, New York, NY 10013-2473, USA

www.cambridge.org
Information on this title: www.cambridge.org/9780521676564

© John Gerring 2007

This publication is in copyright. Subject to statutory exception
and to the provisions of relevant collective licensing agreements,
no reproduction of any part may take place without the written
permission of Cambridge University Press.

First published 2007
Reprinted 2007 (twice), 2008 (thrice), 2009

Printed in the United States of America

A catalog record for this publication is available from the British Library.

Library of Congress Cataloging in Publication Data

Gerring, John, 1962–
Case study research : principles and practices / John Gerring.
  p. cm.
Includes bibliographical references and index.
ISBN-13 (invalid) 978-0-521-85928-8 (hardback)
ISBN-10 0-521-85928-X (hardback)
ISBN-13 978-0-521-67656-4 (pbk.)
ISBN-10 0-521-67656-8 (pbk.)
1. Social sciences – Research – Methodology. 2. Case method. I. Title.
H62.G47   2007
001.4'32 – dc22   2006051819

ISBN 978-0-521-85928-8 hardback
ISBN 978-0-521-67656-4 paperback

Cambridge University Press has no responsibility for the persistence or
accuracy of URLs for external or third-party Internet Web sites referred to in
this publication and does not guarantee that any content on such Web sites is,
or will remain, accurate or appropriate. Information regarding prices, travel
timetables, and other factual information given in this work are correct at
the time of first printing, but Cambridge University Press does not guarantee
the accuracy of such information thereafter.

For Liz, Kirk, Nicole, and Anthony,
who are hereby exempted from the usual familial obligation
to pretend to have read Uncle John's latest book.

Historical knowledge and generalization (i.e., classificatory and nomothetic) knowledge... differ merely in the relative emphasis they put upon the one or the other of the two essential and complementary directions of scientific research: in both cases we find a movement from concrete reality to abstract concepts and from abstract concepts back to concrete reality – a ceaseless pulsation which keeps science alive and forging ahead.

– Florian Znaniecki (1934: 25)

Contents

Acknowledgments

I began thinking seriously about this project while conducting a workshop on case studies at Bremen University, sponsored by the Transformations of the State Collaborative Research Center (CRC). I owe special thanks to my hosts in Bremen: Ingo Rohlfing, Peter Starke, and Dieter Wolf. Subsequently, the various parts of the project were presented at the Third Congress of the Working Group on Approaches and Methods in Comparative Politics, Liege, Belgium; at the annual meetings of the Institute for Qualitative Research (IQRM), Arizona State University; at the Centro de Investigación y Docencia Económicas (CIDE); and at the annual meetings of the American Political Science Association. I am thankful for comments and suggestions from participants at these gatherings.

The book evolved from a series of projects: articles in the *American Political Science Review, Comparative Political Studies*, and *International Sociology*; chapters in the *Oxford Handbook of Comparative Politics* and the *Oxford Handbook of Political Methodology*; and papers coauthored with Rose McDermott, Jason Seawright, and Craig Thomas.[1] I am grateful to these coauthors, and to the publishers of these papers, for permission to adapt these works for use in the present volume.

For detailed feedback on various drafts, I owe thanks to Andy Bennett, Tom Burke, Melani Cammett, Kanchan Chandra, Renske Doorenspleet, Colin Elman, Gary Goertz, Shareen Hertel, Staci Kaiser, Bernhard Kittel, Ned Lebow, Jack Levy, Evan Lieberman, Jim Mahoney, Ellen Mastenbroek, Devra Moehler, Howard Reiter, Kirsten Rodine,

---

[1] See Gerring (2004b, 2006, 2007a, 2007b, 2007c); Gerring and McDermott (2005); Gerring and Thomas (2005); Seawright and Gerring (2005).

Ingo Rohlfing, Richard Snyder, Peter Starke, Craig Thomas, Lily Tsai, and David Woodruff. For clarification on various subjects, I am in debt to Bear Braumoeller, Patrick Johnston, Jason Seawright, Jas Sekhon, and Peter Spiegler.

This book also owes a large debt to a recent volume on the same subject, *Case Studies and Theory Development* by Alexander George and Andrew Bennett – cited copiously in footnotes on the following pages. I like to think of these two books as distinct, yet complementary, explorations of an immensely complex subject. Anyone who, upon finishing this text, wishes further enlightenment should turn to George and Bennett.

My final acknowledgment is to the generations of scholars who have written on this subject, whose ideas I appropriate, misrepresent, or warp beyond recognition. (In academic venues, the first is recognized as a citation, the second is known as a reinterpretation, and the third is called original research.) The case study method has a long and largely neglected history, beginning with Frederic Le Play (1806–1882) in France and the so-called Chicago School in the United States, including such luminaries as Herbert Blumer, Ernest W. Burgess, Everett C. Hughes, George Herbert Mead, Robert Park, Robert Redfield, William I. Thomas, Louis Wirth, and Florian Znaniecki. Arguably, the case study was the first method of social science. Depending upon one's understanding of the method, it may extend back to the earliest historical accounts or to mythic accounts of past events.[2] Certainly, it was the dominant method of most of the social science disciplines in the nineteenth and early twentieth centuries.[3] Among contemporary writers, the work of Donald Campbell, David Collier, and Harry Eckstein has been particularly influential on my own thinking about these matters. It is a great pleasure to acknowledge my indebtedness to these scholars.

---

[2] Bernard (1928); Jocher (1928: 203).

[3] Glimpses of this early history can be found in Brooke (1970); Hamel (1993); and in various studies conducted by members of the Chicago School (e.g., Bulmer 1984; Hammersley 1989; Smith and White 1921). A good survey of the concept as it has been used in twentieth-century sociology can be found in Platt (1992). Dufour and Fortin (1992) provide an annotated bibliography, focusing mostly on sociology.

Case Study Research
Principles and Practices

1

The Conundrum of the Case Study

There are two ways to learn how to build a house. One might study the construction of many houses – perhaps a large subdivision or even hundreds of thousands of houses. Or one might study the construction of a particular house. The first approach is a cross-case method. The second is a within-case or *case study* method. While both are concerned with the same general subject – the building of houses – they follow different paths to this goal.

The same could be said about social research. Researchers may choose to observe lots of cases superficially, or a few cases more intensively. (They may of course do both, as recommended in this book. But there are usually trade-offs involved in this methodological choice.)

For anthropologists and sociologists, the key unit is often the social group (family, ethnic group, village, religious group, etc.). For psychologists, it is usually the individual. For economists, it may be the individual, the firm, or some larger agglomeration. For political scientists, the topic is often nation-states, regions, organizations, statutes, or elections.

In all these instances, the case study – of an individual, group, organization or event – rests implicitly on the existence of a micro-macro link in social behavior.[1] It is a form of cross-level inference. Sometimes, in-depth knowledge of an individual example is more helpful than fleeting knowledge about a larger number of examples. We gain better understanding of the whole by focusing on a key part.

---

[1] Alexander et al. (1987).

Two centuries after Frederic Le Play's pioneering work, the various disciplines of the social sciences continue to produce a vast number of case studies, many of which have entered the pantheon of classic works. The case study research design occupies a central position in anthropology, archaeology, business, education, history, medicine, political science, psychology, social work, and sociology.[2] Even in economics and political economy, fields not usually noted for their receptiveness to case-based work, there has been something of a renaissance. Recent studies of economic growth have turned to case studies of unusual countries such as Botswana, Korea, and Mauritius.[3] Debates on the relationship between trade policy and growth have likewise combined cross-national regression evidence with in-depth (quantitative and qualitative) case analysis.[4] Work on ethnic politics and ethnic conflict has exploited within-country variation or small-N cross-country comparisons.[5] By the standard of praxis,

---

[2] For examples, surveys of the case study method in various disciplines and subfields, see: anthropology/archeaology (Bernhard 2001; Steadman 2002); business, marketing, organizational behavior, public administration (Bailey 1992; Benbasat, Goldstein, and Mead 1987; Bock 1962; Bonoma 1985; Jensen and Rodgers 2001); city and state politics (Nicholson-Crotty and Meier 2002); comparative politics (Collier 1993; George and Bennett 2005: Appendix; Hull 1999; Nissen 1998); education (Campoy 2004; Merriam 1988); international political economy (Odell 2004; Lawrence, Devereaux, and Watkins 2005); international relations (George and Bennett 2005: Appendix; Maoz 2002; Maoz et al. 2004; Russett 1970); medicine, public health (Jenicek 2001; Keen and Packwood 1995; Mays and Pope 1995; "Case Records from the Massachusetts General Hospital," a regular feature in the *New England Journal of Medicine*; Vandenbroucke 2001); psychology (Brown and Lloyd 2001; Corsini 2004; Davidson and Costello 1969; Franklin, Allison, and Gorman 1997; Hersen and Barlow 1976; Kaarbo and Beasley 1999; Kennedy 2005; Robinson 2001). For cross-disciplinary samplers, see Hamel (1993) and Yin (2004). For general discussion of the methodological properties of the case study (focused mostly on political science and sociology), see Brady and Collier (2004); Burawoy (1998); Campbell (1975/1988); Eckstein (1975); Feagin, Orum, and Sjoberg (1991); George (1979); George and Bennett (2005); Gomm, Hammersley, and Foster (2000); Lijphart (1975); McKeown (1999); Platt (1992); Ragin (1987, 1997); Ragin and Becker (1992); Stake (1995); Stoecker (1991); Van Evera (1997); Yin (1994); and the symposia in *Comparative Social Research* 16 (1997). An annotated bibliography of works (primarily in sociology) can be found in Dufour and Fortin (1992).

[3] Acemoglu, Johnson, and Robinson (2003); Chernoff and Warner (2002); Rodrik (2003). See also studies focused on particular firms or regions, e.g., Coase (1959, 2000) and Libecap (1989).

[4] Srinivasan and Bhagwati (1999); Stiglitz (2002, 2005); Vreeland (2003).

[5] Abadie and Gardeazabal (2003); Chandra (2004); Miguel (2004); Posner (2004). For additional examples of case-based work in political economy, see Abadie and Gardeazabal (2003); Alston (2005); Bates et al. (1998); Bevan, Collier, and Gunning (1999); Chang and Golden (in process); Fisman (2001); Huber (1996); Piore (1979); Rodrik (2003); Udry (2003); and Vreeland (2003).

therefore, it would appear that the method of the case study is solidly ensconced, perhaps even thriving. Arguably, we are witnessing a movement in the social sciences away from a variable-centered approach to causality and toward a case-based approach.[6]

Contributing to this movement is a heightened skepticism toward cross-case econometrics.[7] It no longer seems self-evident that nonexperimental data drawn from nation-states, cities, social movements, civil conflicts, or other complex phenomena should be treated in standard regression formats. The complaints are myriad, and oft-reviewed.[8] They include: (a) the problem of arriving at an adequate specification of a causal model, given a plethora of plausible models, and the associated problem of modeling interactions among these covariates;[9] (b) identification problems (which cannot always be corrected by instrumental variable techniques);[10] (c) the problem of "extreme" counterfactuals (i.e., extrapolating or interpolating results from a general model where the extrapolations extend beyond the observable data points);[11] (d) problems posed by influential cases;[12] (e) the arbitrariness of standard significance tests;[13] (f) the misleading precision of point estimates in the context of "curve-fitting" models;[14] (g) the problem of finding an appropriate estimator and

---

[6] This classic distinction has a long lineage. See, e.g., Abbott (1990); Abell (1987); Bendix (1963); Meehl (1954); Przeworski and Teune (1970: 8–9); Ragin (1987; 2004: 124); and Znaniecki (1934: 250–1).

[7] Of the cross-country growth regression, a standard technique in economics and political science, a recent authoritative review notes: "The weight borne by such studies is remarkable, particularly since so many economists profess to distrust them. The cross-sectional (or panel) assumption that the same model and parameter set applies to Austria and Angola is heroic; so too is the neglect of dynamics and path dependency implicit in the view that the data reflect stable steady-state relationships. There are huge cross-country differences in the measurement of many of the variables used. Obviously important idiosyncratic factors are ignored, and there is no indication of how long it takes for the cross-sectional relationship to be achieved. Nonetheless the attraction of simple generalizations has seduced most of the profession into taking their results seriously" (Winters, McCullock, and McKay 2004: 78).

[8] For general discussion of the following points, see Achen (1986); Ebbinghaus (2005); Freedman (1991); Kittel (1999, 2005); Kittel and Winner (2005); Manski (1993); Winship and Morgan (1999); and Winship and Sobel (2004).

[9] Achen (2002, 2005); Leamer (1983); Sala-i-Martin (1997).

[10] Bartels (1991); Bound, Jaeger, and Baker (1995); Diprete and Gangl (2004); Manski (1993); Morgan (2002a, 2002b); Reiss (2003); Rodrik (2005); Staiger and Stock (1997).

[11] King and Zeng (2004a, 2004b).

[12] Bollen and Jackman (1985).

[13] Gill (1999).

[14] Chatfield (1995).

modeling temporal autocorrelation in pooled time-series datasets;[15] (h) the difficulty of identifying causal mechanisms;[16] and, last but certainly not least, (i) the ubiquitous problem of faulty data (measurement error).[17] Many of the foregoing difficulties may be understood as the by-product of causal variables that offer limited variation through time, cases that are extremely heterogeneous, and "treatments" that are correlated with many possible confounders.

A second factor militating in favor of case-based analysis is the development of a series of alternatives to the standard linear/additive model of cross-case analysis, thus establishing a more variegated set of tools to capture the complexity of social behavior.[18] Charles Ragin and associates have explored ways of dealing with situations where different combinations of factors lead to the same set of outcomes, a set of techniques known as qualitative comparative analysis (QCA).[19] Andrew Abbott has worked out a method that maps causal sequences across cases, known as optimal sequence matching.[20] Bear Braumoeller, Gary Goertz, Jack Levy, and Harvey Starr have defended the importance of necessary-condition arguments in the social sciences, and have shown how these arguments might be analyzed.[21] James Fearon, Ned Lebow, Philip Tetlock, and others have explored the role of counterfactual thought experiments in the analysis of individual case histories.[22] Andrew Bennett, Colin Elman, and Alexander George have developed typological methods for analyzing cases.[23] David Collier, Jack Goldstone, Peter Hall, James Mahoney, and Dietrich Rueschemeyer have worked to revitalize the comparative and comparative-historical methods.[24] And scores of researchers have attacked the problem of how to convert the relevant details of a temporally constructed narrative into standardized formats so that cases can be meaningfully compared.[25] While not all of these techniques are, strictly

---

[15] Kittel (1999, 2005); Kittel and Winner (2005).

[16] George and Bennett (2005).

[17] Herrera and Kapur (2005).

[18] On this topic, see the landmark volume edited by Brady and Collier (2004).

[19] Drass and Ragin (1992); Hicks (1999: 69–73); Hicks et al. (1995); Ragin (1987, 2000); several chapters by Ragin in Janoski and Hicks (1993); "Symposium: qualitative comparative analysis (QCA)" (2004).

[20] Abbott (2001); Abbott and Forrest (1986); Abbott and Tsay (2000).

[21] Braumoeller and Goertz (2000); Goertz (2003); Goertz and Levy (forthcoming); Goertz and Starr (2003).

[22] Fearon (1991); Lebow (2000); Tetlock and Belkin (1996).

[23] Elman (2005); George and Bennett (2005: Chapter 11).

[24] Collier (1993); Collier and Mahon (1993); Collier and Mahoney (1996); Goldstone (1997); Hall (2003); Mahoney (1999); Mahoney and Rueschemeyer (2003).

[25] Abbott (1992); Abell (1987, 2004); Buthe (2002); Griffin (1993).

speaking, case study techniques (they sometimes involve a rather large number of cases), they move us closer to a case-based understanding of causation insofar as they aim to preserve the texture and detail of individual cases, features that are often lost in large-N cross-case analyses.

A third factor inclining social scientists toward case-based methods is the recent marriage of rational-choice tools with single-case analysis, sometimes referred to as an *analytic narrative*.[26] Whether the technique is qualitative or quantitative, or some mix of both, scholars equipped with economic models are turning to case studies in order to test the theoretical predictions of a general model, to investigate causal mechanisms, and/or to explain the features of a key case.

Finally, epistemological shifts in recent decades have enhanced the attractiveness of the case study format. The "positivist" model of explanation, which informed work in the social sciences through most of the twentieth century, tended to downplay the importance of causal mechanisms in the analysis of causal relations. Famously, Milton Friedman argued that the only criterion for evaluating a model was to be found in its accurate prediction of outcomes. The verisimilitude of the model, its accurate depiction of reality, was beside the point.[27] In recent years, this explanatory trope has come under challenge from "realists," who claim (among other things) that causal analysis should pay close attention to causal mechanisms.[28] Within political science and sociology, the identification of a specific mechanism – a causal pathway – has come to be seen as integral to causal analysis, regardless of whether the model in question is formal or informal or whether the evidence is qualitative or quantitative.[29] Given this newfound (or at least newly self-conscious) interest in mechanisms, it is hardly surprising that social scientists would turn to case studies as a mode of causal investigation.

The Paradox

For all the reasons just stated, one might suppose that the case study holds an honored place among methods currently taught and practiced

---

[26] The term, attributed to Walter W. Stewart by Friedman and Schwartz (1963: xxi), was later popularized by Bates et al. (1998), and has since been adopted more widely (e.g., Rodrik 2003). See also Bueno de Mesquita (2000) and Levy (1990–91).

[27] Friedman (1953). See also Hempel (1942) and Popper (1934/1968).

[28] Bhaskar (1978); Bunge (1997); Glennan (1992); Harre (1970); Leplin (1984); Little (1998); Sayer (1992); Tooley (1988).

[29] Dessler (1991); Elster (1998); George and Bennett (2005); Hedstrom and Swedberg (1998); Mahoney (2001); McAdam, Tarrow, and Tilly (2001); Tilly (2001).

in the social sciences. But this is far from evident. Indeed, the case study research design is viewed by most methodologists with extreme circumspection. A work that focuses its attention on a single example of a broader phenomenon is apt to be described as a "mere" case study, and is often identified with loosely framed and nongeneralizable theories, biased case selection, informal and undisciplined research designs, weak empirical leverage (too many variables and too few cases), subjective conclusions, nonreplicability, and causal determinism.[30] To some, the term *case study* is an ambiguous designation covering a multitude of "inferential felonies."[31]

Arguably, many of the practitioners of this method are prone to invoking its name in vain – as an all-purpose excuse, a license to do whatever a researcher wishes to do with a chosen topic. Zeev Maoz notes,

There is a nearly complete lack of documentation of the approach to data collection, data management, and data analysis and inference in case study research. In contrast to other research strategies in political research where authors devote considerable time and effort to document the technical aspects of their research, one often gets the impression that the use of case study [sic] absolves the author from any kind of methodological considerations. Case studies have become in many cases a synonym for free-form research where everything goes and the author does not feel compelled to spell out how he or she intends to do the research, why a specific case or set of cases has been selected, which data are used and which are omitted, how data are processed and analyzed, and how inferences were derived from the story presented. Yet, at the end of the story, we often find sweeping generalizations and "lessons" derived from this case.[32]

To say that one is conducting a case study sometimes seems to imply that normal methodological rules do not apply; that one has entered a different methodological or epistemological (perhaps even ontological)

---

[30] Achen and Snidal (1989); Geddes (1990, 2003); Goldthorpe (1997); King, Keohane, and Verba (1994); Lieberson (1985: 107–15; 1992; 1994); Lijphart (1971: 683–4); Odell (2004); Sekhon (2004); Smelser (1973: 45, 57). It should be underlined that these writers, while critical of the case study format, are not necessarily opposed to case studies per se; that is to say, they should not be classified as *opponents* of the case study. More than an echo of current critiques can be found in earlier papers, e.g., Lazarsfeld and Robinson (1940) and Sarbin (1943, 1944). In psychology, Kratochwill (1978: 4–5) writes: "Case study methodology was typically characterized by numerous sources of uncontrolled variation, inadequate description of independent, dependent variables, was generally difficult to replicate. While this made case study methodology of little scientific value, it helped to generate hypotheses for subsequent research...." See also Hersen, Barlow (1976: Chapter 1) and Meehl (1954).
[31] Achen and Snidal (1989: 160).
[32] Maoz (2002: 164–5).

zone. As early as 1934, Willard Waller described the case study approach as an essentially *artistic* process.

> Men who can produce good case studies, accurate and convincing pictures of people and institutions, are essentially artists; they may not be learned men, and sometimes they are not even intelligent men, but they have imagination and know how to use words to convey truth.[33]

The product of a good case study is *insight*, and insight is

> the unknown quantity which has eluded students of scientific method. That is why the really great men of sociology had no "method." They had a method; it was the search for insight. They went "by guess and by God," but they found out things.[34]

Decades later, a methods textbook describes case studies as a product of "the mother wit, common sense and imagination of person doing the case study. The investigator makes up his procedure as he goes along."[35]

The quasi-mystical qualities associated with the case study persist to this day. In the field of psychology, a gulf separates "scientists" engaged in cross-case research from "practitioners" engaged in clinical research, usually focused on individual cases.[36] In the fields of political science and sociology, case study researchers are acknowledged to be on the soft side of increasingly hard disciplines. And across fields, the persisting case study orientations of anthropology, education, law, social work, and various other fields and subfields relegate them to the nonrigorous, nonsystematic, nonscientific, nonpositivist end of the academic spectrum.

Apparently, the methodological status of the case study is still highly suspect. Even among its defenders there is confusion over the virtues and vices of this ambiguous research design. Practitioners continue to ply their trade but have difficulty articulating what it is they are doing, methodologically speaking. The case study survives in a curious methodological limbo.

---

[33] Waller (1934: 296–7).
[34] Ibid.
[35] Simon (1969: 267), quoted in Platt (1992: 18).
[36] Hersen and Barlow (1976: 21) write that in the 1960s, when this split developed, "clinical procedures were largely judged as unproven, the prevailing naturalistic research was unacceptable to most scientists concerned with precise definition of variables, cause-effect relationships. On the other hand, the elegantly designed, scientifically rigorous group comparison design was seen as impractical, incapable of dealing with the complexities, idiosyncrasies of individuals by most clinicians."

This leads to a paradox: although much of what we know about the empirical world has been generated by case studies, and case studies continue to constitute a large proportion of the work generated by the social science disciplines (as demonstrated in the previous section), the case study *method* is generally unappreciated – arguably, because it is poorly understood.

How can we make sense of the profound disjuncture between the acknowledged contributions of this genre to the various disciplines of social science and its maligned status within these disciplines? If case studies are methodologically flawed, why do they persist? Should they be rehabilitated, or suppressed? How fruitful *is* this style of research?

Situating This Book

This book aims to provide a general understanding of the case study as well as the tools and techniques necessary for its successful implementation. The subtitle reflects my dual concerns with general principles as well as with specific practices.

The first section explores some of the complexities embedded in the topic. Chapter Two provides a definition of the case study and the logical entailments of this definition. A great deal flows from this definition, so this is not a chapter that should be passed over quickly. Chapter Three addresses the methodological strengths and weaknesses of case study research, as contrasted with cross-case research. Case studies are useful in some research contexts, but not in all. We need to do better in identifying these different circumstances.

The second section of the book addresses the practical question of how one might go about constructing a case study. Chapter Four addresses preliminary issues. Chapter Five outlines a variety of strategies for choosing cases. Chapter Six proposes an experimental template for understanding case study research design. Chapter Seven presents a rather different sort of approach called process tracing. An epilogue provides a short discussion of case studies whose purpose is to explain a single outcome, rather than a class of outcomes. (This is understood as a *single-outcome study*, to distinguish it from the garden-variety case study.) A glossary provides a lexicon of key terms.

A number of differences between the book in your hands and other books exploring the same general topic should be signaled at the outset. First, unlike some texts, this one does not intend to provide a comprehensive review of methodological issues pertaining to social science research.

My intention, rather, is to hone in on those issues that pertain specifically to case study research. Issues that apply equally to single-case and cross-case analysis are ignored, or are treated only in passing.[37] Philosophy-of-science issues are almost entirely bypassed, except where they impinge directly upon case study research.

Second, I focus on the role of case studies in facilitating *causal* analysis. This is not intended to denigrate the interpretive case study or the essentially descriptive task of gathering evidence – for example, through ethnography, interviews, surveys, or primary and secondary accounts. If I give these matters short shrift, it is only because they are well covered by other authors.[38]

Third, rather than focusing on a single field or subfield of the social sciences, I take a broad, cross-disciplinary view of the topic. My conviction is that the methodological issues entailed by the case study method are general, rather than field-specific. Moreover, by examining basic methodological issues in widely varying empirical contexts we sometimes gain insights into these issues that are not apparent from a narrower perspective. Examples are drawn from all fields of the social sciences, and occasionally from the natural sciences. To be sure, the discussion betrays a pronounced tilt toward my own discipline, political science, and toward two subfields where case studies have been particularly prominent – comparative politics and international relations. However, the arguments should be equally applicable to anthropology, business, economics, history, law, medicine, organizational behavior, public health, social work, and sociology – indeed, to any field in the social sciences.

The reader should be aware that the examples chosen for discussion in this book often privilege work that has come to be understood as classic or paradigmatic – that is, works that have elicited commentary from other writers. The inclusion of an exemplar should not be taken as an indication that I endorse the writer's findings, or even her methodological choices.

---

[37] I have assumed, for example, that the reader is aware of various injunctions such as the following: (1) One's use of sources – written, oral, or dataset – should be intelligent, taking into account possible biases and omissions; (2) whatever procedures the writer follows (qualitative or quantitative, library work or field research) should be described in enough detail to be replicable; (3) the author should consider plausible alternatives to the argument that she presents, those presented by the literature on a topic as well as those that might suggest themselves to a knowledgeable reader. These standard-issue topics are covered elsewhere, e.g., in Gerring (2001); King, Keohane, and Verba (1994); and in numerous handbooks devoted to qualitative or quantitative research.

[38] See text citations in Chapter Four as well as the extensive bibliography at the end of this work.

It means only that a work serves as "a good example of X." The point of the example is thus to illustrate specific methodological issues, not to portray the state of research in a given field.

Indeed, many of my examples will be familiar to readers of other methodological texts, where these examples have been chewed over. The replication of familiar examples should serve to enhance methodological understanding of difficult points, as recurrence to familiar cases enhances clarity and consensus in the law. A case-based method rests on an in-depth knowledge of key cases, through which general points are elucidated and evaluated. It is altogether fitting, I might add, that a book on the case study method should assume a case-based heuristic.[39]

Foregrounding the Arguments

Although this purports to be a textbook on the case study, it is also inevitably an argument about what the case study should be. All methods texts have this two-faced quality, even if the writer is not explicit about her arguments. I wish to be as explicit as possible. What follows, therefore, is a brief résumé of larger arguments that circulate throughout the book.

Qualitative and Quantitative

Traditionally, the case study has been associated with qualitative methods of analysis. Indeed, the notion of a case study is sometimes employed as a broad rubric covering a host of nonquantitative approaches – ethnographic, clinical, anecdotal, participant-observation, process-tracing, historical, textual, field research, and so forth. I argue that this offhand usage should be understood as a methodological affinity, not a definitional entailment. To study a single case intensively need not limit an investigator to qualitative techniques. Granted, large-N cross-case analysis is always quantitative, since there are (by construction) too many cases to handle in a qualitative way. Yet case study research may be either quant or qual, or some combination of both, as emphasized in the following chapter and in various examples sprinkled throughout the book. Moreover, there is no reason that case study work cannot accommodate formal mathematical

---

[39] I do not mean to suggest that cases written for teaching purposes (e.g., at the Harvard Business School [Roberts 2002]), which are entirely descriptive (though they are intended to allow students to reach specific conclusions), are similar to case studies written for analytic purposes. This book is focused on the second, not the first.

models, which may help to elucidate the relevant parameters operative within a given case.[40]

Consider that the purpose of a statistical sample is to reveal elements of a broader population. "The fundamental idea of statistics," writes Bradley Efron, "is that useful information can be accrued from individual small bits of data."[41] In this respect, the function of a sample is no different from the function of a case study. If the within-case evidence drawn from a case study can be profitably addressed with quantitative techniques, these techniques must be assimilated into the case study method. Indeed, virtually all case studies produced in the social sciences today include some quantitative and qualitative components, and some of the most famous case studies – including *Middletown* and *Yankee City* and the pioneering family studies by Frederic Le Play – include a substantial portion of quantitative analysis.[42] The *purely* narrative case study, one with no numerical analysis whatsoever, may not even exist. And I am quite sure that there is no purely quantitative case study, utterly devoid of prose.

Therefore, this book endeavors to speak to audiences who are versed in qualitative methods, as well as to those who are versed in quantitative methods. This means finding a common vocabulary that will traverse these estranged camps, and it means suggesting links across these two methodological zones, wherever they may exist. This is more easily accomplished in some situations than in others. I appeal to the reader's forbearance in dealing with contexts where our diverse lexicons do not match up neatly or where qual/quant parallels are suggestive, but not exact.

Experimental and Observational

The virtues of the experimental method have been recognized by virtually every methodological treatise since the time of Francis Bacon. However, not much is made of this fact in the social sciences, where the ambit of truly experimental methods has been quite limited (with the notable exception of the discipline of psychology). This is beginning to change.[43] But the general assumption remains that because experimental work is impossible

---

[40] See, e.g., Houser and Freeman (2001) and Pahre (2005).

[41] Efron (1982: 341), quoted in King (1989: 12).

[42] Brooke (1970); Lynd and Lynd (1929/1956); Warner and Lunt (1941).

[43] For discussions of the experimental model of social science research, see Achen (1986); Campbell (1988); Cook and Campbell (1979); Freedman (1991); Green and Gerber (2001); McDermott (2002); Winship and Morgan (1999); and Winship and Sobel (2004). The first person to advocate a quasi-experimental approach to case studies (to my knowledge) was Eckstein (1975). See also Lee (1989).

in most research settings, the experimental ideal is of little consequence for practicing anthropologists, economists, political scientists, and sociologists. The pristine beauty of the true experiment is therefore regarded as a utopian ideal that can hardly be preserved if the real work of social science is to proceed.

I believe this dichotomization of research methods into experimental and observational categories to be a mistake. Not only is the dichotomy ambiguous, but it serves little purpose. There is no *point* in drawing a sharp line between experimental and observational work, since both aim (or ought to aim) toward the same methodological ideals and both face the same obstacles in this quest. Indeed, we gain purchase on the tasks of research design – all research designs – by integrating the criteria employed in "experimental" work with the criteria applicable to "observational" work. The virtues of the experimental method extend to all methods, in varying degrees, and it is these degrees that ought to occupy the attention of practitioners and methodologists.

I argue that many of the characteristic virtues and flaws of case study research designs can be understood according to the degree to which they conform to, or deviate from, the true experiment. The experiment thus provides a useful template for discussion of methodological issues in observational research, an ideal type against which to judge the utility of all research designs. Often, the strongest defense of a case study is that it is quasi-experimental in nature. This is because the experimental ideal is often better approximated within a small number of cases that are closely related to one another, or by a single case observed over time, than by a large sample of heterogeneous units.

Case Studies and Cross-Case Studies

A final argument concerns the traditional dichotomy between single-case and cross-case evidence. Often, these modes of analysis are conceptualized as being in opposition to each other. Work is classified as case study or large-N cross-case; researchers are lumped into one or the other school; journals adopt one or the other profile. It is not surprising that a degree of skepticism – and occasionally, outright hostility – has crept into relations between these disparate approaches to the empirical world.

However, rather than thinking of these methodological options as opponents, I suggest that we think of them as complements. Researchers may do both and, arguably, *must* engage both styles of evidence. At the very least, the process of case selection involves a consideration of the cross-case characteristics of a group of potential cases. Cases chosen for case study analysis are identified by their status (extreme, deviant, and so forth) relative to an assumed population of cases. Thus, while we continue to categorize studies as predominantly case-oriented or variable-oriented, it is inappropriate to regard these two approaches as rival enterprises.[44]

My own experience in these matters is that reflection upon cross-case patterns, far from being a hindrance to case study research, is, to the contrary, a helpful tool. It helps one to formulate useful insights, to separate those that are limited in range from those that might travel to other regions. And it certainly helps one to select cases and to explain the significance of those cases (see Chapter Five). The more one knows about the population, the more one knows about the cases, and vice versa. Hence, the virtue of cross-level research designs.[45]

By way of provocation, I shall insist there is no such thing as a case study, *tout court*. To conduct a case study implies that one has also conducted cross-case analysis, or at least thought about a broader set of cases. Otherwise, it is impossible for an author to answer the defining question of all case study research: what is this a case *of*? So framed, this book should be of interest to scholars in both the "cross-case" and "case study" camps. Indeed, my hope is that this book will contribute to breaking down the rather artificial boundaries that have separated these genres within the social sciences. Properly constituted, there is no reason that case study results cannot be synthesized with results gained from cross-case analysis, and vice versa.

[44] This distinction is drawn from Ragin (1987; 2004: 124). It is worth noting that Ragin's distinctive method (QCA) is also designed to overcome this traditional dichotomy.

[45] Achen and Shively (1995); Berg-Schlosser and De Meur (1997); Moaz and Mor (1999); Wong (2002). For a skeptical view of cross-level research, see Lieberson (1985: 107–15).

PART I

THINKING ABOUT CASE STUDIES

Narrow debates pertaining to specific methods can often be resolved by an appeal to context (which method is appropriately applied in setting A?), or by an investigation of the mathematical properties underlying different statistical methods (e.g., which technique of modeling serial autocorrelation is consistent with our understanding of a phenomenon and with the evidence at hand?). Broader methodological debates, however, are always and necessarily about *concepts*. How should we define key terms (e.g., "case," "causation," "process-tracing")? What is the most useful way to carve up the lexical terrain?[1]

It will be seen that these questions of definition are inextricable from the broader questions of social science methodology. For it is with these key terms that we make sense of the subject matter. Thus, while the first part of the book is prefatory to the practical advice offered in Part Two, it is certainly not incidental. It is impossible to conduct case studies without also conceptualizing the case study and its place in the toolbox of social research. In thinking this matter through, a degree of abstraction is inevitable. I have endeavored to leaven the generalities with specific examples, wherever possible.

Chapter Two asks what a case study is, and how it might be differentiated from other styles of research. This chapter is definitional. It deals with the various meanings that have been attached to, or are implied by, the case study research design.

---

[1] For discussion of concept formation in the social sciences see Adcock (2005); Collier and Mahon (1993); Gerring (2001: Chapters 3–4); and Sartori (1984).

Building on this scaffolding, Chapter Three inquires into the strengths and weaknesses of the case study method, as contrasted with cross-case methods. Under what conditions is a case study approach most useful, most revealing, or most suspect?

2

What Is a Case Study?

The Problem of Definition

The key term of this book is, admittedly, a definitional morass. To refer to a work as a "case study" might mean: (a) that its method is qualitative, small-N,[1] (b) that the research is holistic, thick (a more or less comprehensive examination of a phenomenon),[2] (c) that it utilizes a particular type of evidence (e.g., ethnographic, clinical, nonexperimental, non-survey-based, participant-observation, process-tracing, historical, textual, or field research),[3] (d) that its method of evidence gathering is naturalistic (a "real-life context"),[4] (e) that the topic is diffuse (case and context are difficult to distinguish),[5] (f) that it employs triangulation ("multiple sources of evidence"),[6] (g) that the research investigates the properties of a single observation,[7] or (h) that the research investigates the properties of a single phenomenon, instance, or example.[8]

Evidently, researchers have many things in mind when they talk about case study research. Confusion is compounded by the existence of a

---

[1] Eckstein (1975); George and Bennett (2005); Lijphart (1975); Orum, Feagin, and Sjoberg (1991: 2); Van Evera (1997: 50); Yin (1994).

[2] Goode and Hart (1952: 331; quoted in Mitchell 1983: 191); Queen (1928: 226); Ragin (1987, 1997); Stoecker (1991: 97); Verschuren (2003).

[3] George and Bennett (2005); Hamel (1993); Hammersley and Gomm (2000); Yin (1994).

[4] Yin (2003: 13).

[5] Yin (1994: 123).

[6] Ibid.

[7] Campbell and Stanley (1963: 7); Eckstein (1975: 85).

[8] This is probably the most common understanding of the term. George and Bennett (2005: 17), for example, define a case as "an instance of a class of events." (Note that elsewhere in the same chapter they infer that the analysis of that instance will be small-N, i.e., qualitative.) See also Odell (2001: 162) and Thies (2002: 353).

large number of near-synonyms – single unit, single subject, single case, $N = 1$, case-based, case-control, case history, case method, case record, case work, within-case, clinical research, and so forth.[9] As a result of this profusion of terms and meanings, proponents and opponents of the case study marshal a wide range of arguments but do not seem any closer to agreement than when this debate was first broached several decades ago. Jennifer Platt notes that "much case study theorizing has been conceptually confused, because too many different themes have been packed into the idea 'case study.'"[10]

How, then, should the case study be understood? The first six options enumerated above (a–f) seem inappropriate as general definitions of the topic, since each implies a substantial shift in meaning relative to established usage. One cannot substitute case study for *qualitative, ethnographic, process-tracing, holistic, naturalistic, diffuse*, or *triangulation* without feeling that something has been lost in translation. These terms are perhaps better understood as describing certain kinds of case studies, not the topic at large. A seventh option, (g), equates the case study with the study of a single observation, the $N = 1$ research design. This is logically impossible, as I will argue. The eighth option, (h), centering on *phenomenon, instance*, or *example* as the key term, is correct as far as it goes but also ambiguous. Imagine asking someone, "What is your instance?" or "What is your phenomenon?" A case study presupposes a relatively bounded phenomenon, an implication that none of these terms captures.

Can this concept be reconstructed in a clearer, more productive fashion? I begin this chapter by stipulating a series of definitions. I then present a typology of research designs, understood according to the patterns of spatial and temporal evidence that they draw upon. A final section addresses a central definitional question, namely, whether case studies should be understood as exclusively "small-N" analyses.

---

[9] Davidson and Costello (1969); Franklin, Allison, and Gorman (1997); Hersen and Barlow (1976); Kazdin (1982); Kratochwill (1978).

[10] Platt (1992: 48). Elsewhere in this perceptive article, Platt (1992: 37) comments: "the diversity of the themes which have been associated with the term, and the vagueness of some of the discussion, causes some difficulty. . . . In practice, 'case study method' in its heyday [in the interwar years] seems to have meant some permutation of the following components: life history data collected by any means, personal documents, unstructured interview data of any kind, the close study of one or a small number of cases whether or not any attempt was made to generalize from them, any attempt at holistic study, and non-quantitative data analysis. These components have neither a necessary logical nor a regular empirical connection with each other."

Definitions

For purposes of methodological discussion, it is essential to develop a vocabulary that is consistent and clear. In arriving at definitions for key terms, I rely on ordinary usage (within the language region of social science) as much as possible. However, because ordinary usage is often ambiguous, encompassing a range of meanings for a given term (as we have seen above for "case"), some concept reconstruction is unavoidable. At the end of this discussion, I hope it will be clear why this particular way of defining terms might be useful, at least for methodological purposes.[11]

Case connotes a spatially delimited phenomenon (a unit) observed at a single point in time or over some period of time. It comprises the type of phenomenon that an inference attempts to explain. Thus, in a study that attempts to elucidate certain features of nation-states, cases are comprised of nation-states (across some temporal frame); in a study that attempts to explain the behavior of individuals, cases are comprised of individuals, and so forth. Each case may provide a single observation or multiple (within-case) observations.

For students of political science, the archetypal case is the dominant political unit of our time, the nation-state. However, this is a matter of convention. The study of smaller social and political units (regions, cities, villages, communities, social groups, families) or specific institutions (political parties, interest groups, businesses) is equally common in many social science disciplines.[12] In psychology, medicine, and social work the notion of a case study is usually linked to clinical research, where individuals are the preferred units of analysis.[13] Whatever one's chosen unit, the methodological issues attached to the case study have nothing to do with the size of the cases. A case may be created out of any phenomenon so long as it has identifiable boundaries and comprises the primary object of an inference.

Note that the spatial boundaries of a case are often more apparent than its temporal boundaries. We know, more or less, where a country begins and ends, while we may have difficulty explaining *when* a country

---

[11] In the following analysis, I take a "minimal" approach to definition (Gerring 2001: Chapter 4; Gerring and Barresi 2003). Scholars embedded in a particular research setting may choose somewhat different terms and meanings.

[12] For discussion of subnational studies in political science, see Snyder (2001).

[13] Corsini (2004); Davidson and Costello (1969); Hersen and Barlow (1976); Franklin, Allison, and Gorman (1997); Robinson (2001). For discussion of the meaning of the term "case study," see Benbasat, Goldstein, and Mead (1987: 371); Cunningham (1997); Merriam (1988); and Verschuren (2003).

begins and ends. Yet some temporal boundaries must be assumed. This is particularly important when cases consist of discrete events – crises, revolutions, legislative acts, and so forth – within a single unit. Occasionally, the temporal boundaries of a case are more obvious than its spatial boundaries. This is true when the phenomena under study are eventful but the unit undergoing the event is amorphous. For example, if one is studying terrorist attacks it may not be clear how the spatial unit of analysis should be understood, but the events themselves may be well bounded.

A *case study* may be understood as the intensive study of a single case where the purpose of that study is – at least in part – to shed light on a larger class of cases (a population). *Case study research* may incorporate several cases, that is, multiple case studies. However, at a certain point it will no longer be possible to investigate those cases intensively. At the point where the emphasis of a study shifts from the individual case to a sample of cases, we shall say that a study is *cross-case*. Evidently, the distinction between case study and cross-case study is a matter of degree. The fewer cases there are, and the more intensively they are studied, the more a work merits the appellation "case study." Even so, this proves to be a useful distinction, and much follows from it. Indeed, the entire book rests upon it. All empirical work may be classified as either case study (comprising one or a few cases) or cross-case study (comprising many cases).

An additional implication of the term "case study" is that the unit(s) under special focus is not perfectly representative of the population, or is at least questionable. Unit homogeneity across the sample and the population is not assured. If, for example, one is studying a single H_2O molecule, it may be reasonable to assume that the behavior of that molecule is identical to that of all other H_2O molecules. Under the circumstances, one would not refer to such an investigation as a "case study," regardless of how intensive the investigation of that single molecule might be. In social science settings one rarely faces phenomena of such consistency, so this is not an issue of great practical significance. Nonetheless, intrinsic to the concept is an element of doubt about the bias that may be contained in a sample of one or several.

A few additional terms may now be formally defined.

An *observation* is the most basic element of any empirical endeavor. Conventionally, the number of observations in an analysis is referred to with the letter N. (Confusingly, N may also be used to designate the number of cases in a study, a usage that is usually clear from context.) A single observation may be understood as containing several dimensions, each of which may be measured (across disparate observations) as a *variable*.

Where the proposition is causal, these may be subdivided into dependent (Y) and independent (X) variables. The dependent variable refers to the outcome of an investigation. The independent variable refers to the explanatory (causal) factor, that which the outcome is supposedly dependent on.

A case may consist of a single observation (N = 1). This would be true, for example, in a cross-sectional analysis of multiple cases. In a case study, however, the case under study always provides more than one observation. These may be constructed diachronically (by observing the case or some subset of within-case units over time) or synchronically (by observing within-case variation at a single point in time), as discussed below.

This is a clue to the fact that case studies and cross-case studies usually operate at different levels of analysis. The case study is typically focused on within-case variation (if there is a cross-case component, it is probably secondary in importance to the within-case evidence). The cross-case study, as the name suggests, is typically focused on cross-case variation (if there is also within-case variation, it is probably secondary in importance to the cross-case evidence). They have the same object in view – the explanation of a population of cases – but they go about this task differently.

A *sample* consists of whatever cases are subjected to formal analysis; they are the immediate subject of a study or case study. (Confusingly, the term "sample" may also refer to the observations under study. But at present, we treat the sample as consisting of cases.) In a case study, the sample is small, by definition, consisting of the single case or handful of cases that the researcher has under her lens. Usually, however, when one uses the term "sample" one is implying that the number of cases is large. Thus, "sample-based work" will be understood as referring to large-N cross-case methods – the opposite of case study work. To reiterate, the feature distinguishing the case study format from a sample-based (or "cross-case") research design is the number of cases falling within the sample – one or a few versus many – and the corresponding thoroughness with which each case is studied. Case studies, like large-N samples, seek to represent, in all ways relevant to the proposition at hand, a population of cases. A series of case studies might therefore be referred to as a sample if they are relatively brief and relatively numerous; it is a matter of emphasis and of degree. The more case studies one has, the less intensively each one is studied, and the more confident one is in their representativeness (of some broader population), the more likely one is to describe them as a sample rather than as a series of case studies. For practical reasons – unless, that is, a study is extraordinarily long – the case study research format is usually limited to a dozen cases or fewer. A single case is not unusual.

Granted, in some circumstances a single study may combine the two elements – an intensive case study and a more superficial analysis conducted on a larger sample. These additional cases are often brought into the analysis in a peripheral way – typically, in an introductory or concluding section of the paper or the book. Often, these peripheral cases are surveyed through a quick reading of the secondary literature or through a statistical analysis. Sometimes, the status of these informal cases is left implicit (they are not theorized as part of the formal research design). This may be warranted in circumstances where the relevant comparison or contrast between the formal case(s) under intensive study and the peripheral cases is obvious. Thus, studies of American exceptionalism, in enumerating features of the American experience, often assume that the United States is different from European countries in relevant respects.[14] In this situation, the additional cases – the UK, France, Germany, and so on – provide the necessary background for whatever arguments are being made about America. They are present, in the sense that they carry an important burden in the analysis, but perhaps they are not formally accounted for in the author's research design. For our purposes, what is significant is that most works combine case study and cross-case study components, whether or not the latter are explicit. Methodologically, these approaches are distinct, even though they may be integrated into a single work. (Indeed, this is a good way of approaching many subjects.)

Continuing with our review of key terms, the sample of cases (large or small) rests within a *population* of cases to which a given proposition refers. The population of an inference is thus equivalent to the breadth or scope of a proposition. (I use the terms *proposition, hypothesis, inference*, and *argument* interchangeably.) Note that most samples are not exhaustive; hence the use of the term "sample," referring to *sampling* from a larger population. Occasionally, however, the sample equals the population of an inference; all potential cases are studied.

For those familiar with the rectangular form of a dataset, it may be helpful to conceptualize observations as rows, variables as columns, and cases as either groups of observations or individual observations. Several possibilities are illustrated in the tables presented here: two cases (Table 2.1), multiple cross-sectional cases (Table 2.2), and time-series cross-sectional cases (Table 2.3).

---

[14] Amenta (1991).

TABLE 2.1. *Case study dataset with two cases*

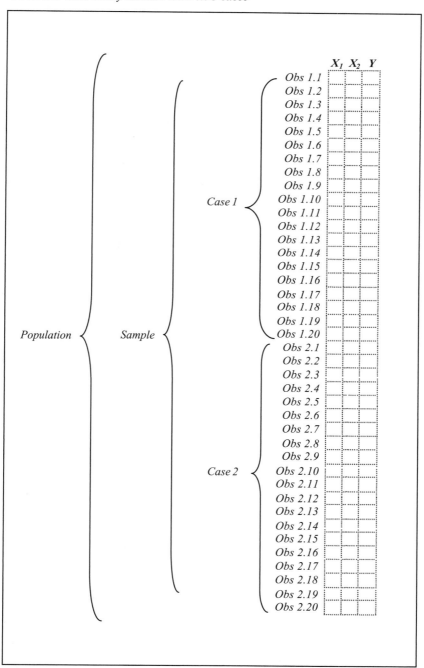

Population = 1; Sample = 1; Cases = 2; Observations (N) = 40; Variables = 3.

TABLE 2.2. *Cross-case cross-sectional dataset with forty cases*

		X_1	X_2	Y
Case 1	Obs 1			
Case 2	Obs 2			
Case 3	Obs 3			
Case 4	Obs 4			
Case 5	Obs 5			
Case 6	Obs 6			
Case 7	Obs 7			
Case 8	Obs 8			
Case 9	Obs 9			
Case 10	Obs 10			
Case 11	Obs 11			
Case 12	Obs 12			
Case 13	Obs 13			
Case 14	Obs 14			
Case 15	Obs 15			
Case 16	Obs 16			
Case 17	Obs 17			
Case 18	Obs 18			
Case 19	Obs 19			
Case 20	Obs 20			
Case 21	Obs 21			
Case 22	Obs 22			
Case 23	Obs 23			
Case 24	Obs 24			
Case 25	Obs 25			
Case 26	Obs 26			
Case 27	Obs 27			
Case 28	Obs 28			
Case 29	Obs 29			
Case 30	Obs 30			
Case 31	Obs 31			
Case 32	Obs 32			
Case 33	Obs 33			
Case 34	Obs 34			
Case 35	Obs 35			
Case 36	Obs 36			
Case 37	Obs 37			
Case 38	Obs 38			
Case 39	Obs 39			
Case 40	Obs 40			

Population { *Sample* { ... }

Population = 1; Sample = 1; Cases = 40; Observations (N) = 40; Variables = 3.

TABLE 2.3. *Time-series cross-sectional dataset*

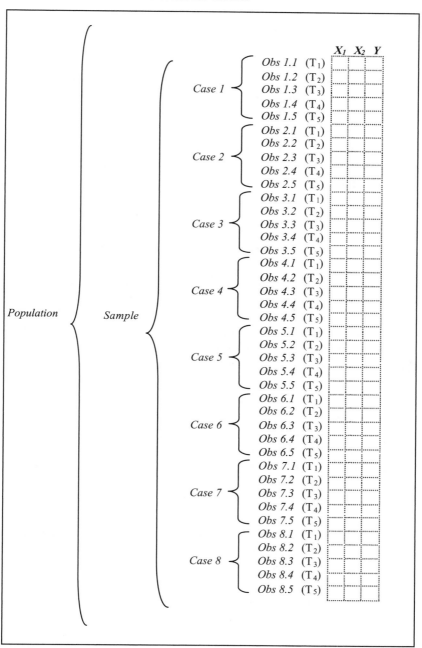

Population = 1; Sample = 1; Cases = 8; Observations (N) = 40; Time (T) = 1–5; Variables = 3.

It must be appreciated that all these terms are definable only by reference to a particular proposition and a corresponding research design. A country may function as a case, an observation, or a population. It all depends upon what one is arguing. In a typical cross-country time-series regression analysis, cases are countries and observations are country-years.[15] However, shifts in the level of analysis of a proposition necessarily change the referential meaning of all terms in the semantic field. If one moves down one level of analysis, the new population lies within the old population, the new sample within the old sample, and so forth. Population, case, and observation are nested within each other. Since most social science research occurs at several levels of analysis, these terms are generally in flux. Nonetheless, they have distinct meanings within the context of a single proposition and its associated research design.

Consider a survey-based analysis of respondents within a single country, under several scenarios. Under the first scenario, the proposition of interest pertains to individual-level behavior. It is about how individuals behave. As such, cases are defined as individuals, and this is properly classified as a *cross-case* study. Now, let us suppose that the researcher wishes to use this same survey-level data drawn from a single country to elucidate an inference pertaining to countries, rather than to individuals. Under this scenario, each poll respondent constitutes a within-case observation. If there is only one country, or a few countries, under investigation – and the inference, as before, pertains to multiple countries – then this study is properly classified as a *case study*. If many countries are under study (with or without individual-level data), then it is properly classified as a *cross-case* study. Again, the key questions are (a) how many cases are studied and (b) how intensively are they studied – with the understanding that a "case" embodies the unit of concern in the central inference.

To complicate matters further, the status of a work may change as it is digested and appropriated by a community of scholars. A *meta-analysis* is a systematic attempt to integrate the results of individual studies into a quantitative analysis, pooling individual cases drawn from each study into a single dataset (with various weightings and restrictions). The ubiquitous *literature review* or *case study survey* aims at the same objective in a less synoptic fashion. Both statistical meta-analyses and narrative literature reviews assimilate a series of studies, treating them as case studies in some larger project – whether or not this was the intention of the original authors.[16]

---

[15] See, e.g., Przeworski et al. (2000).
[16] Lipsey and Wilson (2001); Lucas (1974).

A Typology of Covariational Research Designs

In order to better understand what a case study is, one must comprehend what it is not. The distinctiveness of the case study may be clarified by placing it within a broader set of methodological options. Here, I shall classify research designs according to (a) the number of cases that they encompass (one, several, or many), (b) the kind of X/Y variation that they exploit (spatial or temporal), and (c) the location of that variation (cross-case or within-case). This produces a typology with ten possible cells, as depicted in Table 2.4.

Variations on the case study format occupy five of these ten cells, designated by the shaded regions in Table 2.4. Type 2 represents variation in a single case over time (diachronic analysis). Type 3 represents within-case variation at a single point in time (synchronic analysis). Type 4 combines synchronic and diachronic analysis, and is perhaps the most common approach in case study work. Thus, Robert Putnam's classic study of Italy, *Making Democracy Work*, exploits variation across regions and over time in order to test the causal role of social capital.[17]

It is common to combine several cases in a single study. If the cases are comprised of large territorial units, then this combination may be referred to as the "comparative" method (if the variation of interest is primarily synchronic) or the "comparative-historical" method (if the variation of interest is both synchronic and diachronic).[18] It should be pointed out that these terms are used primarily within the subfield of comparative politics. Other terms, such as "most-similar" and "most-different," may be used as well. Thus, while a case is always singular, a case study work or research design often refers to a study that includes several cases.

The larger point is that the evidentiary basis upon which case studies rely is plural, not singular. Indeed, there are five possible styles of covariational evidence in a case study. Usually, they are intermingled – different sorts of analysis will be employed at different stages of the analysis – so that it is often difficult to categorize a study as falling neatly into a single cell in Table 2.4.

The bottom half of Table 2.4 lays out various cross-case research designs, where the most important element of the empirical analysis involves comparisons across *many* cases (more than a handful). Cross-case

---

[17] Putnam (1993).

[18] On the comparative method see Collier (1993); Lijphart (1971, 1975); Przeworski and Teune (1970); Richter (1969); and Smelser (1976). On the comparative-historical method see Mahoney and Rueschemeyer (2003). On the history of the comparative method, a term that harkens back to Bryce (1921), see Lasswell (1931).

TABLE 2.4. *Research designs: A covariational typology*

Cases	Spatial Variation	Temporal Variation	
		No	*Yes*
One — None		1. [Logically impossible]	2. Single-case study (diachronic)
One — Within-case		3. Single-case study (synchronic)	4. Single-case study (synchronic + diachronic)
Several — Cross-case & within-case		5. Comparative method	6. Comparative-historical
Many — Cross-case		7. Cross-sectional	8. Time-series cross-sectional
Many — Cross-case & within-case		9. Hierarchical	10. Hierarchical time-series

Note: Shaded cells are case study research designs.

analysis without any explicit temporal component (type 7) is usually classified as cross-sectional, even though a temporal component is simulated with independent variables that are assumed to precede the dependent variable. An example was illustrated in Table 2.2. When an explicit temporal component is included, we often refer to the analysis as time-series cross-sectional (TSCS) or pooled time-series (type 8). This format was illustrated in Table 2.3. When one examines across-case and within-case variation in the same research design, one is said to be employing a hierarchical model (type 9). Finally, when all forms of covariation are enlisted in a single research design, the resulting method may be described as a hierarchical time-series design (type 10).[19]

It bears repeating that I have listed the methods most commonly identified with these research designs not with the intention of distinguishing labels but rather with the intention of illustrating various types of causal

---

[19] It will be noted that, like most case studies, hierarchical models involve a movement across levels of analysis. However, while a case study moves *down* from the primary level of analysis (to within-case cases), a hierarchical model moves *up*. Thus, if classrooms are the primary unit of analysis in a study, one might employ a hierarchical model to control for the effects of larger cases – schools, districts, regions, and so forth. But one would not employ individual students as cases in such an analysis (not, that is, without changing the unit of analysis for the entire study).

evidence. The classification of a research design always depends upon the particular proposition that a researcher intends to prove. Potentially, each of the foregoing cross-case methods might also be employed in the capacity of a case study. (That is, a case study may enlist cross-sectional, time-series cross-sectional, hierarchical, or hierarchical time-series techniques.) It all depends upon the proposition in question (i.e., what sort of phenomena it is about, and hence what sort of phenomena constitutes "cases") and on the degree of analytic focus devoted to the individual cases.

The N Question

Traditionally, the case study has been identified with qualitative methods and cross-case analysis with quantitative methods. This is how Franklin Giddings put the matter in his 1924 textbook, in which he contrasted two fundamentally different procedures:

> In the one we follow the distribution of a particular trait, quality, habit or other phenomenon as far as we can. In the other we ascertain as completely as we can the number and variety of traits, qualities, habits, or what not, combined in a particular instance. The first of these procedures has long been known as the statistical method.... The second procedure has almost as long been known as the case method.[20]

In the intervening decades, this disjunction has become ever more ensconced: a contrast between "stats" and "cases," "quant" and "qual." Those who work with numbers are apt to distrust case study methods, while those who work with narratives are likely to be favorably disposed.

I believe that this distinction is not intrinsic, that is, definitional. What distinguishes the case study method from all other methods is its reliance on evidence drawn from a single case and its attempt, at the same time, to illuminate features of a broader set of cases. It follows from this that the number of observations (N) employed by a case study may be either small or large, and consequently may be evaluated in a qualitative or quantitative fashion.[21]

---

[20] Giddings (1924: 94). See also Meehl (1954); Rice (1928: Chapter 1); and Stouffer (1941: 349).

[21] This section explains and elaborates on a theme first articulated by Lundberg (1941), followed by Campbell (1975/1988) – itself a revision of Campbell's earlier perspective (Campbell and Stanley 1963). Historical ballast for this view may be garnered from the field of experimental research in psychology, commonly dated to the publication of Gustav Theodor Fechner's *Elemente der Psychophysik* in 1860. In this work, Hersen and

In order to see why this might be so, let us consider how a case study of a single event – say, the French Revolution – works. Intuitively, such a study provides an N of 1 (France). If one were to broaden the analysis to include a second revolution (e.g., the American Revolution), it would be common to describe the study as comprising two observations. Yet this is a gross distortion of what is really going on. The event known as the French Revolution provides *at least* two observations, for it will be observed over time to see what changed and what remained the same. These patterns of covariation offer essential empirical clues. They also construct multiple observations from an individual case. So $N = 2$, at the very least (e.g., before and after a revolution), in a case study of type 2 (in Table 2.4).

If, instead, there is no temporal variation – if, for example, the French Revolution is examined at a single point in time – then the investigation is likely to focus on cross-sectional covariational patterns *within* that case, a case study of type 3 (in Table 2.4). If the primary unit of analysis is the nation-state, then within-case cases might be constructed from provinces, localities, groups, or individuals. The possibilities for within-case analysis are, in principle, infinite. In their pathbreaking study of the International Typographers Union, Lipset, Trow, and Coleman note the variety of within-case evidence, which included union locals, union shops (within each local), and individual members of the union.[22] It is not hard to see why within-case N often swamps cross-case N. This is bound to be true wherever individuals comprise within-case observations. A single national survey will produce a much larger sample than any conceivable cross-country analysis. Thus, in many circumstances case studies of type 3 comprise a larger N than cross-sectional analyses or time-series

Barlow (1976: 2–3) report, Fechner developed "measures of sensation through several psychophysical methods. With these methods, Fechner was able to determine sensory thresholds, just noticeable differences (JNDs) in various sense modalities. What is common to these methods is the repeated measurement of a response at different intensities or different locations of a given stimulus in an individual subject... It is interesting to note that Fechner was one of the first to apply statistical methods to psychological problems. Fechner noticed that judgments of [JNDs] in the sensory modalities varied somewhat from trial to trial. To quantify this variation, or 'error' in judgment, he borrowed the normal law of error, demonstrated that these 'errors' were normally distributed around a mean, which then became the 'true' sensory threshold. This use of descriptive statistics anticipated the application of these procedures to groups of individuals at the turn of the century when traits of capabilities were also found to be normally distributed around a mean." Hersen and Barlow note that Fechner, the pioneer, "was concerned with variability *within* the subject." See also Queen (1928).

[22] Lipset, Trow, and Coleman (1956: 422).

cross-sectional analyses. For example, a recent review of natural resource management studies found that the N of a study varies inversely with its geographic scope. Specifically, case studies focused on single communities tend to have large samples, since they often employ individual-level observations; cross-case studies are more likely to treat communities as comprising observations, and hence have a smaller N.[23] This is a common pattern.

Evidently, if a case study *combines* temporal and within-case variation, as in case studies of type 4, then its potential N increases accordingly. And if cross-case analysis is added to this, as in the comparative method or the comparative-historical method (types 5 and 6 in Table 2.4), then one realizes a further enlargement in potential observations.

These facts hold true regardless of whether the method is experimental or nonexperimental. It is also true of counterfactual reasoning, which typically consists of four observations – the actual (as it happened) before and after observations, and the before and after observations as reconstructed through counterfactual reasoning (i.e., with an imagined intervention). In short, the case study does not preclude a large N. It simply precludes a large *cross-case* N, by definition. Indeed, many renowned case studies are data-rich and include extensive, and occasionally quite sophisticated, quantitative analysis. Frederic Le Play's work on working-class families incorporated hundreds of case studies.[24] Robert and Helen Lynd's study of Muncie, Indiana, featured surveys of hundreds of respondents in "Middletown."[25] *Yankee City*, another pioneering community study, included interviews with 17,000 people.[26]

What, then, of the infamous $N = 1$ research design that haunts the imaginations of social scientists everywhere?[27] This hypothetical research design occupies the empty cell in Table 2.4. The cell is empty because it represents a research design that is not logically feasible. A single case observed at a single point in time without the addition of within-case observations offers no evidence whatsoever of a causal proposition. In trying to intuit a causal relationship from this snapshot one would be engaging in a truly random operation, since an infinite number of lines might be drawn through that one data point. I do not think there are any

---

[23] Poteete and Ostrom (2005: 11).

[24] Brooke (1970).

[25] Lynd and Lynd (1929/1956).

[26] Warner and Lunt (1941).

[27] Achen and Snidal (1989); Geddes (1990); Goldthorpe (1997); King, Keohane, and Verba (1994); Lieberson (1985: 107–15; 1992, 1994).

examples of this sort of investigation in social science research. Thus, I regard it as a myth rather than a method.[28]

The point becomes even clearer if we consider the case study in relation to a time-series cross-section (TSCS) research design, as illustrated in Table 2.3. Let us imagine that cases are comprised of countries and that temporal units are years; hence, the unit of analysis is the country-year. In Table 2.3, each case has five observations and thus represents a single country observed over five years (T_{1-5}). Now, consider the possibility of constructing a case study from just one of these observations – a single country at a single point in time. This seems an unlikely prospect, unless of course there is significant within-case variation during that year. Perhaps this country, during those twelve months, offers a critical juncture in which the variables of theoretical interest undergo a significant change. Whether the temporal era is short or long (and we can imagine much shorter and much longer temporal periods), the significant feature of most case studies is that they look at periods of change, and these periods of change produce (or are regarded as producing) distinct observations – classically "before" (pre-) and "after" (post-) observations. Alternatively, it may be possible to exploit spatial (cross-sectional) evidence in that country at that particular time – for example, with extensive documentary records or a systematic survey. In these circumstances, one can easily imagine a case study being constructed from a single observation in a time-series cross-section research design. But this can be accomplished only by subdividing the original observation into multiple observations. N is no longer equal to 1.

The skeptical reader may regard this conclusion as a semantic quibble, of little import to the real world of research. If so, she might consider the following quite common research scenario. An ethnographic study provides a thick description, in prose, of a particular setting which is intended to uncover certain features of other settings (not studied). The prose stretches for five hundred pages in a draft manuscript and is rather

[28] The one possible exception is the deviant case that disproves a deterministic proposition. However, the utility of the deviant case rests upon a broader population of cases that lies in the background of a case study focused on a single case. Thus, the N of such a study, I would argue, is greater than one – even if no within-case evidence is gathered. The more important point is perhaps the following. No one has ever conducted a case study analysis that consists of only a single observation. If the point of the case study is to demonstrate that a single case of such-and-such a type exists (perhaps with the goal of falsifying a deterministic proposition), then it is likely to take a good deal of work to establish the facts of that case. This work consists of multiple within-case observations. Again, the N is much higher than one.

repetitive; certain patterns are repeated again and again. In an effort to reduce the sheer volume of descriptive material, as well as to attain a more synthetic analysis, the researcher begins to code the results of her labors into standardized categories: she counts. Has she, by committing the act of numeracy, now converted a case study into some other type of study? (If so, what shall we call it?) Note that the object of her study does not vary, even though the prose is now combined with some form of quantitative analysis, which may be simple or sophisticated. The introduction of statistical analysis does not – should not – disqualify a study as a "case study."

The Style of Analysis

To be sure, *non*–case study work is by definition quantitative ("statistical") in nature. This is so because whenever one is attempting to incorporate a large number of cases into a single analysis, it will be necessary to reduce the evidence to a small number of dimensions. One cannot explore 1,000 cases on their own terms (i.e., in detail). (One might simply accumulate case study after case study in a compendious multivolume work. However, in order to reach any meaningful conclusions about this pile of data it will be necessary to reduce the informational overload, which is why God gave us statistics.)

With case study evidence, the situation is evidently more complicated. Case studies may employ a great variety of techniques – both quantitative and qualitative – for the gathering and analysis of evidence. This is one of the intriguing qualities of case-study research and lends that research its characteristic flexibility. Thus, it seems fair to say that there is an elective affinity between the case study format and qualitative, small-N work, even though the latter is not definitionally entailed. Let us explore why this might be so.

Case study research, by definition, is focused on a single, relatively bounded unit. That single unit may, or may not, afford opportunities for large-N within-case analysis. Within-case evidence is sometimes quite extensive, as when individual-level variation bears upon a group-level inference. But not always.

Consider the following classic studies, each of which focuses on the attitudes and characteristics of American citizens. *The American Voter*, a collaborative effort by Angus Campbell, Philip Converse, Warren Miller, and Donald Stokes, examines public opinion on a wide range of topics that are thought to influence electoral behavior through the instrument of a nationwide survey of the general public.[29] *The People's Choice*, by Paul Lazarsfeld, Bernard Berelson, and Hazel Gaudet, is a longitudinal panel study focusing on 600 citizens living in Erie County, Ohio, who were polled at monthly intervals during the 1940 presidential campaign to determine what influences the campaign may have had on their choice of candidates.[30] *Middletown*, by Robert and Helen Lynd, examines life in a midsized city, including such topics as earning a living, making a home, training the young, using leisure, taking part in religious practices, and taking part in community activities (these are the sections into which the book is divided). The Lynds and their accomplices rely on a great variety of evidence, including in-depth interviews, surveys, direct observation, secondary accounts, registers of books checked out of the library, and so forth.[31] *Political Ideology*, by Robert Lane, attempts to uncover the sources of political values in a subsection of the American public, represented by fifteen subjects who are interviewed intensively by the author. These subjects are male, white, married, fathers, between the ages of twenty-five and fifty-four, working-class and white-collar, native-born, of varying religions, and living in an (unnamed) city on the eastern seaboard.[32]

A summary of some of the methodological features of these four studies is contained in Table 2.5. Note that the first two studies (*The American Voter* and *The People's Choice*) are classified as cross-case and the second pair (*Middletown* and *Political Ideology*) as case studies. What is it that drives this distinction? Clearly, it is not the type of subjects under study (all focus primarily on individuals), the number of observations (which range from small-N to large-N), or the breadth of the population (all purport to describe features of the same country). The style of analysis differs in one respect: only in the case studies does qualitative analysis comprise a significant portion of the research. This, in turn, is a product of the number of cases under investigation. Where hundreds of individuals are being studied at once, there is no opportunity to evaluate cases in a qualitative

---

[29] Campbell et al. (1960).

[30] Lazarsfeld, Berelson, and Gaudet (1948). A larger poll, with 2,000 respondents, was taken initially, as a way of establishing a baseline for the chosen panel of 600. In addition, special attention was paid to those whose vote choice changed during the course of the panel. These might be looked upon as a series of case studies nested within the larger panel study. However, because this sort of analysis plays only a secondary role in the overall analysis, it seems fair to characterize this research design as "cross-case."

[31] Lynd and Lynd (1929/1956).

[32] Lane (1962).

TABLE 2.5. *Case study and cross-case study research designs compared*

	Study	Subjects	Cases	Largest Sample	Analysis	Population
Cross-case study	*The American Voter* (Campbell et al., 1960)	Citizens of the United States	1,000+ (individuals)	1,000+	Quant	Americans
	The People's Choice (Lazarsfeld 1948)	Citizens of Erie County, OH	600 (individuals)	2,000	Quant	Americans
Case study	*Middletown* (Lynd and Lynd. 1929/1956)	Citizens of Muncie, IN	1 (cities)	300+	Quant & Qual	American cities
	Political Ideology (Lane 1962)	Working men of "Eastport"	15 (individuals)	15	Qual	American working class

All categories (subjects, cases, analysis, population) refer to the primary inferences produced by the study in question.

manner. By contrast, where a single case (as in *Middletown*) or a small number of cases (as in *Political Ideology*) is under study, qualitative analysis is usually de rigueur – though it may be combined with quantitative analysis (as in *Middletown*).

The reader will notice that subtle differences in the research objective of a study can shift it from one category to another. If, for example, Robert and Helen Lynd decided to treat their surveys as representative of *individuals* in the general public (across the United States), rather than as representative of *cities* in the United States, then *Middletown* would take on the methodological features of *The People's Choice*: it would become a cross-case study. Indeed, this is a plausible reading of some portions of that study.

Importantly, the technique of analysis employed in a case study is not simply a function of the sheer number of within-case observations available in that unit. It is, more precisely, a function of the number of *comparable* observations available within that unit. Consider Robert Lane's intensive interviews. Clearly, lots of "data" was recovered from these lengthy discussions. However, the respondents' answers were not coded so as to conform to standardized variables. Hence, they cannot be handled within a dataset format, usually referred to as a "sample" (although we have occasionally employed this term in a broader sense). Of course, Lane could have chosen to recode these interviews to allow for a quantitative analysis, reducing the diversity of the original information in order to conform to uniform parameters. It is not clear that much would have been gained by doing so. In the event, his study is limited to qualitative forms of analysis.

This issue is treated at length in a later chapter. For the moment, note the fact that case study research often provides a piece of evidence pertaining to A, another piece of evidence pertaining to B, and a third pertaining to C. There may be many observations (in total), and they may all be relevant to a central causal argument, even though they are not directly comparable to one another. These are referred to in Chapter Seven as *noncomparable* observations.

In summary, large-N cross-case research is quantitative, by definition. This much conforms to usual perceptions. However, case study research may be either qualitative or quantitative, or both, depending upon the sort of within-case evidence that is available and relevant to the question at hand. Consequently, the traditional association of case study work with qualitative methods is correctly regarded as a methodological affinity, not a definitional entailment. It is true sometimes, but not all the time.

3

What Is a Case Study Good For?

Case Study versus Large-N Cross-Case Analysis

In Chapter Two, I argued that the case study approach to research is most usefully defined as an intensive study of a single unit or a small number of units (the cases), for the purpose of understanding a larger class of similar units (a population of cases). This was put forth as a minimal definition of the topic.[1] In this chapter, I proceed to discuss the *non*definitional attributes of the case study – attributes that are often, but not invariably, associated with the case study method. These will be understood as methodological affinities flowing from our minimal definition of the concept.[2]

The case study research design exhibits characteristic strengths and weaknesses relative to its large-N cross-case cousin. These trade-offs derive, first of all, from basic research goals such as (1) whether the study is oriented toward hypothesis generating or hypothesis testing, (2) whether internal or external validity is prioritized, (3) whether insight into causal mechanisms or causal effects is more valuable, and (4) whether the scope of the causal inference is deep or broad. These trade-offs also hinge on the shape of the empirical universe, that is, on (5) whether the population of cases under study is heterogeneous or homogeneous, (6) whether

---

[1] My intention was to include only those attributes commonly associated with the case study method that are *always* implied by our use of the term, excluding those attributes that are sometimes violated by standard usage. For further discussion of minimal definitions, see Gerring (2001: Chapter 4); Gerring and Barresi (2003); and Sartori (1976).

[2] These additional attributes might also be understood as comprising an ideal-type ("maximal") definition of the topic (Gerring 2001: Chapter 4; Gerring and Barresi 2003). Recent evaluations of the strengths and weaknesses of case study research can be found in Flyvbjerg (2004); Levy (2002a); and Verschuren (2001).

TABLE 3.1. *Case study and cross-case research designs: considerations*

	Affinity	
	Case Study	Cross-Case Study
Research goals		
1. Hypothesis	Generating	Testing
2. Validity	Internal	External
3. Causal insight	Mechanisms	Effects
4. Scope of proposition	Deep	Broad
Empirical factors		
5. Population of cases	Heterogeneous	Homogeneous
6. Causal strength	Strong	Weak
7. Useful variation	Rare	Common
8. Data availability	Concentrated	Dispersed
Additional factors		
9. Causal complexity	Indeterminate	
10. State of the field	Indeterminate	

the causal relationship of interest is strong or weak, (7) whether useful variation on key parameters within that population is rare or common, and (8) whether available data is concentrated or dispersed. Along each of these dimensions, case study research has an affinity for the first factor, and cross-case research has an affinity for the second, as summarized in Table 3.1.

I argue that other issues impinging upon the research format, such as (9) causal complexity and (10) the state of research in a given field, are indeterminate in their implications. Sometimes these factors militate toward a case study research design; at other times, toward a cross-case research design.

To reiterate, the eight trade-offs depicted in Table 3.1 represent methodological *affinities*, not invariant laws. Exceptions can be found to each one. Even so, these general tendencies are often noted in case study research and have been reproduced in multiple disciplines and subdisciplines over the course of many decades.

It should be stressed that each of these trade-offs carries a ceteris paribus caveat. Case studies are more useful for generating new hypotheses, *all other things being equal*. The reader must bear in mind that nine additional factors also rightly influence a writer's choice of research design, and they may lean in the other direction. Ceteris is not always paribus. One should not jump to conclusions about the research design appropriate to a given setting without considering the entire range of issues involved – some of which may be more important than others.

Hypothesis: Generating versus Testing

Social science research involves a quest for new theories as well as a testing of existing theories; it is comprised of both "conjectures" and "refutations."[3] Regrettably, social science methodology has focused almost exclusively on the latter. The conjectural element of social science is usually dismissed as a matter of guesswork, inspiration, or luck – a leap of faith, and hence a poor subject for methodological reflection.[4] Yet it will readily be granted that many works of social science, including most of the acknowledged classics, are seminal rather than definitive. Their classic status derives from the introduction of a new idea or a new perspective that is subsequently subjected to more rigorous (and refutable) analysis. Indeed, it is difficult to devise a program of falsification the first time a new theory is proposed. Path-breaking research, almost by definition, is protean. Subsequent research on that topic tends to be more definitive insofar as its primary task is limited to verify or falsify a preexisting hypothesis. Thus, the world of social science may be usefully divided according to the predominant goal undertaken in a given study, either hypothesis *generating* or hypothesis *testing*. There are two moments of empirical research, a "lightbulb" moment and a skeptical moment, each of which is essential to the progress of a discipline.[5]

Case studies enjoy a natural advantage in research of an exploratory nature. Several millennia ago, Hippocrates reported what were, arguably, the first case studies ever conducted. They were fourteen in number.[6] Darwin's insights into the process of human evolution came after his

---

[3] Popper (1963).

[4] Karl Popper (quoted in King, Keohane, and Verba 1994: 14) writes: "there is no such thing as a logical method of having new ideas.... Discovery contains 'an irrational element,' or a 'creative intuition.'" One recent collection of essays and interviews takes new ideas as its special focus (Munck and Snyder 2006), though it may be doubted whether there are generalizable results.

[5] Gerring (2001: Chapter 10). The trade-off between these two styles of research is implicit in Achen and Snidal (1989); the authors criticize the case study for its deficits in the latter genre but also acknowledge the benefits of the case study along the former dimension (ibid., 167–8). Reichenbach also distinguishes between a "context of discovery" and a "context of justification." Likewise, Peirce's concept of *abduction* recognizes the importance of a generative component in science.

[6] Bonoma (1985: 199). Some of the following examples are discussed in Patton (2002: 245).

travels to a few select locations, notably Easter Island. Freud's revolutionary work on human psychology was constructed from a close observation of fewer than a dozen clinical cases. Piaget formulated his theory of human cognitive development while watching his own two children as they passed from childhood to adulthood. Levi-Strauss's structuralist theory of human cultures built on the analysis of several North and South American tribes. Douglass North's neoinstitutionalist theory of economic development was constructed largely through a close analysis of a handful of early developing states (primarily England, the Netherlands, and the United States).[7] Many other examples might be cited of seminal ideas that derived from the intensive study of a few key cases.

Evidently, the sheer number of examples of a given phenomenon does not, by itself, produce insight. It may only confuse. How many times did Newton observe apples fall before he recognized the nature of gravity? This is an apocryphal example, but it illustrates a central point: case studies may be more useful than cross-case studies when a subject is being encountered for the first time or is being considered in a fundamentally new way. After reviewing the case study approach to medical research, one researcher finds that although case reports are commonly regarded as the lowest or weakest form of evidence, they are nonetheless understood to comprise "the first line of evidence." The hallmark of case reporting, according to Jan Vandenbroucke, "is to recognize the unexpected." This is where discovery begins.[8]

The advantages that case studies offer in work of an exploratory nature may also serve as impediments in work of a confirmatory/disconfirmatory nature. Let us briefly explore why this might be so.[9]

Traditionally, scientific methodology has been defined by a segregation of conjecture and refutation. One should not be allowed to contaminate the other.[10] Yet in the real world of social science, inspiration is often associated with perspiration. "Lightbulb" moments arise from a close engagement with the particular facts of a particular case. Inspiration is more likely to occur in the laboratory than in the shower.

The circular quality of conjecture and refutation is particularly apparent in case study research. Charles Ragin notes that case study research

---

[7] North and Weingast (1989); North and Thomas (1973).

[8] Vandenbroucke (2001: 331).

[9] For discussion of this trade-off in the context of economic growth theory, see Temple (1999: 120).

[10] Geddes (2003); King, Keohane, and Verba (1994); Popper (1934/1968).

is all about "casing" – defining the topic, including the hypothesis(es) of primary interest, the outcome, and the set of cases that offer relevant information vis-à-vis the hypothesis.[11] A study of the French Revolution may be conceptualized as a study of revolution, of social revolution, of revolt, of political violence, and so forth. Each of these topics entails a different population and a different set of causal factors. A good deal of authorial intervention is necessary in the course of defining a case study topic, for there is a great deal of evidentiary leeway. Yet the subjectivity of case study research allows for the generation of a great number of hypotheses, insights that might not be apparent to the cross-case researcher who works with a thinner set of empirical data across a large number of cases and with a more determinate (fixed) definition of cases, variables, and outcomes. It is the very fuzziness of case studies that grants them an advantage in research at the exploratory stage, for the single-case study allows one to test a multitude of hypotheses in a rough-and-ready way. Nor is this an entirely conjectural process. The relationships discovered among different elements of a single case have a prima facie causal connection: they are all at the scene of the crime. This is revelatory when one is at an early stage of analysis, for at that point there is no identifiable suspect and the crime itself may be difficult to discern. The fact that *A*, *B*, and *C* are present at the expected times and places (relative to some outcome of interest) is sufficient to establish them as independent variables. Proximal evidence is all that is required. Hence, the common identification of case studies as "plausibility probes," "pilot studies," "heuristic studies," "exploratory" and "theory-building" exercises.[12]

A large-N cross-case study, by contrast, generally allows for the testing of only a few hypotheses but does so with a somewhat greater degree of confidence, as is appropriate to work whose primary purpose is to test an extant theory. There is less room for authorial intervention because evidence gathered from a cross-case research design can be interpreted in a limited number of ways. It is therefore more reliable. Another way of stating the point is to say that while case studies lean toward Type 1 errors (falsely rejecting the null hypothesis), cross-case studies lean toward Type 2 errors (failing to reject the false null hypothesis). This explains why case studies are more likely to be paradigm-generating, while cross-case studies toil in the prosaic but highly structured field of normal science.

[11] Ragin (1992b).
[12] Eckstein (1975); Ragin (1992a, 1997); Rueschemeyer and Stephens (1997).

I do not mean to suggest that case studies never serve to confirm or disconfirm hypotheses. Evidence drawn from a single case may falsify a necessary or sufficient hypothesis, as will be discussed. Additionally, case studies are often useful for the purpose of elucidating causal mechanisms, and this obviously affects the plausibility of an X/Y relationship. However, general theories rarely offer the kind of detailed and determinate predictions on within-case variation that would allow one to reject a hypothesis through pattern matching (without additional cross-case evidence). Theory testing is not the case study's strong suit. The selection of "crucial" cases is at pains to overcome the fact that the cross-case N is minimal (see Chapter Five). Thus, one is unlikely to reject a hypothesis, or to consider it definitively proved, on the basis of a single case.

Harry Eckstein himself acknowledged that his argument for case studies as a form of theory confirmation was largely hypothetical. At the time of writing, several decades ago, he could not point to any social science study where a crucial case study had performed the heroic role assigned to it.[13] I suspect that this is still more or less true. Indeed, it is true even of experimental case studies in the natural sciences. "We must recognize," note Donald Campbell and Julian Stanley,

that continuous, multiple experimentation is more typical of science than once-and-for-all definitive experiments. The experiments we do today, if successful, will need replication and cross-validation at other times under other conditions before they can become an established part of science. . . . [E]ven though we recognize experimentation as the basic language of proof . . . we should not expect that 'crucial experiments' which pit opposing theories will be likely to have clear-cut outcomes. When one finds, for example, that competent observers advocate strongly divergent points of view, it seems likely on a priori grounds that both have observed something valid about the natural situation, and that both represent a part of the truth. The stronger the controversy, the more likely this is. Thus we might expect in such cases an experimental outcome with mixed results, or with the balance of truth varying subtly from experiment to experiment. The more mature focus . . . avoids crucial experiments and instead studies dimensional relationships and interactions along many degrees of the experimental variables.[14]

A single case study is still a single-shot affair – a single example of a larger phenomenon.

The trade-off between hypothesis generating and hypothesis testing helps us to reconcile the enthusiasm of case study researchers and the skepticism of case study critics. They are both right, for the looseness of

---

[13] Eckstein (1975).
[14] Campbell and Stanley (1963: 3).

case study research is a boon to new conceptualizations just as it is a bane to falsification.

Validity: Internal versus External

Questions of validity are often distinguished according to those that are *internal* to the sample under study and those that are *external* (i.e., applying to a broader – unstudied – population). The latter may be conceptualized as a problem of representativeness between sample and population. Cross-case research is always more representative of the population of interest than case study research, so long as some sensible procedure of case selection is followed (presumably some version of random sampling, as discussed in Chapter Five). Case study research suffers problems of representativeness because it includes, by definition, only a small number of cases of some more general phenomenon. Are the men chosen by Robert Lane typical of white, immigrant, working-class American males?[15] Is Middletown representative of other cities in America?[16] These sorts of questions forever haunt case study research. This means that case study research is generally weaker with respect to external validity than its cross-case cousin.

The corresponding virtue of case study research is its internal validity. Often, though not invariably, it is easier to establish the veracity of a causal relationship pertaining to a single case (or a small number of cases) than for a larger set of cases. Case study researchers share the bias of experimentalists in this respect: they tend to be more disturbed by threats to within-sample validity than by threats to out-of-sample validity. Thus, it seems appropriate to regard the trade-off between external and internal validity, like other trade-offs, as intrinsic to the cross-case/single-case choice of research design.

Causal Insight: Causal Mechanisms versus Causal Effects

A third trade-off concerns the sort of insight into causation that a researcher intends to achieve. Two goals may be usefully distinguished. The first concerns an estimate of the causal *effect*; the second concerns the investigation of a causal *mechanism* (i.e., a pathway from X to Y).

---

[15] Lane (1962).
[16] Lynd and Lynd (1929/1956).

When I say "causal effect," I refer to two things: (a) the magnitude of a causal relationship (the expected effect on Y of a given change in X across a population of cases) and (b) the relative precision or uncertainty of that point estimate.[17] Evidently, it is difficult to arrive at a reliable estimate of causal effects across a population of cases by looking at only a single case or a small number of cases. (The one possible exception would be an experiment in which a given case can be tested repeatedly, returning to a virgin condition after each test. But here one faces inevitable questions about the representativeness of that much-studied case.)[18] Thus, the estimate of a causal effect is almost always grounded in cross-case evidence.

It is now well established that causal arguments depend not only on measuring causal effects, but also on the identification of a causal mechanism.[19] That is, X must be connected with Y in a plausible fashion; otherwise, it is unclear whether a pattern of covariation is truly causal in nature, or what the causal interaction might be. Moreover, without a clear understanding of the causal pathway(s) at work in a causal relationship, it is impossible to specify the model accurately, to identify possible instruments for the regressor of interest (if there are problems of endogeneity), or to interpret the results.[20] Thus, causal mechanisms are presumed in every estimate of a mean (average) causal effect.

In the task of investigating causal mechanisms, cross-case studies are often not so illuminating. It has become a common criticism of large-N cross-national research – for example, into the causes of growth, democracy, civil war, and other national-level outcomes – that such studies demonstrate correlations between inputs and outputs without clarifying the reasons for those correlations (i.e., clear causal pathways). We learn,

---

[17] The correct estimation of a causal effect rests upon the optimal choice among possible estimators. It therefore follows from the previous discussion that sample-based analyses are also essential for choosing among different estimators – as judged by their relative efficiency and bias, among other desiderata. See Kennedy (2003) for a discussion of these issues.

[18] Note that the intensive study of a single unit may be a perfectly appropriate way to estimate causal effects *within that unit*. Thus, if one is interested in the relationship between welfare benefits and work effort in the United States, one might obtain a more accurate assessment by examining data drawn from the United States alone, rather than cross-nationally. However, since the resulting generalization does not extend beyond the unit in question, this is not a case study in the usual sense.

[19] Achen (2002); Dessler (1991); Elster (1998); George and Bennett (2005); Gerring (2005); Hedstrom and Swedberg (1998); Mahoney (2001); Tilly (2001).

[20] In a discussion of instrumental variables in two-stage least squares analysis, Angrist and Krueger (2001: 8) note that "good instruments often come from detailed knowledge of the economic mechanism, institutions determining the regressor of interest."

for example, that infant mortality is strongly correlated with state failure;[21] but it is quite another matter to interpret this finding, which is consistent with a number of different causal mechanisms. Sudden increases in infant mortality might be the product of famine, of social unrest, of new disease vectors, of government repression, and of countless other factors, some of which might be expected to impact the stability of states, and others of which are more likely to be a result of state instability.

Case studies, if well constructed, may allow one to peer into the box of causality to locate the intermediate factors lying between some structural cause and its purported effect. Ideally, they allow one to "see" X and Y interact – Hume's billiard ball crossing the table and hitting a second ball.[22] Barney Glaser and Anselm Strauss point out that in field work "general relations are often discovered *in vivo*; that is, the field worker literally sees them occur."[23] When studying decisional behavior, case study research may offer insight into the intentions, the reasoning capabilities, and the information-processing procedures of the actors involved in a given setting. Thus, Dennis Chong uses in-depth interviews with a very small sample of respondents in order to better understand the process by which people reach decisions about civil liberties issues. Chong comments:

One of the advantages of the in-depth interview over the mass survey is that it records more fully how subjects arrive at their opinions. While we cannot actually observe the underlying mental process that gives rise to their responses, we can witness many of its outward manifestations. The way subjects ramble, hesitate, stumble, and meander as they formulate their answers tips us off to how they are thinking and reasoning through political issues.[24]

Similarly, the investigation of a single case may allow one to test the causal implications of a theory, thus providing corroborating evidence for a causal argument. This is sometimes referred to as pattern matching (see Chapter Seven).

One example of case study evidence calling into question a general theoretical argument on the basis of an investigation of causal mechanisms concerns the theory of rational deterrence. Deterrence theory, as

---

[21] Goldstone et al. (2000).

[22] This has something to do with the existence of process-tracing evidence, a matter to be discussed later. But it is not necessarily predicated on this sort of evidence. Sensitive time-series data, another specialty of the case study, is also relevant to the question of causal mechanisms.

[23] Glaser and Strauss (1967: 40).

[24] Chong (1993: 868). For other examples of in-depth interviewing, see Hochschild (1981) and Lane (1962).

it was understood in the 1980s, presupposes a number of key assumptions, namely, that "actors have exogenously given preferences and choice options, and [that] they seek to optimize preferences in light of other actors' preferences and options..., [that] variation in outcomes is to be explained by differences in actors' opportunities..., and [that] the state acts as if it were a unitary rational actor."[25] A generation of case studies, however, suggests that, somewhat contrary to theory, (a) international actors often employ "shortcuts" in their decision-making processes (i.e., they do not make decisions de novo, based purely on an analysis of preferences and possible consequences); (b) a strong cognitive bias exists because of "historical analogies to recent important cases that the person or his country has experienced firsthand" (e.g., "Somalia = Vietnam"); (c) "accidents and confusion" are often manifest in international crises; (d) a single important value or goal often trumps other values (in a hasty and ill-considered manner); and (e) actors' impressions of other actors are strongly influenced by their self-perceptions (information is highly imperfect). In addition to these cognitive biases, there is a series of psychological biases.[26] In sum, while the theory of deterrence may still hold, the causal pathways contained in this theory seem to be considerably more variegated than previous work based on cross-case research had led us to believe. In-depth studies of particular international incidents have been helpful in uncovering these complexities.[27]

Dietrich Rueschemeyer and John Stephens offer a second example of how an examination of causal mechanisms may call into question a general theory based on cross-case evidence. The thesis of interest concerns the role of British colonialism in fostering democracy among post-colonial regimes. In particular, the authors investigate the diffusion hypothesis, that democracy was enhanced by "the transfer of British governmental and representative institutions and the tutoring of the colonial people in the ways of British government." On the basis of in-depth analysis of several cases, the authors report:

We did find evidence of this diffusion effect in the British settler colonies of North America and the Antipodes; but in the West Indies, the historical record points to a different connection between British rule and democracy. There the British colonial administration opposed suffrage extension, and only the white elites were

---

[25] Achen and Snidal (1989: 150).

[26] Jervis (1989: 196). See also George and Smoke (1974).

[27] George and Smoke (1974: 504). For another example of case study work that tests theories based upon predictions about causal mechanisms, see McKeown (1983).

'tutored' in the representative institutions. But, critically, we argued on the basis of the contrast with Central America, British colonialism did prevent the local plantation elites from controlling the local state and responding to the labor rebellion of the 1930s with massive repression. Against the adamant opposition of that elite, the British colonial rulers responded with concessions which allowed for the growth of the party-union complexes rooted in the black middle and working classes, which formed the backbone of the later movement for democracy and independence. Thus, the narrative histories of these cases indicate that the robust statistical relation between British colonialism and democracy is produced only in part by diffusion. The interaction of class forces, state power, and colonial policy must be brought in to fully account for the statistical result.[28]

Whether or not Rueschemeyer and Stephens are correct in their conclusions need not concern us here. What is critical, however, is that any attempt to deal with this question of causal mechanisms is heavily reliant on evidence drawn from case studies. In this instance, as in many others, the question of causal pathways is simply too difficult, requiring too many poorly measured or unmeasurable variables, to allow for accurate cross-sectional analysis.[29]

To be sure, causal mechanisms do not always require explicit attention. They may be quite obvious. And in other circumstances, they may be amenable to cross-case investigation. For example, a sizeable literature addresses the causal relationship between trade openness and the welfare state. The usual empirical finding is that more open economies are associated with greater social welfare spending. The question then

---

[28] Rueschemeyer and Stephens (1997: 62).

[29] A third example of case study analysis focused on causal mechanisms concerns policy delegation within coalition governments. Michael Thies (2001) tests two theories about how parties delegate power. The first, known as *ministerial government*, supposes that parties delegate ministerial portfolios in toto to one of their members (the party whose minister holds the portfolio). The second theory, dubbed *managed delegation*, supposes that members of a multiparty coalition delegate power, but also actively monitor the activity of ministerial posts held by other parties. The critical piece of evidence used to test these rival theories is the appointment of junior ministers (JMs). If JMs are from the same party as the minister, we can assume that the ministerial government model is in operation. If the JMs are from different parties, Thies infers that a managed delegation model is in operation, where the JM is assumed to perform an oversight function regarding the activity of the bureau in question. This empirical question is explored across four countries – Germany, Italy, Japan, and the Netherlands – providing a series of case studies focused on the internal workings of parliamentary government. (I have simplified the nature of the evidence in this example, which extends not only to the simple presence or absence of cross-partisan JMs but also to a variety of additional process-tracing clues.) Other good examples of within-case research that shed light on a broader theory can be found in Canon (1999); Martin (1992); Martin and Swank (2004); and Young (1999).

LIBRARY, UNIVERSITY OF CHESTER

becomes why such a robust correlation exists. What are the plausible interconnections between trade openness and social welfare spending? One possible causal path, suggested by David Cameron,[30] is that increased trade openness leads to greater domestic economic vulnerability to external shocks (due, for instance, to changing terms of trade). If that is true, one should find a robust correlation between annual variations in a country's terms of trade (a measure of economic vulnerability) and social welfare spending. As it happens, the correlation is not robust, and this leads some commentators to doubt whether the putative causal mechanism proposed by David Cameron and many others is actually at work.[31] Thus, in instances where an intervening variable can be effectively operationalized across a large sample of cases, it may be possible to test causal mechanisms without resorting to case study investigation.[32]

Even so, the opportunities for investigating causal pathways are generally more apparent in a case study format. Consider the contrast between formulating a standardized survey for a large group of respondents and formulating an in-depth interview with a single subject or a small set of subjects, such as that undertaken by Dennis Chong in the previous example. In the latter situation, the researcher is able to probe into details that would be impossible to delve into, let alone anticipate, in a standardized survey. She may also be in a better position to make judgments as to the veracity and reliability of the respondent. Tracing causal mechanisms is about cultivating sensitivity to a local context. Often, these local contexts are essential to cross-case testing. Yet the same factors that render case studies useful for micro-level investigation also make them less useful for measuring mean (average) causal effects. It is a classic trade-off.

Scope of Proposition: Deep versus Broad

The utility of a case study mode of analysis is in part a product of the scope of the causal argument that a researcher wishes to prove or demonstrate. Arguments that strive for great breadth are usually in greater need of cross-case evidence; causal arguments restricted to a small set of cases can more plausibly subsist on the basis of a single-case study. The extensive/intensive trade-off is fairly commonsensical.[33] A case study of France probably

---

[30] Cameron (1978).

[31] Alesina, Glaeser, and Sacerdote (2001).

[32] For additional examples of this nature, see Feng (2003); Papyrakis and Gerlagh (2003); and Ross (2001).

[33] Eckstein (1975: 122).

offers more useful evidence for an argument about Europe than for an argument about the whole world. Propositional breadth and evidentiary breadth generally go hand in hand.

Granted, there are a variety of ways in which single-case studies can credibly claim to provide evidence for causal propositions of broad reach – for example, by choosing cases that are especially representative of the phenomenon under study ("typical" cases) or by choosing cases that represent the most difficult scenario for a given proposition and are thus biased against the attainment of certain results ("crucial" cases), as discussed in Chapter Five. Even so, a proposition with a narrow scope is more conducive to case study analysis than a proposition with a broad purview, all other things being equal. The breadth of an inference thus constitutes one factor, among many, in determining the utility of the case study mode of analysis. This is reflected in the hesitancy of many case study researchers to invoke determinate causal propositions with great reach – "covering laws," in the idiom of philosophy of science.

By the same token, one of the primary virtues of the case study method is the depth of analysis that it offers. One may think of depth as referring to the detail, richness, completeness, wholeness, or the degree of variance in an outcome that is accounted for by an explanation. The case study researcher's complaint about the thinness of cross-case analysis is well taken; such studies often have little to say about individual cases. Otherwise stated, cross-case studies are likely to explain only a small portion of the variance with respect to a given outcome. They approach that outcome at a very general level. Typically, a cross-case study aims only to explain the occurrence/nonoccurrence of a revolution, while a case study might also strive to explain specific features of that event – why it occurred when it did and in the way that it did. Case studies are thus rightly identified with "holistic" analysis and with the "thick" description of events.[34]

Whether to strive for breadth or depth is not a question that can be answered in any definitive way. All we can safely conclude is that researchers invariably face a choice between knowing more about less, or less about more. The case study method may be defended, as well as criticized, along these lines.[35] Indeed, arguments about the "contextual sensitivity" of case studies are perhaps more precisely (and fairly) understood as arguments about depth and breadth. The case study researcher who

---

[34] My use of the term "thick" is somewhat different from the usage in Geertz (1973).
[35] See Ragin (2000: 22).

feels that cross-case research on a topic is insensitive to context is usually not arguing that *nothing at all* is consistent across the chosen cases. Rather, the case study researcher's complaint is that much more could be said – accurately – about the phenomenon in question with a reduction in inferential scope.[36]

Indeed, I believe that a number of traditional issues related to case study research can be understood as the product of this basic trade-off. For example, case study research is often lauded for its holistic approach to the study of social phenomena in which behavior is observed in natural settings. Cross-case research, by contrast, is criticized for its construction of artificial research designs that decontextualize the realm of social behavior by employing abstract variables that seem to bear slight relationship to the phenomena of interest.[37] These associated congratulations and critiques may be understood as a conscious choice on the part of case study researchers to privilege depth over breadth.

The Population of Cases: Heterogeneous versus Homogeneous

The choice between a case study and cross-case style of analysis is driven not only by the goals of the researcher, as just reviewed, but also by the shape of the empirical universe that the researcher is attempting to understand. Consider, for starters, that the logic of cross-case analysis is premised on some degree of cross-unit comparability (unit homogeneity). Cases must be similar to each other in whatever respects might affect the causal relationship that the writer is investigating, or such differences must be controlled for. Uncontrolled heterogeneity means that cases are "apples and oranges"; one cannot learn anything about underlying causal processes by comparing their histories. The underlying factors of interest mean different things in different contexts (conceptual stretching), or the X/Y relationship of interest is different in different contexts (unit heterogeneity).

Case study researchers are often suspicious of large-sample research, which, they suspect, contains heterogeneous cases whose differences cannot easily be modeled. "Variable-oriented" research is said to involve unrealistic "homogenizing assumptions."[38] In the field of international

---

[36] Ragin (1987: Chapter 2). Herbert Blumer's (1969: Chapter 7) complaints, however, are more far-reaching.

[37] Orum, Feagin, and Sjoberg (1991: 7).

[38] Ragin (2000: 35). See also Abbott (1990); Bendix (1963); Meehl (1954); Przeworski and Teune (1970: 8–9); Ragin (1987; 2004: 124); Znaniecki (1934: 250–1).

relations, for example, it is common to classify cases according to whether they are deterrence failures or deterrence successes. However, Alexander George and Richard Smoke point out that "the separation of the dependent variable into only two subclasses, deterrence success and deterrence failure," neglects the great variety of ways in which deterrence can fail. Deterrence, in their view, has many independent causal paths (causal equifinality), and these paths may be obscured when a study lumps heterogeneous cases into a common sample.[39]

Another example, drawn from clinical work in psychology, concerns heterogeneity among a sample of individuals. Michel Hersen and David Barlow explain:

Descriptions of results from 50 cases provide a more convincing demonstration of the effectiveness of a given technique than separate descriptions of 50 individual cases. The major difficulty with this approach, however, is that the category in which these clients are classified most always becomes unmanageably heterogeneous. 'Neurotics,' [for example],... may have less in common than any group of people one would choose randomly. When cases are described individually, however, a clinician stands a better chance of gleaning some important information, since specific problems and specific procedures are usually described in more detail. When one lumps cases together in broadly defined categories, individual case descriptions are lost and the ensuing report of percentage success becomes meaningless.[40]

Under circumstances of extreme case-heterogeneity, the researcher may decide that she is better off focusing on a single case or a small number of relatively homogeneous cases. Within-case evidence, or cross-case evidence drawn from a handful of most-similar cases, may be more useful than cross-case evidence, even though the ultimate interest of the investigator is in a broader population of cases. Suppose one has a population of very heterogeneous cases, one or two of which undergo quasi-experimental transformations. Probably, one gains greater insight into causal patterns throughout the population by examining these cases in detail than by undertaking a large-N cross-case analysis. By the same token, if the cases available for study are relatively homogeneous, then the methodological argument for cross-case analysis is correspondingly strong. The inclusion of additional cases is unlikely to compromise the results of the investigation, because these additional cases are sufficiently similar to provide useful information.

[39] George and Smoke (1974: 514).
[40] Hersen and Barlow (1976: 11).

The issue of population heterogeneity/homogeneity may be under-stood, therefore, as a trade-off between N (observations) and K (vari-ables). If, in the quest to explain a particular phenomenon, each potential case offers only one observation and also requires one control variable (to neutralize heterogeneities in the resulting sample), then one loses degrees of freedom with each additional case. There is no point in using cross-case analysis or in extending a two-case study to further cases. If, on the other hand, each additional case is relatively cheap – if no control variables are needed, or if the additional case offers more than one useful observation (through time) – then a cross-case research design may be warranted.[41] To put the matter more simply, when adjacent cases are unit-homogeneous, the addition of more cases is easy, for there is no (or very little) het-erogeneity to model. When adjacent cases are heterogeneous, additional cases are expensive, for every added heterogeneous element must be cor-rectly modeled, and each modeling adjustment requires a separate (and probably unverifiable) assumption. The more background assumptions are required in order to make a causal inference, the more tenuous that inference is. This is not simply a question of attaining statistical signifi-cance. The ceteris paribus assumption at the core of all causal analysis is brought into question (see Chapter 6). In any case, the argument between case study and cross-case research designs is not about causal complexity per se (in the sense in which this concept is usually employed), but rather about the trade-off between N and K in a particular empirical realm, and about the ability to model case-heterogeneity through statistical legerdemain.[42]

Before concluding this discussion, it is important to point out that researchers' judgments about case comparability are not, strictly speak-ing, matters that can be empirically verified. To be sure, one can look – and ought to look – for empirical patterns among potential cases. If those patterns are strong, then the assumption of case comparability seems reasonably secure; and if they are not, then there are grounds for doubt. However, debates about case comparability usually concern borderline instances. Consider that many phenomena of interest to social scientists are not rigidly bounded. If one is studying democracies, there is always

---

[41] Shalev (1998).

[42] To be sure, if adjacent cases are *identical*, the phenomenon of interest is *invariant*. In that case the researcher gains nothing at all by studying more examples of a phenomenon, for the results obtained with the first case will simply be replicated. However, virtually all phenomena of interest to social scientists has some degree of heterogeneity (cases are not identical), some stochastic element. Thus, the theoretical possibility of identical, invariant cases is rarely met in practice.

a question of how to define a democracy, and therefore of determining how high or low the threshold for inclusion in the sample should be. Researchers have different ideas about this, and these ideas can hardly be tested in a rigorous fashion. Similarly, there are long-standing disputes about whether it makes sense to lump poor and rich societies together in a single sample, or whether these constitute distinct populations. Again, the borderline between poor and rich (or "developed" and "undeveloped") is blurry, and the notion of hiving off one from the other for separate analysis questionable, and unresolvable on purely empirical grounds. There is no safe (or "conservative") way to proceed. A final sticking point concerns the cultural/historical component of social phenomena. Many case study researchers feel that to compare societies with vastly different cultures and historical trajectories is meaningless. Yet many cross-case researchers feel that to restrict one's analytic focus to a single cultural or geographic region is highly arbitrary, and equally meaningless. In these situations, it is evidently the choice of the researcher how to understand case homogeneity/heterogeneity across the potential populations of an inference. Where do like cases end and unlike cases begin?

Because this issue is not, strictly speaking, empirical, it may be referred to as an *ontological* element of research design. An ontology is a vision of the world as it really is, a more or less coherent set of assumptions about how the world works, a research *Weltanschauung* analogous to a Kuhnian paradigm.[43] While it seems odd to bring ontological issues into a discussion of social science methodology, it may be granted that social science research is not a purely empirical endeavor. What one finds is contingent upon what one looks for, and what one looks for is to some extent contingent upon what one expects to find. Stereotypically, case study researchers tend to have a "lumpy" vision of the world; they see countries, communities, and persons as highly individualized phenomena. Cross-case researchers, by contrast, have a less differentiated vision of the world; they are more likely to believe that things are pretty much the same everywhere, at least as respects basic causal processes. These basic assumptions, or ontologies, drive many of the choices made by researchers when scoping out appropriate ground for research.

Causal Strength: Strong versus Weak

Regardless of whether the population is homogeneous or heterogeneous, relationships are easier to study if the true causal effect is strong, rather

---

[43] Gutting (1980); Hall (2003); Kuhn (1962/1970); Wolin (1968).

than weak. Causal "strength" refers here to the magnitude and consistency of X's effect on Y across a population of cases. (It involves both the shape of the evidence at hand and whatever priors might be relevant to an interpretation of that evidence.) Where X_1 has a strong effect on Y it will be relatively easy to study this relationship. Weak relationships, by contrast, are often difficult to discern. This much is commonsensical, and applies to all research designs.

For our purposes, what is significant is that weak causal relationships are particularly opaque when encountered in a case study format. Thus, there is a methodological affinity between weak causal relationships and large-N cross-case analysis, and between strong causal relationships and case study analysis.

This point is clearest at the extremes. The strongest species of causal relationships may be referred to as *deterministic*, where X is assumed to be necessary and/or sufficient for Y's occurrence. A necessary and sufficient cause accounts for all of the variation on Y. A sufficient cause accounts for all of the variation in certain instances of Y. A necessary cause accounts, by itself, for the absence of Y. In all three situations, the relationship is usually assumed to be perfectly consistent, that is, invariant. There are no exceptions.

It should be clear why case study research designs have an easier time addressing causes of this type. Consider that a deterministic causal proposition can be *dis*proved with a single case.[44] For example, the reigning theory of political stability once stipulated that only in countries that were relatively homogeneous, or where existing heterogeneity was mitigated by cross-cutting cleavages, would social peace endure.[45] Arend Lijphart's case study of the Netherlands, a country with reinforcing social cleavages and very little social conflict, disproved this deterministic theory on the basis of a single case.[46] (One may dispute whether the original theory is correctly understood as deterministic. However, if it *is*, then it has been decisively refuted by a single case study.) *Proving* an invariant causal argument generally requires more cases. However, it is not nearly as complicated as proving a probabilistic argument, for the simple reason that one assumes invariant relationships; consequently, the single case under study carries more weight. Stochastic variation is ruled out.

[44] Dion (1998).

[45] Almond (1956); Bentley (1908/1967); Lipset (1960/1963); Truman (1951).

[46] Lijphart (1968); see also Lijphart (1969). For additional examples of case studies disconfirming general propositions of a deterministic nature, see Allen (1965); Lipset, Trow, and Coleman (1956); Njolstad (1990); and the discussion in Rogowski (1995).

Magnitude and consistency – the two components of causal strength – are usually matters of degree. It follows that the more tenuous the connection between X and Y, the more difficult it will be to address in a case study format. This is because the causal mechanisms connecting X with Y are less likely to be detectable in a single case when the total impact is slight or highly irregular. It is no surprise, therefore, that the case study research design has, from the very beginning, been associated with causal arguments that are deterministic, while cross-case research has been associated with causal arguments that are assumed to be slight and highly probabilistic.[47] (Strictly speaking, magnitude and consistency are independent features of a causal relationship. However, because they tend to covary, and because we tend to conceptualize them in tandem, I treat them as components of a single dimension.)

Now, let us consider an example drawn from the other extreme. There is generally assumed to be a weak relationship between regime type and economic performance. Democracy, if it has any effect on economic growth at all, probably has only a slight effect over the near to medium term, and this effect is probably characterized by many exceptions (cases that do not fit the general pattern). This is because many things other than democracy affect a country's growth performance, and because there may be a significant stochastic component in economic growth (factors that cannot be modeled in a general way). Because of the diffuse nature of this relationship it will probably be difficult to gain insight by looking at a single case. Weak relationships are difficult to observe in one instance. Note that even if there seems to be a strong relationship between democracy and economic growth in a given country, it may be questioned whether this case is typical of the larger population of interest, given that we have already stipulated that the typical magnitude of this relationship is diminutive and irregular. Of course, the weakness of democracy's presumed relationship to growth is also a handicap in cross-case analysis. A good deal of criticism has been directed toward studies of this type, where findings are rarely robust.[48] Even so, it seems clear that if there *is* a relationship between democracy and growth, it is more likely to be perceptible in a cross-case setting. The positive hypothesis, as well as the null hypothesis, is better approached in a sample rather than in a case.

[47] Znaniecki (1934). See also the discussion in Robinson (1951).
[48] Kittel (1999, 2005); Kittel and Winner (2005); Levine and Renelt (1992); Temple (1999).

Useful Variation: Rare versus Common

When analyzing causal relationships, we must be concerned not only with the strength of an X/Y relationship but also with the distribution of evidence across available cases. Specifically, we must be concerned with the distribution of *useful variation* – understood as variation (temporal or spatial) on relevant parameters that might yield clues about a causal relationship. It follows that where useful variation is rare – that is, limited to a few cases – the case study format recommends itself. Where, on the other hand, useful variation is common, a cross-case method of analysis may be more defensible.

Consider a phenomenon like social revolution, an outcome that occurs very rarely. The empirical distribution on this variable, if we count each country-year as an observation, consists of thousands of nonrevolutions and just a few revolutions. Intuitively, it seems clear that the few "revolutionary" cases are of great interest. We need to know as much as possible about them, for they exemplify all the variation that we have at our disposal. In this circumstance, a case study mode of analysis is difficult to avoid, though it might be combined with a large-N cross-case analysis. As it happens, many outcomes of interest to social scientists are quite rare, so the issue is by no means trivial.[49]

By way of contrast, consider a phenomenon like turnover, understood as a situation where a ruling party or coalition is voted out of office. Turnover occurs within most democratic countries on a regular basis, so the distribution of observations on this variable (incumbency/turnover) is relatively even across the universe of country-years. There are lots of instances of both outcomes. Under these circumstances a cross-case research design seems plausible, for the variation across cases is evenly distributed.

Another sort of variation concerns that which might occur *within* a given case. Suppose that only one or two cases within a large population exhibit quasi-experimental qualities: the factor of special interest (X)

---

[49] Consider the following topics and their – extremely rare – instances of variation: early industrialization (England, the Netherlands); fascism (Germany, Italy); the use of nuclear weapons (United States); world war (World War I, World War II); single nontransferable vote electoral systems (Jordan, Taiwan, Vanuatu, pre-reform Japan); electoral system reforms within established democracies (France, Italy, Japan, New Zealand, Thailand). The problem of "rareness" is less common where parameters are scalar rather than dichotomous. But there are still plenty of examples of phenomena whose distributions are skewed by a few outliers, e.g., population (China, India); personal wealth (Bill Gates, Warren Buffett); ethnic heterogeneity (Papua New Guinea).

varies, and there is no corresponding change in other factors that might affect the outcome. (The quasi-experimental qualities of the case may be the result of a manipulated treatment or a treatment that occurs naturally. These issues are explored in Chapter Six.) Clearly, we are likely to learn a great deal from studying this particular case – perhaps a lot more than we might learn from studying hundreds of additional cases that deviate from the experimental ideal. But again, if many cases have this experimental quality, there is little point in restricting ourselves to a single example; a cross-case research design may be justified.

A final sort of variation concerns the characteristics exhibited by a case relative to a particular theory that is under investigation. Suppose that a case provides a "crucial" test for a theory: it fits that theory's predictions so perfectly and so precisely that no other explanation could plausibly account for the performance of the case. If no other crucial cases present themselves, then an intensive study of this particular case is de rigueur. Of course, if many such cases lie within the population, then it may be possible to study them all at once (with some sort of numeric reduction of the relevant parameters).

The general point here is that the distribution of useful variation across a population of cases matters a great deal in the choice between case study and cross-case research designs. (Many of the issues discussed in Chapters Five and Six are relevant to this discussion of what constitutes "useful variation." Thus, I have touched upon these issues only briefly in this section.)

Data Availability

I have left the most prosaic factor for last. Sometimes, one's choice of research design is driven by the quality and quantity of information that is currently available, or could easily be gathered, on a given question. This is a practical matter and is separate from the actual shape of the empirical universe. It concerns, rather, what we know about the former at a given point in time.[50] The question of evidence may be posed as follows: how much do we know about the cases at hand that might be relevant to the causal question of interest, and how precise, certain, and case-comparable is that data? An evidence-rich environment is one where all relevant factors are measurable, where these measurements are

---

[50] Of course, what we know about the potential cases is not independent of the underlying reality; it is, nonetheless, not entirely dependent on that reality.

relatively precise, where they are rendered in comparable terms across cases, and where one can be relatively confident that the information is indeed accurate. An evidence-poor environment is the opposite.

The question of available evidence impinges upon choices in research design when one considers its distribution across a population of cases. If relevant information is concentrated in a single case, or if it is contained in incommensurable formats across a population of cases, then a case study mode of analysis is almost unavoidable. But if it is evenly distributed across the population – that is, if we are equally well-informed about all cases – and is case-comparable, then there is little to recommend a narrow focus. (I employ data, evidence, and information as synonyms in this section.)

Consider the simplest sort of example, where information is truly limited to one or a few cases. Accurate historical data on infant mortality and other indices of human development are currently available for only a handful of countries (these include Chile, Egypt, India, Jamaica, Mauritius, Sri Lanka, the United States, and several European countries).[51] This data problem is not likely to be rectified in future years, as it is exceedingly difficult to measure infant mortality except by public or private records. Consequently, anyone studying this general subject is likely to rely heavily on these cases, where in-depth analysis is possible and profitable. Indeed, it is not clear whether *any* large-N cross-case analysis is possible prior to the twentieth century. Here, a case study format is virtually prescribed, and a cross-case format proscribed.

Other problems of evidence are more subtle. Let us dwell for the moment on the question of data comparability. In their study of social security spending, Mulligan, Gil, and Sala-i-Martin note that

> although our spending and design numbers are of good quality, there are some missing observations and, even with all the observations, it is difficult to reduce the variety of elderly subsidies to one or two numbers. For this reason, case studies are an important part of our analysis, since those studies do not require numbers that are comparable across a large number of countries. Our case study analysis utilizes data from a variety of country-specific sources, so we do not have to reduce 'social security' or 'democracy' to one single number.[52]

Here, the incommensurability of the evidence militates in favor of a case study format. In the event that the authors (or subsequent analysts) discover a coding system that provides reasonably valid cross-case measures

---

[51] Gerring (2006c).
[52] Mulligan, Gil, Sala-i-Martin (2002: 13).

of social security, democracy, and other relevant concepts, then our state of knowledge about the subject is changed, and a cross-case research design is rendered more plausible.

Importantly, the state of evidence on a topic is never entirely fixed. Investigators may gather additional data, recode existing data, or discover new repositories of data. Thus, when discussing the question of evidence, one must consider the quality and quantity of evidence that *could* be gathered on a given question, given sufficient time and resources. Here it is appropriate to observe that collecting new data, and correcting existing data, is usually easier in a case study format than in a large-N cross-case format. It will be difficult to rectify data problems if one's cases number in the hundreds or thousands. There are simply too many data points to allow for this.

One might consider this issue in the context of recent work on democracy. There is general skepticism among scholars with respect to the viability of extant global indicators intended to capture this complex concept (e.g., the data gathered by Freedom House and by the Polity dataset).[53] Measurement error, aggregation problems, and questions of conceptual validity are rampant. When dealing with a single country or a single continent, it is possible to overcome some of these faults by manually recoding the countries of interest.[54] The case study format often gives the researcher an opportunity to fact check, to consult multiple sources, to go back to primary materials, and to overcome whatever biases may affect the secondary literature. Needless to say, this is not a feasible approach for an individual investigator if one's project encompasses every country in the world. The best one can usually manage, under the circumstances, is some form of convergent validation (by which different indices of the same concept are compared) or small adjustments in the coding intended to correct for aggregation problems or measurement error.[55]

For the same reason, the collection of original data is typically more difficult in cross-case analysis than in case study analysis, involving greater expense, greater difficulties in identifying and coding cases, learning foreign languages, traveling, and so forth. Whatever can be done for a set of cases can usually be done more easily for a single case.

---

[53] Bollen (1993); Bowman, Lehoucq, and Mahoney (2005); Munck and Verkuilen (2002); Treier and Jackman (2005).

[54] Bowman, Lehoucq, and Mahoney (2005).

[55] Bollen (1993); Treier and Jackman (2005).

It should be kept in mind that many of the countries of concern to anthropologists, economists, historians, political scientists, and sociologists are still terra incognita. Outside the OECD, and with the exception of a few large countries that have received careful attention from scholars (e.g., India, Brazil, China), most countries of the world are not well covered by the social science literature. Any statement that one might wish to make about, say, Botswana will be difficult to verify if one has recourse only to secondary materials. And these – very limited – secondary sources are not necessarily of the most reliable sort. Thus, if one wishes to say something about political patterns obtaining in roughly 90 percent of the world's countries, and if one wishes to go beyond matters that can be captured in standard statistics collected by the World Bank and the IMF and other agencies (and these can also be very sketchy when lesser-studied countries are concerned), one is more or less obliged to conduct a case study. Of course, one could, in principle, gather similar information across all relevant cases. However, such an enterprise faces formidable logistical difficulties. Thus, for practical reasons, case studies are sometimes the most defensible alternative when the researcher is faced with an information-poor environment.

However, this point is easily turned on its head. Datasets are now available to study many problems of concern to the social sciences. Thus, it may not be necessary to collect original information for one's book, article, or dissertation. Sometimes in-depth single-case analysis is more time-consuming than cross-case analysis. If so, there is no informational advantage to a case study format. Indeed, it may be easier to utilize existing information for a cross-case analysis, particularly when a case study format imposes hurdles of its own – travel to distant climes, risk of personal injury, expense, and so forth. It is interesting to note that some observers consider case studies to be "relatively *more* expensive in time and resources."[56]

Whatever the specific logistical hurdles, it is a general truth that the shape of the evidence – that which is currently available and that which might feasibly be collected by an author – often has a strong influence on an investigator's choice of research design. Where the evidence for particular cases is richer and more accurate, there is a strong prima facie argument for a case study format focused on those cases. Where, by contrast, the relevant evidence is equally good for all potential cases, and is

[56] Stoecker (1991: 91).

comparable across those cases, there is no reason to shy away from cross-case analysis. Indeed, there may be little to gain from case study formats.

Causal Complexity

Not all factors that impinge upon the choice of research designs have clear affinities to case study or cross-case study research. Others are indeterminate in their implications. Whether these factors favor the focused analysis of a few cases or a relatively superficial analysis of many cases depends upon issues that are difficult to generalize about.

Let us begin with the vexed question of *causal complexity*. Case study researchers often laud their favored method for its better grasp of complex causes,[57] while critics claim that the more complex the causal relationship, the more necessary is cross-case evidence.[58] Intuitively, both positions seem plausible, and much evidently depends upon the interpretation of "complexity," which might refer to probabilistic (rather than invariant) causal patterns, necessary and/or sufficient causes, nonlinear relationships, multiple causes ("equifinality"), nonadditive causal interrelationships, causal sequences (where causal order affects the outcome of interest), a large number of plausible causes (the problem of overdetermination), and many other things besides. Indeed, "complexity," as the term is used in social science circles, seems to refer to any feature of a causal problem that does not fit snugly with standard assumptions of linearity, additivity, and independence. As such, it is a red herring, for it has no determinate meaning.

Some kinds of causal complexity, like necessary and sufficient conditions, may militate in favor of a case study research design, as argued earlier in this chapter (see the section on causal strength). Others, I will argue, are indeterminate. That is, sometimes complex causal relationships are rendered visible in case study research, and we are able to parse out the independent causal effects of each factor (which may depend on their position in an extended causal chain). This is what case study research does, if it is done well and if the chosen case is amenable to that style of research. But oftentimes, this is simply not feasible. Similarly, sometimes one is able to model complex causal relationships in a cross-case setting, and sometimes not. In short, it all depends.

[57] Abbott (1990); George and Bennett (2005); Ragin (1987: 54; 2000: Chapter 4); Rueschemeyer (2003).
[58] Goldthorpe (1997); King, Keohane, and Verba (1994); Lieberson (1985).

Let us explore an example. Suppose one is interested in the influence of fiscal pressures on social revolution – the idea that as governments get more strapped for cash, they are likely to seek to raise taxes, which, in turn, may spark revolt. A nice (confirming) case study would show precisely that, without any interfering (confounding) factors. It would be eventful, in a quasi-experimental way (see Chapter Six). An intervention (treatment) would occur – increasing budget deficits, followed by increasing taxes – and the result could be observed. However, a bad (confirming) case would show that lots of things were happening at the same time that could also have caused revolution. As it happens, lots of things do tend to happen together during critical junctures like revolutions, and so it is often quite difficult to tease out real and spurious causal effects. In statistical terms, this may be understood as a problem of collinearity. Now, let us suppose that you have at your disposal 100 countries, with annual measurements of fiscal pressure, tax instruments, as well as various confounders (controls). Collinearity is still a formidable problem. But with a great deal of cross-case evidence, there is at least a fighting chance that it can be overcome, while there is little chance of overcoming it in most case study settings. (Indeed, some statisticians have looked upon the problem of collinearity as a problem of data insufficiency.)

The general point remains. "Complexity," by itself (keeping in mind that complexity can mean many things), does not favor either a case study or a cross-case approach to causal analysis.

The State of the Field

Another sort of contextual consideration concerns the state of research on a given topic within a field. Social scientists are accustomed to the idea that research occurs within the context of an ongoing tradition. All work is dependent for the identification of topic, argument, and evidence on this research tradition. What we need to know, and hence ought to study, is to some extent contingent upon what is already known. It follows from this that the utility of case study research relative to non–case study research is to some extent the product of the state of research within a given field. A field dominated by case studies may have little need for another case study. A field where cross-case studies are hegemonic may be desperately in need of in-depth studies focused on understudied cases.

Indeed, much of the debate over the utility of the case study method has little to do with the method itself and more to do with the state of current research in a particular field. If both case study and cross-case methods have much to recommend them (an implicit assumption of this book), then both ought to be pursued – perhaps not in equal measure, but at least with equal diligence and respect. There is no virtue, and potentially great harm, in pursuing one approach to the exclusion of the other, or in ghettoizing the practitioners of the minority approach. The triangulation essential to social scientific advance demands the employment of a variety of (viable) methods, including the case study. But there is little that we can say about this desideratum in general, since it depends on the shape of an individual field or subfield.

PART II

DOING CASE STUDIES

In the opening pages of this book, I highlighted the rather severe disjuncture that has opened up between an often-maligned methodology and a heavily practiced method. The case study is disrespected, but nonetheless regularly employed. Indeed, it remains the workhorse of most disciplines and subfields in the social sciences, as demonstrated in Chapter One. How, then, can one make sense of this discrepancy between methodological theory and methodological praxis? This was the question animating Part One of the book.

The torment of the case study begins with its definitional penumbra, as described in Chapter Two. Frequently, this key term is conflated with a disparate set of methodological traits that are not definitionally entailed. Our first task, therefore, was to craft a narrower and more useful concept for purposes of methodological discussion. The case study, I argued, is best defined as an intensive study of a single case (or a small set of cases) with an aim to generalize across a larger set of cases of the same general type. If the inference pertains to nation-states, then a case study would focus on one or several nation-states (while a cross-case study would focus on many nation-states at once). If the inference pertains to individuals, then a case study would focus on one or several individuals (while a cross-case study would focus on many individuals at once). And so forth.

It follows from this definition that case studies may be small- or large-N (since a single case may provide few or many observations), qualitative or quantitative, experimental or observational, synchronic or diachronic. It also follows that the case study research design comports with any macrotheoretical framework or paradigm – for example, behavioralism, rational choice, institutionalism, or interpretivism. It is not epistemologically distinct.[1] What differentiates the case study from the cross-case study is simply its way of defining observations, not its analysis of those observations or its method of modeling causal relations. The case study research design constructs its observations from a single case or a small number of cases, while cross-case research designs construct observations across multiple cases. Cross-case and case study research operate, for the most part, at different levels of analysis.

In other respects, the predicament of the case study is not merely definitional but inheres in the method itself. To study a single case with intent to shed light upon other cases brings in its train several methodological ambiguities. First, the concept of a case study is dependent upon the particular proposition that one has in mind, a proposition that may change through time (as the study is digested by the academic community) or even within a given study (as the author changes her level of analysis). Second, the boundaries of a case are sometimes – despite the researcher's best efforts – open-ended. This is particularly true of temporal boundaries, which may extend into the future and into the past in rather indefinite ways. Third, case studies usually build upon a variety of covariational evidence; there is no single type of case study, but rather *five* (see Table 2.4).

The travails of the case study are rooted, additionally, in an insufficient appreciation of the methodological trade-offs that this method calls forth, as discussed in Chapter Three. At least eight characteristic strengths and weaknesses must be considered (see Table 3.1). Ceteris paribus, case studies are more useful when the purpose of research is hypothesis generating rather than hypothesis testing, when internal validity is given preference over external validity, when insight into causal mechanisms is prioritized over insight into causal effects, when propositional depth is prized over breadth, when the population is heterogeneous rather than homogeneous, when causal relationships are strong rather than weak, when useful variation on key parameters is rare rather than commonplace, and when good-quality evidence is concentrated rather than dispersed. Causal complexity and the existing state of a field of research may also influence a researcher's choice to adopt a single-case or cross-case research design, though their methodological implications are equivocal.

The objective of the first section of the book was to restore a sense of meaning, purpose, and integrity to the case study method. It is hoped that

---

[1] Epistemological differences between case study and cross-case work are a theme in Orum, Feagin, and Sjoberg (1991: 22).

by offering a more carefully bounded definition of the method it might be rescued from some of its ambiguities. It is also hoped that the characteristic strengths of this method, as well as its limitations, will be more apparent to producers and consumers of case study research. The case study is a useful tool for some research objectives and in some research settings, but not all.

In the second section of the book, I turn to practical questions of research design. How does one employ the intensive study of a single case, or a small number of cases, to shed light on a broader class of cases?

Chapter Four addresses preliminary issues pertaining to this quest. Chapter Five examines the problem of case selection. Chapter Six examines the problem of internal validity through the prism of experimental research designs. Chapter Seven approaches the problem of internal validity through the use of a rather different approach called process tracing. The epilogue addresses research design elements of single-outcome studies – where a single outcome, rather than a broader class of outcomes, is of primary interest.

4

Preliminaries

Before entering into a discussion of specific research design techniques, it is important to insert a preliminary discussion of several factors that overshadow all research design issues in case study work. These include evidence-gathering techniques, the formulation of a hypothesis, degrees of falsifiability, the tension between particularizing and generalizing objectives in a case study, the identification of a population that the case study purports to represent, and the importance of cross-level research. Although these six issues affect all empirical work in the social sciences, they are particularly confusing in the context of case study work, and consequently merit our close attention.

The Evidence

The case study, I argued in Chapter Two, should not be defined by a distinctive method of data collection but rather by the goals of the research relative to the scope of the research terrain. Evidence for a case study may be drawn from an existing dataset or set of texts or may be the product of original research by the investigator. Written sources may be primary or secondary. Evidence may be quantitative, qualitative, or a mixture of both – as when qualitative observations are coded numerically so as to create a quantitative variable.[1] Evidence may be drawn from experiments (discussed in Chapter Six), from "ethnographic"

---

[1] Kritzer (1996); Stoker (2003); Theiss-Morse et al. (1991).

field research,[2] from unstructured interviews, or from highly structured surveys.[3]

In short, there are many ways to collect evidence ("data"), and none of these methods is unique to the case study. Techniques differ greatly from discipline to discipline, subfield to subfield, and topic to topic – and rightly so. To be sure, the more intensive the evidence-gathering method, the more difficult it will be to implement that technique across multiple cases. In this respect, ethnographic research is rightly identified as a case study method. Even so, there is no theoretical limit to the number of ethnographies that may be conducted by an individual, or by a group of individuals (perhaps working on a subject over several generations). Once that number has extended beyond the point where qualitative analysis is possible, some form of mathematical reduction is more or less required if an integrative approach to the population is desired. Where, for example, a great deal of textual data exists, analysts usually have recourse to content or discourse analysis.[4]

Getting the facts right is essential to doing good case study research. However, since the methods of data collection are legion, there is little that one can say, in general, about this problem.[5]

One issue deserves emphasis, however. All data requires interpretation, and in this respect all techniques of evidence gathering are *interpretive*.[6]

---

[2] The literature on ethnography (including participant observation and field research) is immense. For a brief discussion of early work in this genre, see Hamel (1993). Contemporary works in the social sciences include Becker (1958); Burawoy, Gamson, and Burton (1991); Denzin and Lincoln (2000); Emerson (1981, 2001); Fenno (1978: 249–93; 1986; 1990); Hammersley and Atkinson (1983); Jessor, Colby, and Shweder (1996); Patton (2002: 339–428); and Smith and Kornblum (1989). The technique known as ethnomethodology is laid out in Garfinkel (1967). Helper (2000) discusses the potential of field research in economics. Examples of ethnographic research in the "hard science" fields of criminology, medical science, and psychology include Athens (1997); Bosk (1981); Estroff (1985); and Katz (1999) – all cited in Rosenbaum (2004: 3). Practical advice on the conduct of field research, with special attention to foreign locations, can be found in Barrett and Cason (1997) and Lieberman, Howard, and Lynch (2004).

[3] A general introduction to survey research is provided by Dillman (1994). Gubrium and Holstein (2002) offers a comprehensive treatment of interview research.

[4] Discussion of various techniques can be found in Coulthard (1992); Hart (1997); Krippendorff (2003); Laver et al. (2003); Neuendorf (2001); Phillips and Hardy (2002); and Silverman (2001). See also "Symposium: Discourse, Content Analysis" (2004).

[5] For research on primary and secondary documents, see Thies (2002). See also Bloch (1941/1953); Elton (1970); George and Bennett (2005); Lustick (1996); Thompson (1978); Trachtenberg (2005); and Winks (1969).

[6] Interpretivist (a.k.a. hermeneutic or *Verstehen*) methods refer broadly to evidence-gathering techniques that are focused on the intentions and subjective meanings contained

Rarely, if ever, does the evidence speak for itself. There may be such things as "brute facts" – for example, Caesar crossed the Rubicon in 51B.C.[7] However, in a study oriented toward the discovery of general causes one is required to invest such acts with meaning. And this requires judgment on the part of the investigator.

Note that the social sciences are defined by their focus on decisional behavior – actions by human beings and humanly created institutions that are not biologically programmed. Thus, any social scientific explanation involves assumptions about why people do what they do or think what they think, a matter of intentions and motivations. Social science is, of necessity, an interpretive act.

In many settings, actor-centered meanings are more or less self-evident. When people behave in apparently self-interested ways, the researcher may not feel compelled to investigate the intentions of the actors.[8] Buying low and selling high is intentional behavior, but it probably does not require detailed ethnographic research in situations where we know (or can intuit) what is going on. On the other hand, if one is interested in why markets work differently in different cultural contexts, or why persons in some cultures give away their accumulated goods, or why in some other circumstances people do *not* buy low and sell high (when it would appear to be in their interest to do so), one is obliged to move beyond readily apprehensible ("obvious") motivations such as self-interest.[9] In these situations – encompassing many of the events that social scientists have interested themselves in – careful attention to meaning, as understood by the actors themselves, is essential.[10] Howard Becker explains:

To understand an individual's behaviour, we must know how he perceives the situation, the obstacles he believed he had to face, the alternatives he saw

in social actions. See Gadamer (1975); Geertz (1973, 1979a, 1979b); Gibbons (1987); Hirsch (1967); Hirschman (1970); Hoy (1982); MacIntyre (1971); Rabinow and Sullivan (1979); Taylor (1985); von Wright (1971); Winch (1958); and Yanow and Schwartz-Shea (2006).

[7] The term originates with Anscombe (1958), though her usage is somewhat different from my own. For a similar use of the term, see Neta (2004).

[8] To be sure, self-interested behavior (beyond the level of self-preservation) is also, on some level, socially constructed. Yet if we are interested in understanding the effect of pocketbook voting on election outcomes, there is little to be gained by investigating the origins of money and material goods as a motivating force in human behavior. Some things we can afford to take for granted. For a useful discussion, see Abrami and Woodruff (2004).

[9] Geertz (1978).

[10] Davidson (1963); Ferejohn (2004); Rabinow and Sullivan (1979); Stoker (2003); Taylor (1970).

opening up to him. We cannot understand the effects of the range of possibilities, delinquent subcultures, social norms and other explanations of behaviour which are commonly invoked, unless we consider them from the actor's point of view.[11]

This is the interpretivist's quest – to understand behavior from the actor's point of view – and it is an enlightening quest wherever the actor's point of view does not correspond to common sense.

Thus, evidence in a social-scientific study often involves an act of interpretation. But this is not unique, or even distinct, to the case study format.

The Hypothesis

It is impossible to pose questions of research design until one has at least a general idea of what one's research question is. There is no such thing as case selection or case analysis in the abstract. A research design must have a purpose, and that purpose is defined by the inference that it is intended to demonstrate or prove.

In this book I am concerned primarily with causal inference, rather than inferences that are descriptive or predictive in nature. Thus, all hypotheses involve at least one independent variable (X) and one dependent variable (Y). For convenience, I shall label the causal factor of special theoretical interest X_1, and the control (background) variable, or vector of controls (if there are any), X_2.

If a writer is concerned to explain a puzzling outcome, but has no preconceptions about its causes, then the research will be described as *Y-centered*. If a researcher is concerned to investigate the effects of a particular cause, with no preconceptions about what these effects might be, the research will be described as *X-centered*. If a researcher is concerned to investigate a particular causal relationship, the research will be described as *X_1/Y-centered*, for it connects a particular cause with a particular outcome.[12] X- or Y-centered research is exploratory; its purpose is to generate new hypotheses. X_1/Y-centered research, by contrast, is confirmatory/disconfirmatory; its purpose is to test an existing hypothesis.

Note that to pursue an X_1/Y-centered analysis does *not* imply that the writer is attempting to prove or disprove a monocausal or deterministic

---

[11] Becker (1970: 64), quoted in Hamel (1993: 17).

[12] This expands on Mill (1843/1872: 253), who wrote of scientific inquiry as twofold: "either inquiries into the cause of a given effect or into the effects or properties of a given cause."

argument. The presumed causal relationship between X_1 and Y may be of any sort. X_1 may explain only a small amount of variation in Y. The X_1/Y relationship may be probabilistic. X_1 may refer either to a single variable or to a vector of causal factors. This vector may be an interrelationship (e.g., an interaction term). The only distinguishing feature of X_1/Y-centered analysis is that a specific causal factor(s), a specific outcome, and some pattern of association between the two are stipulated. Thus, X_1/Y-centered analysis presumes a particular hypothesis – a proposition. Y- or X-centered analysis, by contrast, is much more open-ended. Here, one is "soaking and poking" for causes or effects.[13] Invoking a contrast that was introduced in Chapter Three, we may say that Y- or X-centered analysis is hypothesis-generating, while X_1/Y-centered analysis is hypothesis-testing.

As a rule, the more specific and operational a causal hypothesis is, the easier it will be to identify a set of relevant cases. Naturally, the researcher's operating hypothesis may change in the course of her research. Indeed, the exploratory nature of much case-based research is one of the strengths of this research design, as observed in Chapter Three. It would be a mistake to suppose that hypotheses can be immaculately conceived, in isolation from the contaminating influences of the data. This piece of positivist dogma we would do well to forget. It is often preached, but rarely practiced – and, when practiced, rarely to good effect. Usually, a hypothesis arises from an open-ended conversation between a researcher and her evidence. Indeed, one may have only a rough idea of an argument until one has carried out considerable research. Social scientific study is often motivated by a suspicion – the researcher's qualified hunch – that something "funny" is going on here or there. Puzzles are good points of departure. Even so, issues of research design cannot be fully addressed until that initial hunch is formulated as a specific hypothesis.

A quick glance at the real world of social science reveals that few studies are innocently Y- or X-centered. Researchers usually have some presuppositions about what causes Y or about what X causes. In most circumstances, the researcher is well advised to strive for a more fully elaborated hypothesis, one that encompasses both sides of the causal equation. Y- and X-centered analyses are problematic points of departure. They are hard to pin down precisely because one side of the causal equation is open-ended.

---

[13] Fenno (1978).

Recall, also, that the testing of a single hypothesis (yours or someone else's) cannot be conducted in isolation. There are always competitors, even if these competing theories are difficult to identify. (You may have to construct them yourself if the field of inquiry is relatively undeveloped.) A good research design is one that distinguishes the effects of one causal factor from others that might have contributed to a result. If the theory at issue is broader than a single, obvious causal factor (if it can be operationalized in a variety of ways), then a good research design is one that confirms that theory, while disconfirming others – or at least showing that they cannot account for a specific set of results.[14] A good research design eliminates rival explanations. Thus, in thinking through issues of research design, it is helpful to ask oneself the following question: is there an *alternative* way to explain this set of outcomes?

Finally, one must keep in mind that all causal arguments presume a causal mechanism, or a set of mechanisms.[15] A mechanism is that which explains the putative relationship between X_1 and Y. It is the causal pathway, or connecting thread, between X_1 and Y. A specific and determinate causal pathway is the smoking gun of causal analysis. Of course, causal pathways in social research are usually considerably more ambiguous than the smoking gun metaphor suggests. This is why research designs often focus on this difficult, but essential, task. That is to say, in testing rival theories one is also, necessarily, testing rival causal mechanisms, not just the covariational pattern between X_1 and Y. Indeed, we have observed that one of the strengths of the case study is that it often sheds light on causal mechanisms that remain obscure in cross-case analysis (Chapter Three).

Thus, in thinking through research design issues, it is helpful to ask oneself what causal mechanisms a theory stipulates, and whether they are multiple, conjunctural, or take some other complex form. If you are researching in an exploratory mode these same questions must be asked, though in a more open-ended fashion. In either case, evidence drawn

---

[14] Testing really big, abstract theories such as deterrence and realism (both from the political science subfield of international relations) is much more complicated than testing specific hypotheses. The main problem is that macro-theories (a.k.a. frameworks, paradigms) can be operationalized in so many different ways. They are, therefore, difficult to falsify – or, for that matter, to confirm. In this book I am interested only in the testing of fairly specific hypotheses.

[15] Granted, it is possible to make a strong argument for a causal relationship on the basis of covariational evidence alone, particularly if the covariational evidence is experimental. However, that argument will be even stronger if the researcher can also specify a causal mechanism. For further discussion, see Chapter 3.

from the case study should be enlisted to prove, or disprove, the theory at hand. That is, predictions or expectations about causal mechanisms may influence the choice of cases to be studied. "Black boxes" should be replaced with "smoking guns," wherever possible.

Degrees of Falsifiability

Karl Popper sought to classify all scientific propositions according to their degree of falsifiability – that is, the ease with which a proposition could be proven false.[16] This, in turn, may be thought of as a matter of "riskiness." A risky proposition is one that issues multiple precise and determinate empirical predictions, predictions that could not easily be explained by other causal factors (external to the theory of interest) and hence may be interpreted as strong corroborating evidence for the theory at hand.

Falsifiability/riskiness will be discussed in greater detail in the following chapter. For the moment, let us observe that there is a wide range of variation on this dimension. Some case studies generate (or test) propositions that are highly risky. Others are pitched in such abstract or ambiguous terms that they can hardly fail when tested against a larger population of cases (other than the case under intensive study). For example, E. P. Thompson's renowned history *The Making of the English Working Class* (1963) provides a case study of class formation in one national setting (England). This suggests a very general purview, perhaps applicable to all countries in the modern era. Thompson does not offer a specific theory of class formation, aside from the rather hazy notion that the working class participates in its own development. Thus, unless we intuit a great deal (creating a general theory where there is only a suggestion of one), we can derive relatively little that might be applicable to a broader population of cases.

Many case studies examine a loosely defined general topic – war, revolution, gender relations – in a particular setting. Indeed, the narrowest terrains sometimes claim the broadest extensions. Studies of a war are studies of war; studies of a farming community are studies of farming communities everywhere; studies of individuals are studies of leadership or of human nature, and so forth. But such studies may refrain from adopting general theories of war, farming, leadership, or human nature. This would be true, for example, of most case study work in the interpretivist

---

[16] Popper (1934/1968; 1963).

tradition.[17] Similarly, case studies that carry titles like "Ideas Matter," "Institutions Matter," or "Politics Matters" do not generally culminate in risky predictions. They tell us about an instance in which ideas mattered ("ideas mattered *here*"), but do not produce generalizable propositions about the role of ideas. Most work based on the organizing tool of critical junctures and path-dependent sequences is also of this nature, since the path in question is unique while the fact of its being a path applies, in some very general sense, across cases.[18] What all these theoretical frameworks have in common (indeed, about the only thing they have in common) is that they are both broad and vague. They offer a framework which may be used to shed light on a particular case, but not a falsifiable proposition that could be applied to other cases.

By contrast, some case study work moves beyond the analysis of ambiguous causal frameworks to specific propositions. X_1 is said to cause Y across some range of cases and with some set of background conditions. A good example is Ben Reilly's study of the role of electoral systems in ethnically divided societies. Reilly argues, on the basis of several case studies, that single-transferable-vote (STV) electoral systems have a moderating effect on group conflict relative to first-past-the-post (FPP) electoral systems.[19] This sort of case study is risky insofar as it proposes a specific causal hypothesis that can be tested – and potentially falsified – across a broader range of cases.[20]

---

[17] Clifford Geertz (1973: 26), echoing the suspicion of most historians and anthropologists – of all those, presumably, who hold an interpretivist view of the social science enterprise – describes generalizing across cases as *clinical inference*. "Rather than beginning with a set of observations, attempting to subsume them under a governing law, such inference begins with a set of (presumptive) signifiers, attempts to place them within an intelligible frame. Measures are matched to theoretical predictions, but symptoms (even when they are measured) are scanned for theoretical peculiarities – that is, they are diagnosed." For a brief overview of interpretivism, see Gerring (2004a). This genre of case study may be referred to as interpretivist, idiographic, or "contrast of contexts" (Skocpol and Somers 1980).

[18] Collier and Collier (1991/2002); Pierson (2000, 2004).

[19] Reilly (2001). For other examples see Eaton (2003); Elman (1997); Lijphart (1968); and Stratmann and Baur (2002). This is the style of case study analysis associated with David Collier (1993); Harry Eckstein (1975); Alexander George and Andrew Bennett (George and Bennett 2005; George and Smoke 1974); Arend Lijphart (1975); Skocpol and Somers (1980); and Robert Yin (1994). It is probably the dominant style in economics, political science, and sociology.

[20] Arguably, case studies are riskier than cross-case studies if, and insofar as, a theory is generated in the absence of knowledge about a broader set of cases. In this respect, case study work is commendable, from a Popperian perspective. However, I don't advise this sort of "blind" case study work, and doubt that it ever really occurs.

The Particular and the General

I have stipulated that the concept of a case study is, at least to some extent, generalizing. A case study, strictly speaking, must generalize across a set of cases (see Chapter Two).[21] However, the breadth of an inference is obviously a matter of many degrees. No case study (so-called) denies the importance of the case under special focus, and no case study forswears the generalizing impulse altogether. So the particularizing/generalizing distinction is rightly understood as a continuum, not a dichotomy. Case studies typically partake of both worlds. They are studies both of something particular and of something more general.

This tension is apparent in Graham Allison's well-known study – whose subtitle, *Explaining the Cuban Missile Crisis*, invokes a narrow topic, while the title, *Essence of Decision*, suggests a much larger topic (government decision making). Evidently, different propositions within this same work apply to different subjects, a complication that is noted explicitly by the author. The particularizing/generalizing distinction helps to categorize different studies or different moments within the same study.

Not surprisingly, one finds a good deal of disputation about the appropriate scope of inferences generated by case study research. Jack Goldstone argues that case studies are "aimed at providing explanations for particular cases, or groups of similar cases, rather than at providing general hypotheses that apply uniformly to *all* cases in a suspected case-universe."[22] Alexander George and Richard Smoke advise the use of case studies for the formulation of what they call "contingent generalizations" – "if circumstances A then outcome O."[23] Like many case study researchers, they lean toward a style of analysis that investigates differences across cases or across subtypes, rather than commonalities. Harry Eckstein, on the other hand, envisions case studies that confirm (or disconfirm) hypotheses as broad as those provided by cross-case studies.[24]

Sometimes, the particularizing or generalizing quality of a case study is driven by the concerns of the investigator. It is said that some analysts would prefer to explain 90 percent of the variance in a single case, while others would rather explain 10 percent of the variance across

---

[21] In French, the connotation is quite different. *L'Analyse de cas* is understood to mean a single-event study, not a case study of some broader phenomenon.

[22] Goldstone (1997: 108).

[23] George and Smoke (1974: 96). See also George and Bennett (2005: 30–1).

[24] Eckstein (1975).

100 cases. There are lumpers (generalizers) and splitters (particularizers). Economists, political scientists, and sociologists are usually more interested in generalizing than in particularizing, while anthropologists and historians are nowadays more interested in explaining particular contexts. We have already discussed the trade-off between depth and breadth (Chapter Three).

The particularizing/generalizing tug-of-war is also conditioned by the shape of the empirical phenomena. With respect to the topic of social mobility, John Goldthorpe and Robert Erikson note that while some patterns are well explained by cross-case (general) models, others are resistant to those general explanations.

> Our analyses pointed...to the far greater importance of historically formed cultural or institutional features or political circumstances which could not be expressed as variable values except in a quite artificial way. For example, *levels* of social fluidity were not highly responsive to the overall degree of educational inequality within nations, but *patterns* of fluidity did often reflect the distinctive, institutionally shaped character of such inequality in particular nations, such as Germany or Japan. Or again, fluidity was affected less by the presence of a state socialist regime *per se* than by the significantly differing policies actually pursued by the Polish, Hungarian or Czechoslovak regimes on such matters as the collectivization of agriculture or the recruitment of the intelligentsia. In such instances, then, it seemed to us that the retention of proper names and adjectives in our explanatory accounts was as unavoidable as it was desirable, and that little was to be gained in seeking to bring such historically specific effects within the scope of theory of any kind.[25]

This empirical field offers a good example of how a single phenomenon (social mobility) may exhibit features that are both uniform and unique across the chosen cases.

Statistical researchers will be familiar with the technique of "fixed effects," which incorporate a unique intercept for each unit in a time-series cross-section model. This is another way of capturing the notion of diversity-within-uniformity – case specificity coexisting with case generality.

Case study research format generally occupies an in-between methodological zone that is part "idiographic" and part "nomothetic" (I use these terms with extreme circumspection, since they contain so many different meanings). Some studies lean toward the former, others toward the latter.

[25] Goldthorpe (1997: 17).

Indeed, a degree of ambiguity is *inherent* in the enterprise of the case study. Avner Greif offers the following caveat at the conclusion of his analytic narrative of late medieval Genoa:

This study demonstrates the complexity of investigating self-enforcing political systems. Such an investigation requires a detailed examination of the particularities of the time and place under consideration, utilizing a coherent, context-specific model. Thus it may be premature to attempt to generalize based on this study regarding the sources and implications of self-enforcing political systems.[26]

Here a researcher steeped in the nomothetic tradition of economics comes to terms with the fact that generalizations based on his own case study work are highly speculative. It is not clear how far they might extend.[27]

Indeed, it is difficult to write a study of a single case that does not also function as a case study, and vice versa. Nor is it always easy to neatly separate the single-case and cross-case components of a work. The reason for this structural ambiguity is that the utility of the case study rests on its double function. One wishes to know both what is particular to that unit *and* what is general about it, and these elements are often unclear. Thus, in her study of multilateral economic sanctions, Lisa Martin confesses to her readers that

although I have chosen the cases to allow testing the hypotheses [of theoretical interest], other factors inevitably appear that seem to have had a significant influence on cooperation in particular cases. Because few authors have focused on the question of cooperation in cases of economic sanctions, I devote some attention to these factors when they arise, rather than keeping my analysis within the bounds of the hypotheses outlined in [the theory chapter].[28]

---

[26] Greif (1998: 59). Weingast (1998: 153), in the same volume, notes that his case study "does not afford general tests on a series of other cases." See also the introductory and concluding chapters to this influential volume (Bates et al. 1998: 11, 231, 234). On the other hand, Levi elsewhere (1997: 6) insists that "analytic narrative combines detailed research of specific cases with a more general model capable of producing hypotheses about a significant range of cases outside the sample of the particular project."

[27] George and Smoke (1974: 105) offer parallel reflections on their own case studies, focused on deterrence in international relations. "These case studies are of twofold value. First, they provide an empirical base for the theoretical analysis. . . . But second, the case studies are intended to stand in their own right as historical explanations of the outcomes of many of the major deterrence efforts of the Cold War period. They are 'historical' in the sense that they are, of course, retrospective. However, they are also analytical in the sense that we employ a variety of tools, concepts in attempting to explain the *reasons* behind a particular outcome in terms of the inner logic of the deterrence process [a logic that presumably extends across past, present and future]. They are therefore as much 'political science' as they are 'history.' "

[28] Martin (1992: 97).

It should be kept in mind that case studies often tackle subjects about which little was previously known or about which existing knowledge is fundamentally flawed. The case study typically presents original research of some sort. Indeed, it is the opportunity to study a single case in great depth that constitutes one of the primary virtues of the case study method (see Chapter Three).

Consider that if a researcher were to restrict herself only to elements of the case that were generalizable (i.e., if she rigorously maintains a nomothetic mode of analysis), a reader might justifiably complain. Such rigor would clarify the population of the primary inference, but it would also constitute a considerable waste of scholarly energy. Imagine a study of economic growth that focuses on Mauritius as a case study yet refuses to engage causal questions unless they are clearly applicable to other countries (since this work is supposed to function as a case study of a more general phenomenon, growth). No mention of factors specific to the Mauritian case is allowed; all proper nouns are converted into common nouns.[29] Imagine that the fruit of an anthropologist's ten-year study of a remote tribe, never heretofore visited, culminates in the analysis of a particular causal relationship deemed to be generalizable, but at the cost of ignoring all other features of tribal life in the resulting study. One can only suppose that colleagues, mentors, and funding agencies would be unhappy with an ethnography so tightly focused on a general (cross-case) causal issue. Studies of the foregoing sort do not exist, because they are unduly general.

Since it is often difficult to tell which of the many features of a given case are typical of a larger set of cases (and hence fodder for generalizable inferences) and which are particular to the case under study, the appropriate expedient is for the writer to report all facts and hypotheses that might be relevant – in short, to *overreport*. Much of the detail provided by the typical case study may be regarded as "field notes" of plausible utility for future researchers, perhaps having rather different agendas.

In sum, it seems justifiable for case studies to function on two levels simultaneously, the case itself and some broader class of (perhaps difficult-to-specify) cases. The defining characteristic of the case study is its ability to infer a larger whole from a much smaller part. Yet both retain some importance in the final product. Thus, all case studies are to a certain extent betwixt and between. They partake of two worlds: they are

[29] Przeworski and Teune (1970).

particularizing *and* generalizing. (Note that one portion of this book – the epilogue – is focused on work that is strongly particularizing, i.e., where the intent of the author is to elucidate a single outcome rather than a class of outcomes. Elsewhere, I am concerned primarily with the generalizing component of case study research.)

Specifying a Population

Given the structural conflict between the two moments of the case study, it is absolutely crucial that case study writers be as clear as possible about which of their propositions are intended to describe the case under intensive investigation, and which are intended to apply to a broader set of cases. Each inference must have a clear breadth, domain, scope, or population (terms that I use more or less interchangeably).

Regrettably, these matters are often left ambiguous. Studies focused on some element of politics in the United States often frame their analysis as a study of politics – by implication, politics *in general* (everywhere and always).[30] One is left to wonder whether the study pertains only to American politics, to all contemporary polities, or in varying degrees to both. Indeed, the slippage between study and case study may account for much of the confusion that we encounter when reading single-case analyses. Ongoing controversies over the validity of Theda Skocpol's analysis of social revolution, Michael Porter's analysis of industrial competitiveness, Alexander George and Richard Smoke's study of deterrence failure, as well as many other case-based studies, rest in part on the failure of these authors to clarify the scope of their inferences.[31] It is not clear what these studies are *about*. At any rate, it is open to dispute. If, at the end of a study, the population of the primary inference remains ambiguous, so does the hypothesis. It is not falsifiable. Clarifying an inference may involve some sacrifice in narrative flow, but it is rightly regarded as the entry price of social science.

Caution is evidently required when specifying the population of an inference. One does not wish to claim too much. Nor does one wish to claim too little. Mistakes can be made in either direction, as we have observed. In this discussion I shall emphasize the virtues of breadth, for it is my impression that many case study researchers lean toward narrow

[30] See e.g., Campbell et al. (1960).
[31] Skocpol (1979); Porter (1990); George and Smoke (1974). See also discussion in Collier and Mahoney (1996); Geddes (1990); and King, Keohane, and Verba (1994).

propositions – which seem more modest, more conservative – without realizing the costs of doing so.

In discussion of two extraordinarily influential works of comparative history – Barrington Moore's *Social Origins of Dictatorship and Democracy* and Theda Skocpol's *States and Social Revolutions* – Skocpol and Margaret Somers declare that these studies, and others like them, "cannot be readily generalized beyond the cases actually discussed," for they are inductive rather than deductive exercises in causal analysis. Thus, any attempt to project the arguments in these works onto future revolutions, or onto revolutions outside the class of specified outcomes, is foolhardy. The authors defend this limited scope by likening case-based research to a map. "No matter how good the maps were of, say, North America, the pilot could not use the same map to fly over other continents."[32]

The map metaphor is apt for some phenomena, but not for others. It betrays the authors' general assumption that most phenomena of interest to social science are highly variable across contexts, like the roadways and waterways of a continent. Consider the causes of revolutions, as explored by Skocpol in her path-breaking work. Skocpol carefully bounds her conclusions, which are said to apply only to states that are wealthy and independent (through their history) of colonial rule – and hence exclude other revolutionary cases such as Mexico (1910), Bolivia (1952), and Cuba (1959).[33] One's willingness to accept this scope restriction is contingent upon accepting an important premise, namely, that the causes of revolution in poor countries, or in countries with colonial legacies, are different from the causes of revolution in other countries. One must accept the assumption of unit homogeneity among the chosen cases and unit heterogeneity among the class of excluded cases. This is a plausible claim, but it is not beyond question. (Were the causes of revolution really so different in Cuba and Russia?)

Evidently, the plausible scope of an argument depends on the particular argument and on judgments about various cases, inside and outside of the proposed population. When a researcher restricts an inference to a small population of cases, or to the population that she has studied (which may be large or small), she is open to the charge of gerrymandering – establishing a domain on no other basis than that certain cases seem to fit the inference under study. Donald Green and Ian Shapiro call this an "arbitrary

[32] Skocpol and Somers (1980: 195). See also Goldthorpe (2003: 47) and Skocpol (1994).
[33] Skocpol (1979). See also Collier and Mahoney (1996: 81) and George and Bennett (2005: 120).

domain restriction."[34] The breadth of an inference must make sense; there must be an explicable *reason* for including some cases and excluding others. If the inference is about oranges, then all oranges – but no apples – should be included in the population. If it is about fruit, then both apples and oranges must be included. Defining the population – as, for example, (a) oranges or (b) fruit – is thus critical to defining the inference.

The same goes for temporal boundaries. If an inference is limited to a specific period, it is incumbent upon the writer to explain why that period is different from others. It will not do for writers to hide behind the presumption that social science cannot predict the future. Theoretical arguments cannot opt out of predicting future events *if* the future is like the present in ways that are relevant to the theory. Indeed, if future evidence were deemed ineligible for consideration in judging the accuracy of already-existing theories, then writers would have effectively side-stepped any out-of-sample tests (given that, in their construction, many social scientific theories have already exhausted all possible evidence that is currently available).

Ceteris paribus, social science gives preference to broad inferences over narrow inferences. There are several reasons for this disciplinary preference. First, the scope of an inference usually correlates directly with its theoretical significance. Broad empirical propositions are theory-building; narrow propositions usually have less theoretical significance (unless they are subsumable within some larger theoretical framework). Second, broad empirical propositions usually have greater policy relevance, particularly if they extend into the future. They help us to design effective institutions and policies. Finally, the broader the inference, the greater its falsifiability, for the relevant evidence that might be interrogated to establish the truth or falsehood of the inference is multiplied. For all these reasons, hypotheses should be extended as far as is logically justifiable.

Of course, no theory is infinitely extendable. Indeed, the notion of a "universal covering law" is deceptive, since even the most far-reaching social scientific theory has limits. The issue, then, is how to determine the *appropriate* boundaries of a given proposition. An arbitrary scope condition is one that cannot be rationally justified: there is no reason to suppose that the theory might extend to a specified temporal or spatial boundary but no further – or nearer. A theory of revolution that pertains to the eighteenth, nineteenth, and twentieth centuries, but not to the

---

[34] Green and Shapiro (1999).

twenty-first century, must justify this temporal exclusion. It must also justify the decision to lump three quite diverse centuries together in one single population. Similarly, a theory of revolution that pertains to Africa but not to Asia must justify this spatial exclusion. And a theory of revolution that pertains to the whole world must justify this spatial inclusion. It is not clear that the phenomenon of revolution is similar in all cultural and geopolitical arenas.

My point is a simple one: scope conditions may be arbitrarily large, as well as arbitrarily small. The researcher should not "define out," or "define in," temporal or spatial cases that do not fit the prescribed pattern unless she can think of good reasons why this might be so. All populations must not only be specified, but also justified. Upon this justification hinges the plausibility of the theory as well as the identification of a workable research design.

If, after much cogitation, the scope of an inference still seems ineradicably ambiguous, the writer may adopt the following expedient. Usually, it is possible to specify a limited set of cases that a given proposition *must* cover if it is to make any sense at all – presumably, the set of cases that are most similar to the case(s) under study. At the same time, it is often possible to identify a larger population of cases that *may* be included in the circumference of the inference, though their inclusion is more speculative – presumably because they share fewer characteristics with the case(s) under study. If the researcher distinguishes carefully between these two populations, readers will have a clear idea of the *manifest* scope, and the *potential* scope, of a given inference.

Cross-Level Reasoning

The case study (by definition) attempts to tell us about something broader than the immediate subject of investigation. It is a synecdochic style of investigation, studying the whole through intensive focus on one (or several) of its parts. While this inferential step from sample to population is characteristic of all empirical investigations (leaving aside the relatively rare instance of investigations that are able to encompass the whole population of interest), it is particularly problematic wherever the sample is limited to one or several, for reasons explored in the following chapter.

The wide gap between sample and population, while posing an inferential danger, also offers a unique opportunity. In particular, it affords the opportunity for a different style of causal inference, one resting at a lower level of analysis. This means that case study research is, almost invariably, cross-level research. It operates at the level of the principal units of analysis (the cases) as well as within selected cases (within-case evidence). By way of conclusion to this chapter I want to emphasize the ceaseless back-and-forth, cross-level nature of case study research.

Whatever the field, and whatever the tools, case studies and cross-case studies should be viewed as partners in the iterative task of causal investigation. Cross-case arguments draw on within-case assumptions, and within-case arguments draw on cross-case assumptions. Neither works very well when isolated from the other. In most circumstances, therefore, it is advisable to conduct both types of analysis. Each is made stronger by the other.

Christopher Udry testifies to the utility of this interplay in his own area of expertise, development economics.

The hallmark of this work is that it engages the researcher in an interactive process of detailed observation, construction of economic models, data collection, and empirical testing. An initial hypothesis is refined and clarified through detailed observation, which informs the collection of appropriate data. As the economic environment is clarified during the course of fieldwork, the data-collection procedure can be adjusted in response. Finally, the research proceeds to formal statistical analysis and, one hopes, to new hypotheses.... The relatively small scale of the research facilitates this iterative process, particularly with respect to the ability of the researcher to quickly modify data collection.[35]

Ideally, the case study researcher should think carefully about cross-case evidence before conducting the time-consuming effort of an in-depth study focused on a single case. One should have at least a preliminary idea of how one's results are likely to fit into a broader set of cases. In any event, all case studies should at some point be *generalized*. That is, the author should clarify how the intensively studied case represents some broader population of cases. In many instances case study research results in a new proposition (or a significant modification of an existing proposition), one not previously tested in a cross-case sample. If so, it is imperative that the case study researcher reveal, or at the very least suggest, how this new proposition might be operationalized across other cases, what the breadth of the inference is, and what a reasonable cross-case test might consist of. The exploratory case study should culminate in cross-case confirmatory analysis.

Granted, the case study researcher may feel that in light of the in-depth knowledge she has of her case and her comparative ignorance of other

[35] Udry (2003: 107).

cases, it would be unreasonable and irresponsible to speculate on the latter. Misgivings are understandable. However, if properly framed – as a hunch rather than a conclusion – there is no need to refrain from cross-case speculation. These hunches are vital signposts for future research. They bring greater clarity to the inference of primary interest and point the way to a cumulative research agenda. No case study research should be allowed to conclude without at least a nod to how one's case might be situated in a broader universe of cases. Without this cross-case generalization, the case study sits alone. Its insights, regardless of their brilliance, cannot be integrated into a broader field of study.

The larger point, then, is that cross-case analysis is presumed in all case study analysis. The case study is, by definition, a study of some phenomenon broader than the unit under investigation. The more one knows about this broader population of cases, the easier it will be to choose cases and to understand their significance. Similarly, the more one knows about individual cases, the easier it will be to interpret causal patterns that extend across a population of cases, and to construct appropriate causal models.[36] Cross-case and within-case analysis are interdependent. It is difficult to imagine cross-case research that does not draw upon case study work, or case study work that disregards adjacent cases. They are distinct, but synergistic, tools in the analysis of social life.[37]

---

[36] Gordon and Smith (2004).
[37] The same point was made many decades ago by L. L. Bernard (1928: 310), and again by Samuel Stouffer (1941: 357).

5

Techniques for Choosing Cases

Case study analysis focuses on a small number of cases that are expected to provide insight into a causal relationship across a larger population of cases. This presents the researcher with a formidable problem of case selection. Which cases should be chosen?

In large-sample research, case selection is usually handled by some version of randomization. If a sample consists of a large enough number of independent random draws, the selected cases are likely to be fairly representative of the overall population on any given variable. Furthermore, if cases in the population are distributed homogeneously across the ranges of the key variables, then it is probable that some cases will be included from each important segment of those ranges, thus providing sufficient leverage for causal analysis. (For situations in which cases with theoretically relevant values of the variables are rare, a stratified sample that oversamples some subset of the population may be employed.)

A demonstration of the fact that random sampling is likely to produce a representative sample is shown in Figure 5.1, a histogram of the mean values of 500 random samples, each consisting of 1,000 cases. For each case, one variable has been measured: a continuous variable that falls somewhere between zero and one. In the population, the mean value of this variable is 0.5. How representative are the random samples? One good way of judging this is to compare the means of each of the 500 random samples to the population mean. As can be seen in the figure, all of the sample means are very close to the population mean. So random sampling was a success, and each of the 500 samples turns out to be fairly representative of the population.

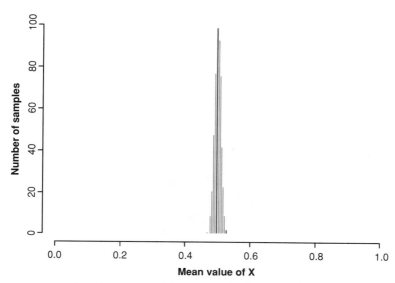

FIGURE 5.1. Sample means of large-sample draws. A histogram showing the mean values of one variable in 500 samples of 1,000 cases each. Population mean = 0.5.

However, in case study research the sample is small (by definition), and this makes randomization problematic. Consider what would happen if the sample size were changed from 1,000 cases to only 5 cases. The results are shown in Figure 5.2. On average, these small-N random samples produce the right answer, so the procedure culminates in results that are unbiased. However, many of the sample means are rather far from the population mean, and some are quite far indeed. Hence, even though this case-selection technique produces representative samples *on average*, any given sample may be wildly unrepresentative. In statistical terms, the problem is that small sample sizes tend to produce estimates with a great deal of variance – sometimes referred to as a problem of precision. For this reason, random sampling is unreliable in small-N research. (Note that in this chapter "N" refers to cases, not observations.) Moreover, there is no guarantee that a few cases, chosen randomly, will provide leverage into the research question that animates an investigation. The sample might be representative, but uninformative.

If random sampling is inappropriate as a selection method in case study research, how, then, is one to choose a sample comprised of one or several cases? Keep in mind that the goals of case selection

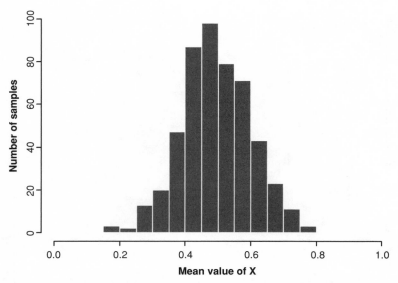

FIGURE 5.2. Sample means of small-sample draws. A histogram showing the mean values of one variable in 500 samples of 5 cases each. Population mean = 0.5.

remain the same regardless of the size of the chosen sample. Large-N cross-case analysis and case study analysis both aim to identify cases that reproduce the relevant causal features of a larger universe (representativeness) and provide variation along the dimensions of theoretical interest (causal leverage). In case study research, however, these goals must be met through purposive (nonrandom) selection procedures. These may be enumerated according to nine techniques, from which we derive nine case study types: *typical, diverse, extreme, deviant, influential, crucial, pathway, most-similar,* and *most-different.*

Table 5.1 summarizes each type, including its general definition, a technique for identifying it within a population of potential cases, its uses, and its probable representativeness. While each of these techniques is normally practiced on one or several cases (the diverse, most-similar, and most-different methods require at least two), all *may* employ additional cases – with the proviso that, at some point, they will no longer offer an opportunity for in-depth analysis and will thus no longer be case studies in the usual sense.

The main point of this chapter is to show how case-selection procedures rest, at least implicitly, upon an analysis of a larger population of potential cases. The case(s) identified for intensive study is chosen from a population, and the reasons for this choice hinge upon the way in which it is

TABLE 5.1. *Techniques of case-selection*

1. Typical
- *Definition*: Cases (one or more) are typical examples of some cross-case relationship.
- *Cross-case technique*: A low-residual case (on-lier).
- *Uses*: Hypothesis testing.
- *Representativeness*: By definition, the typical case is representative.

2. Diverse
- *Definition*: Cases (two or more) illuminate the full range of variation on X_1, Y, or X_1/Y.
- *Cross-case technique*: Diversity may be calculated by (a) categorical values of X_1 or Y (e.g., Jewish, Catholic, Protestant), (b) standard deviations of X_1 or Y (if continuous), or (c) combinations of values (e.g., based on cross-tabulations, factor analysis, or discriminant analysis).
- *Uses*: Hypothesis generating or hypothesis testing.
- *Representativeness*: Diverse cases are likely to be representative in the minimal sense of representing the full variation of the population (though they might not mirror the *distribution* of that variation in the population).

3. Extreme
- *Definition*: Cases (one or more) exemplify extreme or unusual values on X_1 or Y relative to some univariate distribution.
- *Cross-case technique*: A case lying many standard deviations away from the mean of X_1 or Y.
- *Uses*: Hypothesis generating (open-ended probe of X_1 or Y).
- *Representativeness*: Achievable only in comparison to a larger sample of cases.

4. Deviant
- *Definition*: Cases (one or more) deviate from some cross-case relationship.
- *Cross-case technique*: A high-residual case (outlier).
- *Uses*: Hypothesis generating (to develop new explanations of Y).
- *Representativeness*: After the case study is conducted, it may be corroborated by a cross-case test, which includes a general hypothesis (a new variable) based on the case study research. If the case is now an on-lier, it may be considered representative of the new relationship.

5. Influential
- *Definition*: Cases (one or more) with influential configurations of the independent variables.
- *Cross-case technique*: Hat matrix or Cook's distance.
- *Uses*: Hypothesis testing (to verify the status of cases that may influence the results of a cross-case analysis).
- *Representativeness*: Not pertinent, given the goals of the influential-case study.

6. Crucial
- *Definition*: Cases (one or more) are most- or least-likely to exhibit a given outcome.
- *Cross-case technique*: Qualitative assessment of relative crucialness.

(continued)

TABLE 5.1 *(continued)*

- *Uses*: Hypothesis testing (confirmatory or disconfirmatory).
- *Representativeness*: Assessable by reference to prior expectations about the case and the population.

7. Pathway
- *Definition*: Cases (one or more) where X_1, and not X_2, is likely to have caused a positive outcome ($Y = 1$).
- *Cross-case technique*: Cross-tab (for categorical variables) or residual analysis (for continuous variables).
- *Uses*: Hypothesis testing (to probe causal mechanisms).
- *Representativeness*: May be tested by examining residuals for the chosen cases.

8. Most-similar
- *Definition*: Cases (two or more) are similar on specified variables other than X_1 and/or Y.
- *Cross-case technique*: Matching.
- *Uses*: Hypothesis generating or hypothesis testing.
- *Representativeness*: May be tested by examining residuals for the chosen cases.

9. Most-different
- *Definition*: Cases (two or more) are different on specified variables other than X_1 and Y.
- *Cross-case technique*: The inverse of the most-similar method of large-N case selection (see above).
- *Uses*: Hypothesis generating or hypothesis testing (eliminating deterministic causes).
- *Representativeness*: May be tested by examining residuals for the chosen cases.

situated within that population. This is the origin of the terminology just listed – typical, diverse, extreme, and so on. It follows that case-selection procedures in case study research may build upon prior cross-case analysis and depend, at the very least, upon certain assumptions about a broader population. This, in turn, reinforces a central perspective of the book: case study analysis does not exist, and is impossible to conceptualize, in isolation from cross-case analysis.

To be sure, the sort of cross-case analysis that might be possible in a given research context rests on how large the population of potential cases is, on how much information one has about these cases, on what sort of general model might be constructed, and with what degree of confidence that model might be applied. In order for most quantitative (statistical) case-selection techniques to be fruitful, several caveats must be satisfied. First, the inference must pertain to more than several cases; otherwise, statistical analysis is usually problematic. Second, relevant data must be available for that population, or a significant sample of that population, on key variables, and the researcher must feel reasonably confident in the accuracy and conceptual validity of these variables. Third, all the standard considerations of statistical research (e.g., identification, specification, robustness) must be carefully considered and, wherever possible, investigated. I shall not dilate further on these familiar issues except to warn the researcher against the unthinking use of statistical techniques.[1]

When these requirements are not met, the researcher must employ a qualitative approach to case selection. Thus, the point of this chapter is not to insist upon quantitative techniques of case selection in case study research. My purpose, rather, is to elucidate general principles that might guide the process of case selection in case study research, whether the technique is quantitative or qualitative. Some of these principles are already widely known and widely practiced. Others are less common, or less well understood. Most of these methods are viable – indeed, are virtually identical – in qualitative and quantitative contexts. Hence, the statistical sections of this chapter usually simply reformulate the logic of qualitative case-selection procedures as they might be applied to large populations where the foregoing caveats apply.

Typical Case

In order for a focused case study to provide insight into a broader phenomenon, it must be representative of a broader set of cases. It is in this context that one may speak of a *typical-case* approach to case selection. The typical case exemplifies what is considered to be a typical set of values, given some general understanding of a phenomenon. By construction, the typical case is also a representative case; I employ these two terms synonymously.[2] (The antonym, *deviance*, is discussed in a later section.)

Some typical cases serve an exploratory role. Here, the author chooses a case based upon a set of descriptive characteristics and then probes for causal relationships. Robert and Helen Lynd selected a single city "to be

---

[1] Gujarati (2003); Kennedy (2003). Interestingly, the potential of cross-case statistics in helping to choose cases for in-depth analysis is recognized in some of the earliest discussions of the case study method (e.g., Queen 1928: 226).

[2] The latter term is often employed in the psychological literature (e.g., Hersen and Barlow 1976: 24).

as representative as possible of contemporary American life." Specifically, they were looking for a city with

1) a temperate climate; 2) a sufficiently rapid rate of growth to ensure the presence of a plentiful assortment of the growing pains accompanying contemporary social change; 3) an industrial culture with modern, high-speed machine production; 4) the absence of dominance of the city's industry by a single plant (i.e., not a one-industry town); 5) a substantial local artistic life to balance its industrial activity...; and 6) the absence of any outstanding peculiarities or acute local problems which would mark the city off from the midchannel sort of American community.[3]

After examining a number of options, the Lynds decided that Muncie, Indiana, was more representative than, or at least as representative as, other midsized cities in America, thus qualifying as a typical case.

This is an inductive approach to case selection. Note that typicality may be understood according to the mean, median, or mode on a particular dimension; there may be multiple dimensions (as in the foregoing example); and each may be differently weighted (some dimensions may be more important than others). Where the selection criteria are multidimensional and a large sample of potential cases is in play, some form of factor analysis may be useful in identifying the most-typical case(s). Although the Lynds did not employ a statistical model to evaluate potential cases, it is easy to see how they might have done so, at least along the first five criteria. (The final criteria would be difficult to operationalize in a large sample, since it involves "peculiarities" of any sort.)

However, the more common employment of the typical-case method involves a *causal* model of some phenomenon of theoretical interest. Here, the researcher has identified a particular outcome (Y), and perhaps a specific X_1/Y hypothesis, which she wishes to investigate. In order to do so, she looks for a typical example of that causal relationship. Intuitively, one imagines that a case selected according to the mean values of all parameters must be a typical case relative to some causal relationship. However, this is by no means assured.

Suppose that the Lynds were primarily interested in explaining feelings of trust/distrust among members of different social classes (one of the implicit research goals of the *Middletown* study). This outcome is likely to be affected by many factors, only some of which are included in their six selection criteria. So choosing cases with respect to a causal hypothesis

---

[3] Lynd and Lynd (1929/1956), quoted in Yin (2004: 29–30).

involves, first of all, identifying the relevant variables. It involves, secondly, the selection of a case that has "typical" values relative to the overall causal model; it is well explained.

Note that cases with atypical scores on a *particular dimension* (e.g., very high or very low) may still be typical examples of a causal relationship. Indeed, they may be more typical than cases whose values lie close to the mean.

Note also that because the typical case embodies a typical value on some set of variables, the variance of interest to the researcher must lie *within* that case. Specifically, the typical case of some phenomenon may be helpful in exploring causal mechanisms and in solving identification problems (e.g., endogeneity between X_1 and Y, an omitted variable that may account for X_1 *and* Y, or some other spurious causal association). Depending upon the results of the case study, the author may confirm an existing hypothesis, disconfirm that hypothesis, or reframe it in a way that is consistent with the findings of the case study.

Cross-Case Technique

How might one identify a typical case from a large population of potential cases? If the causal relationship involves only a single independent variable and if the relationship is quite strong, it may be possible to identify typical cases simply by eyeballing the evidence. A strong positive association between X_1 and Y means that a case with similar (high, low, or middling) values on X_1 and Y is probably a typical case. However, there are few bivariate causal relationships in social science. Usually, more than one causal factor must be evaluated, even if the additional variables serve only as controls. Moreover, without some overall assessment of the cross-case evidence it may be difficult to say whether the general relationship is positive or negative, strong or weak. Thus, in any large-N sample (i.e., whenever the number of potential cases is great) it is advisable to perform a formal cross-case analysis in order to identify "typical" cases.

Suppose that an arbitrary case in the population, denoted as case *i*, has a known score on each of several relevant variables. For the sake of economy of language, let the variables involved in the relationship be labeled y_i and $x_{1,i}, \ldots x_{K,i}$, where y_i is the score of case *i* on one variable and each of the $x_{K,i}$'s is the score of case *i* on one of the K other variables under consideration. Thus, the relationship involves a total of K + 1 variables. K can be any integer greater than or equal to 1.

With these symbols, the established relationships among the variables can be expressed mathematically. The idea is to find a function, f(), such that the average score of y for cases with some specific set of scores on $x_1 \ldots x_K$ is equal to $f(x_1, \ldots x_K)$. Thus, the function f() should be chosen to capture the key ideas about the relationship of interest. A familiar example may make this discussion clearer.

Often, researchers choose an additive (linear) function to play the role of f(). Using traditional statistical notation, in which the average score of y_i across infinite repetitions of case i is denoted by its expectation, $E(y_i)$, a linear function represents a relationship in which:

$$E(y_i) = \beta_0 + \beta_1 x_{1,i} + \cdots + \beta_K x_{K,i} \qquad (5.1)$$

Each of the β_K's in this equation represents an unknown constant. Regression analysis allows researchers to use known information about the y and $x_1 \ldots x_K$ variables for a set of cases to estimate these unknown constants. Estimates of β_K will be denoted here as b_K.

Using this terminology, we can now develop a formula for the degree to which a particular case is typical in light of a given relationship. A case is "typical" in the terms of small-N methodology to the extent that its score on the y variable is close to the average score on that variable for a case with the same scores on the $x_1 \ldots x_K$ variables, as given by equation 5.1. That is,

$$\text{Typicality}(i) = -\text{abs}[y_i - E(y_i | x_{1,i}, \ldots x_{K,i})] \qquad (5.2)$$
$$= -\text{abs}[y_i - b_0 + b_1 x_{1,i} + \cdots + b_K x_{K,i}]$$

According to this discussion, the typicality of a case with respect to a particular relationship is simply -1 times the absolute value of that case's error term (its residual) in regression analysis. This measure of typicality ranges, in theory, from negative infinity to zero. When a case falls close to the regression line, its typicality will be just below zero. When a case falls far from the regression line, its typicality will be far below zero. Typical cases have small residuals.

In a large-N sample, there will often be many cases with high (i.e., near-zero) typicality scores. In such situations, researchers may elect not to focus on the cases with the highest estimated typicality, for such estimates may not be accurate enough to distinguish among several almost-identical cases. Instead, researchers may choose to randomly select from the set of cases with very high typicality, or to choose from among these cases according to additional criteria, such as those to be discussed here, or by reason of practicality (cost, convenience, etc.). However, scholars should try to avoid selecting from among the set of typical cases in a way that is correlated with relevant omitted variables; such selection procedures complicate the task of causal inference.

Consider the (presumably causal) relationship between economic development and level of democracy.[4] Democracy is understood here as a continuous concept along a twenty-one-point scale, from -10 (most autocratic) to $+10$ (most democratic).[5] Economic development is measured in standard fashion by per capita GDP.[6] Figure 5.3 displays this relationship in the form of a bivariate scatterplot. The classical result is strikingly illustrated: wealthy countries are almost exclusively democratic. (For heuristic purposes, certain simplifying assumptions are adopted. I shall assume, for example, that this measure of democracy is continuous and unbounded.[7] I shall assume, more importantly, that the true relationship between economic development and democracy is log-linear, positive, and causally asymmetric, with economic development treated as exogenous and democracy as endogenous.[8])

Given this general relationship, how might a set of "typical" cases be selected? Recall that the Y variable is simply the democracy score, and there is only one independent variable: logged per capita GDP. Hence, the simplest relevant model is:

$$E(\text{Polity}_i) = \beta_0 + \beta_1 \text{GDP}_i \qquad (5.3)$$

For our purposes, the most important feature of this model is the residuals for each case. Figure 5.4 shows a histogram of these residuals. Obviously, a fairly large number of cases have quite low residuals and therefore might be considered typical. A higher proportion of cases fall far below the regression line than far above it, suggesting that the model may be

[4] Lipset (1959). Whether economic development has only the effect of maintaining democratic regimes (Przeworski et al. 2000) or also of causing regime transitions (Boix and Stokes 2003) is not relevant to the present discussion, where I assume a simple linear relationship between wealth and democracy.

[5] This scoring derives from the Polity2 variable in the Polity IV dataset (Marshall and Jaggers 2005).

[6] Data are drawn from the Penn World Tables dataset (Summers and Heston 1991).

[7] But see Treier and Jackman (2003).

[8] But see Gerring et al. (2005) and Przeworski et al. (2000).

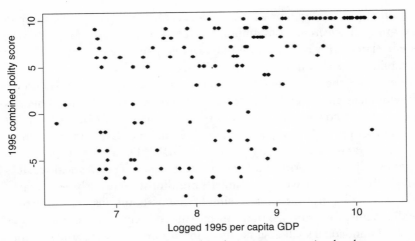

FIGURE 5.3. The presumed relationship between economic development and democracy. A scatterplot showing level of democracy (on the vertical axis) and level of wealth (on the horizontal axis) of all available countries in 1995. N = 131.

incomplete. Hopefully, within-case analysis will be able to shed light on the reasons for the asymmetry.[9]

Because of the large number of cases with quite small residuals, the researcher will have a range of options for selecting typical cases. Indeed, in this example, twenty-six cases have a typicality score between 0 and −1. Any or all of these might reasonably be selected as typical cases with respect to the model described in equation 5.3.

Conclusion

Typicality responds to the first desideratum of case selection, that the chosen case be representative of a population of cases (as defined by the primary inference). Even so, it is important to remind ourselves that a single-minded pursuit of representativeness does not ensure that this desideratum will be achieved. Indeed, the issue of case representativeness is not an issue that can ever be definitively settled in a case study format. When one refers to a "typical case" one is saying, in effect, that the *probability* of a case's representativeness is high, relative to other cases.

Note that the measure of typicality introduced here, the size of a case's residual, can be misleading if the statistical model is misspecified. And

---

[9] In this example, the asymmetry is probably due to the failure of the model to take into account the restricted range of the dependent variable, as discussed earlier.

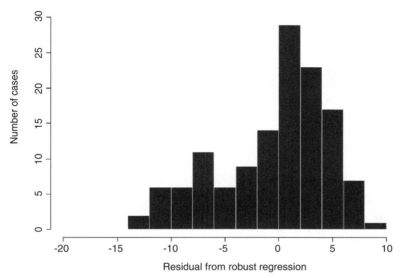

FIGURE 5.4. Potential typical cases. A histogram of the residuals from a robust regression of logged per capita GDP on level of democracy.

it provides little insurance against errors that are purely stochastic. A case may lie directly on the regression line but still be, in some important respect, atypical. For example, it might have an odd combination of values; the interaction of variables might be different from that in other cases; or unusual causal mechanisms might be at work. Most important, an analysis of residuals does not address problems of sample bias. If the large-N sample is not representative of the relevent population then any analysis based on the former is apt to be flawed. Typicality does not ensure representativeness. For these reasons, it is important to supplement a statistical analysis of cases with evidence drawn from the case in question (the case study itself) and with our general knowledge of the world. One should never judge a case solely by its residual. Yet, all other things being equal, a case with a low residual is less likely to be unusual than a case with a high residual, and to this extent the method of case selection outlined here may be a helpful guide to case study researchers faced with a large number of potential cases.

Diverse Case

A second case-selection strategy has as its primary objective the achievement of maximum variance along relevant dimensions. I refer to this as a *diverse-case* method. For obvious reasons, this method requires the selection of a set of cases – at minimum, two – that are intended to represent the full range of values characterizing X_1, Y, or some particular X_1/Y relationship.[10]

Where the individual variable of interest is categorical (on/off, red/black/blue, Jewish/Protestant/Catholic), the identification of diversity is readily apparent. The investigator simply chooses one case from each category. For a continuous variable, the choices are not so obvious. However, the researcher is well advised to choose both extreme values (high and low), and perhaps the mean or median as well. One may also look for break-points in the distribution that seem to correspond to categorical differences among cases. Or one may follow a theoretical hunch about which threshold values count – that is, which ones are likely to produce different values on Y.

Another sort of diverse case takes account of the values of multiple variables (i.e., a vector) rather than a single variable. If these variables are categorical, the identification of causal types rests upon the intersection of each category. Two dichotomous variables produce a matrix with four cells; three dichotomous variables produce a matrix of eight cells, and so forth. If all variables are deemed relevant to the analysis, the selection of diverse cases mandates the selection of one case drawn from within each cell. Let us say that an outcome is thought to be affected by sex, race (black/white), and marital status. Here, a diverse-case strategy of case selection would identify one case within each of these intersecting cells – a total of eight cases. Again, things become more complicated when one or more of the factors is continuous, rather than categorical. Here, the diversity of case values do not fall neatly into cells. Rather, these cells must be created by fiat – for example, high, medium, low.

It will be seen that where multiple variables are under consideration, the logic of diverse-case analysis rests upon the logic of *typological* theorizing – where different combinations of variables are assumed to have effects on an outcome that vary across types. George and Bennett define a typological theory as

---

[10] This method has not been given much attention by qualitative methodologists; hence, the absence of a generally recognized name. It bears some resemblance to J. S. Mill's Joint Method of Agreement and Difference (Mill 1843/1872), which is to say, a mixture of most-similar and most-different analysis, as discussed later. Patton (2002: 234) employs the concept of "maximum variation (heterogeneity) sampling."

a theory that specifies independent variables, delineates them into nominal, ordinal, or interval categories, and provides not only hypotheses on how these variables operate singly, but contingent generalizations on how and under what conditions they behave in specified conjunctions or configurations to produce effects on specified dependent variables. We call specified conjunctions or configurations of the variables "types." A fully specified typological theory provides hypotheses on all of the mathematically possible types relating to a phenomenon, or on the full 'property space,' to use Lazarsfeld's term. Typological theories are rarely fully specified, however, because researchers are usually interested only in the types that are relatively common or that have the greatest implications for theory-building or policy-making.[11]

George and Smoke, for example, wish to explore different types of deterrence failure – by "fait accompli," by "limited probe," and by "controlled pressure." Consequently, they wish to find cases that exemplify each type of causal mechanism.[12]

Diversity may thus refer to a range of variation on X_1 or Y, or to a particular combination of causal factors (with or without a consideration of the outcome). In each instance, the goal of case selection is to capture the full range of variation along the dimension(s) of interest.

Cross-Case Technique

Since diversity can mean many things, its employment in a large-N setting is necessarily dependent upon how it is understood. If it is understood to pertain only to a single variable (X_1 or Y), then the task is fairly simple, as we have discussed. Univariate traits are usually easy to discover in a large-N setting through descriptive statistics or through visual inspection of the data.

Where diversity refers to particular *combinations* of variables, the relevant cross-case technique is some version of stratified random sampling (in a probabilistic setting)[13] or Qualitative Comparative Analysis (in a deterministic setting).[14] If the researcher suspects that a causal relationship is affected not only by combinations of factors but also by their *sequencing*,

---

[11] George and Bennett (2005: 235). See also Elman (2005) and Lazarsfeld and Barton (1951).

[12] More precisely, George and Smoke (1974: 534, 522–36, Chapter 18; see also discussion in Collier and Mahoney 1996: 78) set out to investigate causal pathways and discovered, in the course of their investigation of many cases, these three causal types. But for our purposes what is important is that the final sample include at least one representative of each "type."

[13] See Cochran (1977).

[14] Ragin (2000).

then the technique of analysis must incorporate temporal elements.[15] Thus, the method of identifying causal types rests upon whatever method of identifying causal relationships is presumed to exist.

Note that the identification of distinct case types is intended to identify groups of cases that are internally homogeneous (in all respects that might affect the causal relationship of interest). Thus, the choice of cases *within* each group should not be problematic, and may be accomplished through random sampling. However, if there is suspected diversity within each category, then measures should be taken to assure that the chosen cases are typical of each category. A case study should not focus on an atypical member of a subgroup.

Indeed, considerations of diversity and typicality often go together. Thus, in a study of globalization and social welfare systems, Duane Swank first identifies three distinctive groups of welfare states: "universalistic" (social democratic), "corporatist conservative," and "liberal." Next, he looks within each group to find the most-typical cases. He decides that the Nordic countries are more typical of the universalistic model than the Netherlands, since the latter has "some characteristics of the occupationally based program structure and a political context of Christian Democratic-led governments typical of the corporatist conservative nations."[16] Thus, the Nordic countries are chosen as representative cases within the universalistic case type, and are accompanied in the case-study portion of his analysis by other cases chosen to represent the other welfare state types (corporatist conservative and liberal).

Conclusion

Encompassing a full range of variation is likely to enhance the representativeness of the sample of cases chosen by the researcher. This is a distinct advantage. Of course, the inclusion of a full range of variation may distort the actual distribution of cases across this spectrum. If there are more "high" cases than "low" cases in a population and the researcher chooses only one high case and one low case, the resulting sample of two is not perfectly representative. Even so, the diverse-case method often has stronger claims to representativeness than any other small-N sample (including the typical case). The selection of diverse cases has the additional advantage of introducing variation on the key variables of interest. A set of diverse

---

[15] Abbott (2001); Abbott and Forrest (1986); Abbott and Tsay (2000).
[16] Swank (2002: 11). See also Esping-Andersen (1990).

cases is, by definition, a set of cases that encompasses a range of high and low values on relevant dimensions.

There is, therefore, much to recommend this method of case selection. I suspect that these advantages are commonly understood and are applied on an intuitive level by case study researchers. However, the lack of a recognizable name – and an explicit methodological defense – has made it difficult for case study researchers to identify this method of case selection, and to explain its logic to readers.

Extreme Case

The *extreme-case* method selects a case because of its extreme value on an independent or dependent variable of interest.[17] Thus, studies of domestic violence may choose to focus on extreme instances of abuse.[18] Studies of altruism may focus on those rare individuals who risk their lives to help others (e.g., Holocaust resisters).[19] Studies of ethnic politics may focus on the most heterogeneous societies (e.g., Papua New Guinea) in order to better understand the role of ethnicity in a democratic setting.[20] Studies of industrial policy often focus on the most successful countries (e.g., the NICs),[21] and so forth.[22]

Often an extreme case corresponds to a case that is considered to be prototypical or paradigmatic of some phenomena of interest. This is because concepts are often defined by their extremes, that is, their ideal types. German fascism defines the concept of fascism in part because it offers the most extreme example of that phenomenon. However, the *methodological* value of this case, and others like it, derives from its extremity (along some dimension of interest), not from its theoretical status or its status in the literature on a subject.

The notion of "extreme" may now be defined more precisely. An extreme value is an observation that lies far away from the mean of a given

---

[17] It does not make sense to apply the extreme-case method in a confirmatory/disconfirmatory analysis. If a particular causal relationship is at issue, then both X_1 and Y must be taken into account when choosing cases, as described in the various scenarios that follow. At present, therefore, we shall assume that the researcher has a general question in mind, but not a specific hypothesis.

[18] Browne (1987).

[19] Monroe (1996).

[20] Reilly (2000/2001).

[21] Deyo (1987).

[22] For further examples, see Collier and Mahoney (1996); Geddes (1990); and Tendler (1997).

distribution. For a continuous variable, the distance from the mean may be in either direction (positive or negative). For a dichotomous variable (present/absent), I understand extreme to mean *unusual*. If most cases are positive along a given dimension, then a negative case constitutes an extreme case. If most cases are negative, then a positive case constitutes an extreme case. All things being equal, one is concerned not only with cases where something "happened," but also with cases where something did not. It is the rareness of the value that makes a case valuable, in this context, not its positive or negative value.[23] Thus, if one is studying state capacity, a case of state failure is probably more informative than a case of state endurance simply because the former is more unusual. Similarly, if one is interested in incest taboos, a culture where the incest taboo is absent or weak is probably more useful than a culture where it is present. Fascism is more important than nonfascism; and so forth. There is a good reason, therefore, why case studies of revolution tend to focus on "revolutionary" cases. Theda Skocpol had much more to learn from France than from Austro-Hungary, since France was more unusual than Austro-Hungary within the population of nation-states that Skocpol was concerned to explain.[24] The reason is quite simple: there are fewer revolutionary cases than nonrevolutionary cases; thus, the variation that one wishes to explore as a clue to causal relationships is encapsulated in these cases, viewed against a backdrop of nonrevolutionary cases.

Cross-Case Technique

As stated, extreme cases lie far from the mean of a variable. Extremity (E), for the ith case, can be defined in terms of the sample mean ($\bar{X}$) and the standard deviation (s) for that variable:

$$E_i = \left| \frac{X_i - \bar{X}}{s} \right| \tag{5.4}$$

This definition of extremity is the absolute value of the standardized ("Z") score for the ith case. Cases with a large E_i qualify as extreme. Sometimes, the only criterion is a relative one. The researcher wishes to find the most extreme case(s) available. At other times, it may be helpful

---

[23] Traditionally, methodologists have conceptualized cases as having "positive" or "negative" values (e.g., Emigh 1997; Mahoney and Goertz 2004; Ragin 2000: 60; Ragin 2004: 126).

[24] Skocpol (1979).

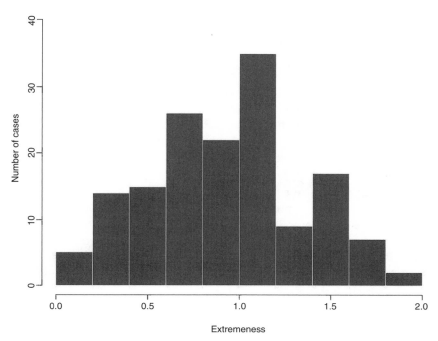

FIGURE 5.5. Potential extreme cases. A histogram of the "extremeness" of all countries on the dimension of democracy, as measured by standard deviations from the mean (absolute value).

to set an arbitrary threshold. Under assumptions of normality, cases with an extremeness score smaller than two would generally not be considered extreme. If the researcher wishes to be more conservative in classifying cases as extreme, a higher threshold may be employed. In general, the choice of threshold is left to the researcher, to be made in a way that is appropriate to the research problem at hand.

The mean of our democracy variable is 2.76, suggesting that the countries in the 1995 dataset tend to be somewhat more democratic than authoritarian (zero is defined as the break-point between democracy and autocracy). The standard deviation is 6.92, implying that there is a fair amount of scatter around the mean.

Figure 5.5 shows a histogram of the extremeness scores for all countries on level of democracy. As can easily be seen, no cases have extremeness scores greater than two. The two countries with the highest scores are Qatar and Saudi Arabia. These countries, which both have a democracy score of −10 for 1995, are probably the two best candidates for extreme-case analysis.

Conclusion

The extreme-case method appears to violate the social science folk wisdom warning us not to "select on the dependent variable."[25] Selecting cases on the dependent variable is indeed problematic if a number of cases are chosen, all of which lie on one end of a variable's spectrum (they are all positive *or* negative), and if the researcher then subjects this sample to cross-case analysis as if it were representative of a population.[26] Results for this sort of analysis would almost assuredly be biased. Moreover, there will be little variation to explain, since the values of each case are explicitly constrained.

However, this is not the proper employment of the extreme-case method. (It is more appropriately labeled an extreme-*sample* method.) The extreme-case method refers back to a larger sample of cases that lie in the background of the analysis and provide a full range of variation as well as a more representative picture of the population. It is a self-conscious attempt to *maximize* variance on the dimension of interest, not to minimize it. If this population of cases is well understood – through the author's own cross-case analysis, through the work of others, or through common sense – then a researcher may justify the selection of a single case exemplifying an extreme value for within-case analysis. If not, the researcher may be well advised to follow a diverse-case method (see the earlier discussion).

By way of conclusion, let us return to the problem of representativeness. In the context of causal analysis, representativeness refers to a case that exemplifies values on X_1 and Y that conform to a general pattern. In a cross-case model, the representativeness of an individual case is gauged by the size of its residual. The representative case is therefore a typical case (as already discussed), not a deviant case (as will be discussed). It will be seen that an extreme case may be typical *or* deviant. There is simply no way to tell, because the researcher has not yet specified a causal proposition. Once such a causal proposition has been specified, we may then ask whether the case in question is similar to some population of cases (in all respects that might affect the X_1/Y relationship of interest). It is at this point that it becomes possible to say, within the context of a cross-case statistical model, whether a case lies near to, or far from, the

---

[25] Geddes (1990); King, Keohane, and Verba (1994). See also discussions in Brady and Collier (2004); Collier and Mahoney (1996); and Rogowski (1995).

[26] The exception would be a circumstance in which the researcher intends to disprove a deterministic argument (Dion 1998).

regression line. However, this sort of analysis means that the researcher is no longer pursuing an extreme-case method. The extreme-case method is purely exploratory – a way of probing possible causes of Y, or possible effects of X_1, in an open-ended fashion. If the researcher has some notion of what additional factors might affect the outcome of interest, or of what relationship the causal factor of interest has to Y, then she ought to pursue one of the other methods explored elsewhere in this chapter. This also implies that an extreme-case method may transform into a different kind of approach as a study evolves, that is, as a more specific hypothesis comes to light. Useful "extreme" cases at the outset of a study may prove less useful at a later stage of analysis.

Deviant Case

The *deviant-case* method selects the case(s) that, by reference to some general understanding of a topic (either a specific theory or common sense), demonstrates a surprising value. Barbara Geddes notes the importance of deviant cases in medical science, where researchers are habitually focused on that which is pathological (according to standard theory and practice). The *New England Journal of Medicine*, one of the premier journals of the field, carries a regular feature entitled "Case Records of the Massachusetts General Hospital." These articles bear titles like the following: "An 80-Year-Old Woman with Sudden Unilateral Blindness" or "A 76-Year-Old Man with Fever, Dyspnea, Pulmonary Infiltrates, Pleural Effusions, and Confusion."[27] Similarly, medical researchers are keen to investigate those rare individuals who have not succumbed, despite repeated exposure, to the AIDS virus.[28] Why are they resistant? What is different about these people? What can we learn about AIDS in other patients by observing people who have built-in resistance to this disease?

Case studies in psychology and sociology are often comprised of deviant (in the social sense) persons or groups. In economics, case studies may consist of countries or businesses that overperform (e.g., Botswana, Microsoft) or underperform (e.g., Britain through most of the twentieth century; Sears in recent decades) relative to some set of expectations. In

---

[27] Geddes (2003: 131). For other examples of case work from the annals of medicine, see "Clinical Reports" in *The Lancet*; "Case Studies" in *The Canadian Medical Association Journal*; and various issues of the *Journal of Obstetrics and Gynecology*, often devoted to clinical cases (discussed in Jenicek 2001: 7). For examples from the subfield of comparative politics, see Kazancigil (1994).
[28] Buchbinder and Vittinghoff (1999); Haynes, Pantaleo, and Fauci (1996).

political science, case studies may focus on countries where the welfare state is more developed (e.g., Sweden) or less developed (e.g., the United States) than one would expect, given a set of general expectations about welfare state development.

In all fields, the deviant case is closely linked to the investigation of theoretical anomalies. Indeed, to say "deviant" is to imply "anomalous."[29] Note that while extreme cases are judged relative to the mean of a single distribution (the distribution of values along a single dimension), deviant cases are judged relative to some general model of causal relations. The deviant-case method selects cases that, by reference to some general cross-case relationship, demonstrate a surprising value. They are "deviant" in that they are poorly explained by the multivariate model. The important point is that deviantness can only be assessed relative to the general (quantitative or qualitative) model employed.

This means that the relative deviantness of a case is likely to change whenever the general model is altered. For example, the United States is a deviant welfare state when this outcome is gauged relative to societal wealth. But it is less deviant – and perhaps not deviant at all – when certain additional (political and societal) factors are included in the model, as discussed in the epilogue. Deviance is model-dependent. Thus, when discussing the concept of the deviant case, it is helpful to ask the following question: *relative to what general model* (or set of background factors) is Case A deviant?

The purpose of a deviant-case analysis is usually to probe for new – but as yet unspecified – explanations. (If the purpose is to disprove an extant theory, I shall refer to the study as a crucial case, as will be discussed later.) Thus, the deviant-case method is only slightly more determinate than the extreme-case method. It, too, is an exploratory form of research. The researcher hopes that causal processes within the deviant case will illustrate some causal factor that is applicable to other (deviant) cases. This means that a deviant-case study usually culminates in a general proposition – one that may be applied to other cases in the population.

Cross-Case Technique

In statistical terms, deviant-case selection is the opposite of typical-case selection. Where a typical case lies as close as possible to the prediction

---

[29] For a discussion of the important role of anomalies in the development of scientific theorizing, see Elman (2003) and Lakatos (1978). For examples of deviant-case research designs in the social sciences, see Amenta (1991); Coppedge (2004); Eckstein (1975); Emigh (1997); and Kendall and Wolf (1949/1955).

of a formal, mathematical representation of the hypothesis at hand, a deviant case lies as far as possible from that prediction. Referring back to the model developed in equation 5.3, we can define the extent to which a case deviates from the predicted relationship as follows:

$$\text{Deviance}(i) = \text{abs}[y_i - E(y_i | x_{1,i}, \ldots x_{K,i})] \tag{5.5}$$
$$= \text{abs}[y_i - b_0 + b_1 x_{1,i} + \cdots + b_K x_{K,i}]$$

Deviance ranges from 0, for cases exactly on the regression line, to a theoretical limit of infinity. Researchers will usually be interested in selecting from the cases with the highest overall estimated deviance.

In our running example, a two-variable model with economic development (X_1) and democracy (Y), the most deviant cases fall below the regression line. This can be seen in Figure 5.4. In fact, all eight cases with a deviance score of more than ten have negative residuals; their scores on the outcome are lower than they "should" be, given their level of development. These eight cases are Croatia, Cuba, Indonesia, Iran, Morocco, Singapore, Syria, and Uzbekistan. Our general model of democracy does not explain these cases very well. Quite possibly, we could develop a better model if we understood what – aside from GDP per capita – might be driving the choice of regime type in these polities. This is the usual purpose for which deviant-case analysis is employed.

Conclusion

As I have noted, the deviant-case method is an exploratory form of analysis. As soon as a researcher's exploration of a particular case has identified a factor to explain that case, it is no longer (by definition) deviant. (The exception would be a circumstance in which a case's outcome is deemed to be accidental or idiosyncratic, and therefore inexplicable by any general model.) If the new explanation can be accurately measured as a single variable (or set of variables) across a larger sample of cases, then a new cross-case model is in order. In this fashion, a case study initially framed as a deviant case is likely to be transformed into some other sort of analysis.

This feature of the deviant-case study also helps to resolve doubts about its representativeness. Evidently, the representativeness of a deviant case is problematic, since the case in question is, by construction, atypical. However, this problem can be mitigated if the researcher generalizes whatever proposition is provided by the case study to other cases. In a large-N model, this is accomplished by the creation of a variable to represent the new hypothesis that the case study has identified. This may require some original coding of cases (in addition to the case under intensive study). However, so long as the underlying information for this coding is available, it should be possible to test the new hypothesis in a cross-case model. If the new variable is successful in explaining the studied case, it should no longer be deviant; or, at the very least, it will be less deviant. In statistical terms, its residual will have shrunk. It is now typical, or at least more typical, and this relieves concerns about possible unrepresentativeness.

Influential Case

Sometimes the choice of a case is motivated solely by the need to verify the assumptions behind a general model of causal relations. Here, the analyst attempts to provide a rationale for disregarding a problematic case, or a set of problematic cases. That is to say, she attempts to show why apparent deviations from the norm are not *really* deviant, or do not challenge the core of the theory, once the circumstances of the special case or cases are fully understood. A cross-case analysis may, after all, be marred by several classes of problems, including measurement error, specification error, errors in establishing proper boundaries for the inference (the scope of the argument), and stochastic error (fluctuations in the phenomenon under study that are treated as random, given available theoretical and empirical resources). If poorly fitting cases can be explained away by reference to these kinds of problems, then the theory of interest is that much stronger. This sort of deviant-case analysis answers the question, "What about Case A (or cases of Type A)? How does that (seemingly disconfirming) case fit the model?"

Because its underlying purpose, as well as the appropriate techniques for case identification, is different from that of the deviant-case study, I offer a new term for this method. The *influential case* is a case that appears at first glance to invalidate a theory, or at least to cast doubt upon a theory. Possibly, upon closer inspection, it does not. Indeed, it may end up confirming that theory – perhaps in some slightly altered form. In this guise, the influential case is the "case that proves the rule."

A simple version of influential-case analysis involves the confirmation of a key case's score on some critical dimension. This is essentially a question of measurement. Sometimes cases are poorly explained simply because they are poorly understood. A close examination of a particular context may reveal that an apparently falsifying case has been miscoded. If so, the initial challenge presented by that case to some general theory has been obviated.

However, the more usual employment of the influential-case method culminates in a substantive reinterpretation of the case – perhaps even of the general model. It is not just a question of measurement. Consider Thomas Ertman's study of state building in Western Europe. As summarized by Gerardo Munck, this study argues

> that the interaction of a) the type of local government during the first period of statebuilding, with b) the timing of increases in geopolitical competition, strongly influences the kind of regime and state that emerge. [Ertman] tests this hypothesis against the historical experience of Europe and finds that most countries fit his predictions. Denmark, however, is a major exception. In Denmark, sustained geopolitical competition began relatively late and local government at the beginning of the statebuilding period was generally participatory, which should have led the country to develop 'patrimonial constitutionalism.' But in fact, it developed 'bureaucratic absolutism.' Ertman carefully explores the process through which Denmark came to have a bureaucratic absolutist state and finds that Denmark had the early marks of a patrimonial constitutionalist state. However, the country was pushed off this developmental path by the influence of German knights, who entered Denmark and brought with them German institutions of local government. Ertman then traces the causal process through which these imported institutions pushed Denmark to develop bureaucratic absolutism, concluding that this development was caused by a factor well outside his explanatory framework.[30]

Ertman's overall framework is confirmed insofar as he has been able to show, by an in-depth discussion of Denmark, that the causal processes stipulated by the general theory hold even in this apparently disconfirming case. Denmark is still deviant, but it is so because of "contingent historical circumstances" that are exogenous to the theory.[31]

The reader will have noted that influential-case analysis is similar to deviant-case analysis. Both focus on outliers, unusual cases (relative to the theory at hand). However, as we shall see, they focus on different kinds of unusual cases. Moreover, the animating goals of these two research designs are quite different. The influential-case analysis begins with the aim of confirming a general model, while the deviant-case study has the aim of generating a new hypothesis that modifies an existing general model. The confusion between these two case-study types stems from the fact that the same case study may fulfill both objectives – qualifying a general model and, at the same time, confirming its core hypothesis.

In their study of Roberto Michels's "iron law of oligarchy," Lipset, Trow, and Coleman choose to focus on an organization – the International

---

[30] Munck (2004: 118). See also Ertman (1997).
[31] Ertman (1997: 316).

Typographical Union – that appears to violate the central presupposition.[32] The ITU, as noted by one of the authors, has "a long-term two-party system with free elections and frequent turnover in office" and is thus anything but oligarchic.[33] Thus, it calls into question Michels's grand generalization about organizational behavior. The authors explain this curious result by the extraordinarily high level of education among the members of this union. Thus, Michels's law is shown to be valid for most organizations, but not all. It is valid with qualifications. Note that the respecification of the original model (in effect, Lipset, Trow, and Coleman introduce a new control variable or boundary condition) involves the exploration of a new hypothesis. In this respect, the use of an influential case to confirm an existing theory is quite similar to the use of a deviant case to unearth a new theory.

Cross-Case Technique

Influential cases in regression are those cases that, if counterfactually assigned a different value on the dependent variable, would most substantially change the resulting estimates. Two quantitative measures of influence are commonly applied in regression diagnostics.[34] The first, often referred to as the "leverage" of a case, derives from what is called the *hat matrix*.[35] Suppose that the scores on the independent variables for all of the cases in a regression are represented by the matrix X, which has N rows (representing each of the N cases) and $K + 1$ columns (representing the K independent variables and allowing for a constant). Further, allow Y to represent the scores on the dependent variable for all of the cases. Therefore, Y will have N rows and only one column.

Using these symbols, the formula for the hat matrix, H, is as follows:

$$H = X(X^T X)^{-1} X^T \tag{5.6}$$

In this equation, the symbol "T" represents a matrix transpose operation, and the symbol "-1" represents a matrix inverse operation.[36] A measure

---

[32] Lipset, Trow, and Coleman (1956).

[33] Lipset (1959: 70).

[34] Belsey, Kuh, and Welsch (2004).

[35] This somewhat curious name derives from the fact that, if the hat matrix is multiplied by the vector containing values of the dependent variable, the result is the vector of fitted values for each case. Typically, the vector of fitted values for the dependent variable is distinguished from the actual vector of values on the dependent variable by the use of the "^" or "hat" symbol. Hence, the hat matrix, which produces the fitted values, can be said to put the hat on the dependent variable.

[36] See Greene (2002) for a brief review.

of the leverage of each case can be derived from the diagonal of the hat matrix. Specifically, the leverage of case i is given by the number in the (i,i) position in the hat matrix, or $H_{i,i}$.[37]

For any X matrix, the diagonal entries in the hat matrix will automatically add up to $K + 1$. Hence, interpretations of the leverage scores for different cases will necessarily depend on the overall number of cases. Clearly, any case with a score near one is a case with a great deal of leverage. In most regression situations, however, no case has a score that high. A standard rule of thumb is to pay close attention to cases with a leverage score higher than $2\ (K + 1)/N$. Cases with a leverage score above this value are good candidates for influential-case selection.

An interesting feature of the hat matrix is that it does not depend on the values of the dependent variable. Indeed, the Y vector does not appear in equation 5.6. This means that the measure of leverage derived from the hat matrix is, in effect, a measure of *potential* influence. It tells us how much difference the case would make in the final estimate if it were to have an unusual score on the dependent variable, but it does not tell us how much difference each case actually made in the final estimate.

Analysts involved in selecting influential cases will sometimes be interested in measures of potential influence, because such measures are relevant in selecting cases when there may be some a priori uncertainty about scores on the dependent variable. Much of the information in such case studies comes from a careful, in-depth measurement of the dependent variable – which may sometimes be unknown, or only approximately known, before the case study begins. The measure of leverage derived from the hat matrix is appropriate for such situations because it does not require actual scores for the dependent variable.

A second commonly discussed measure of influence in statistics is *Cook's distance*. This statistic is a measure of the extent to which the estimates of the β_i parameters would change if a given case were omitted from the analysis. Because regression analysis typically includes more than one β_i parameter, a measure of influence requires some method of combining the differences in each parameter to produce an overall measure of a case's influence. The Cook's distance statistic resolves this dilemma by

---

[37] The discussion here involves the use of the hat matrix in linear regression. Analysts may also be interested in situations that do not resemble linear regression problems, e.g., where the dependent variable is dichotomous or categorical. Sometimes, these situations can be accommodated within the framework of generalized linear models, which includes its own generalization of the hat matrix (McCullagh and Nelder 1989).

taking a weighted sum of the squared parameter differences associated with deleting a specific case. Specifically, the formula for Cook's distance is:

$$\frac{(b_{-i} - b)^\mathrm{T} \mathbf{X}^\mathrm{T} \mathbf{X}(b_{-i} - b)}{(K + 1)MSE} \tag{5.7}$$

In this formula, b represents all of the parameter estimates from the regression using the whole set of cases, and b_{-i} represents the parameter estimates from the regression that excludes the ith case. $\mathbf{X}$, as above, represents the matrix of independent variables. K is the total number of independent variables (not including the constant, which is allowed for in the formula by the use of $K + 1$). Finally, MSE stands for the mean squared error, which is a measure of the amount of variation in the dependent variable not linearly associated with the independent variables.[38]

This somewhat intimidating mathematical notation gives precise expression to the intuitive idea, discussed earlier, of measuring influence as a weighted sum of the differences that result in each parameter estimate when a single case is deleted from the sample. One disadvantage of this formula is that it requires a number of extra regressions to be run in order to compute measures of influence for each case. The overall regression must of course be computed, and then an additional regression, with one case deleted, is required for each case.

Fortunately, matrix-algebraic manipulation demonstrates that the expression for Cook's distance given in equation 5.7 is equivalent to the following, computationally much easier expression:

$$\frac{r_i^2 \mathbf{H}_{i,i}}{(K + 1)(1 - \mathbf{H}_{i,i})} \tag{5.8}$$

In this expression, $\mathbf{H}_{i,i}$ refers to the measure of leverage for the ith case, taken from the diagonal of the hat matrix, as already discussed. K once again represents the number of independent variables. Finally, r_i^2 is a special, modified version of the ith case's regression residual, known as the Studentized residual, which needs to be separately computed.

The Studentized residual is designed so that the residuals for all cases will have the same variance. If the standard regression residual for case i

---

[38] Specifically, the MSE is found by summing the squared residuals from the full regression and then dividing by $N - K - 1$, where N is the number of cases and K is the number of independent variables.

is denoted by ε_i, then the Studentized residual, r_i^2, can be computed as follows. (All symbols in this expression are as previously defined.)

$$r_i = \frac{\varepsilon_i}{\sqrt{MSE(1 - \mathbf{H}_{i,i})}} \tag{5.9}$$

As can be seen from an inspection of equations 5.8 and 5.9, Cook's distance for a case depends primarily on two quantities: the size of the regression residual for that case and the leverage for that case. The most influential cases are those with substantial leverage that lie significantly off the regression line.

Cook's distance for a given case provides a summary of the overall difference that the decision to include that case makes for the parameter estimates. Cases with a large Cook's distance contribute quite a lot to the inferences drawn from the analysis. In this sense, such cases are vital for maintaining analytic conclusions. Discovering a significant measurement error on the dependent variable or an important omitted variable for such a case may dramatically revise estimates of the overall relationships. Hence, it may be reasonable to select influential cases for in-depth study.

To summarize, three statistical concepts have been introduced in this section. The hat matrix provides a measure of leverage, or potential influence. Based solely on each case's scores on the independent variables, the hat matrix tells us how much a change in (or a measurement error on) the dependent variable for that case would affect the overall regression line. Cook's distance goes further, considering scores on both the independent and the dependent variables in order to tell us how much the overall regression estimates would be affected if each case were to be dropped from the analysis. This produces a measure of how much actual influence each case has on the overall regression.

Either the hat matrix or Cook's distance may serve as an acceptable measure of influence for selecting case studies, although the differences just discussed must be kept in mind. In the following examples, Cook's distance will be used as the primary measure of influence because our interest is in whether any particular cases might be influencing the coefficient estimates in our democracy-and-development regression. A third concept, the Studentized residual, was introduced as a necessary element in computing Cook's distance. (The hat matrix is, of course, also a necessary ingredient in Cook's distance.)

Figure 5.6 shows the Cook's distance scores for each of the countries in the 1995 per capita GDP and democracy dataset. Most countries have

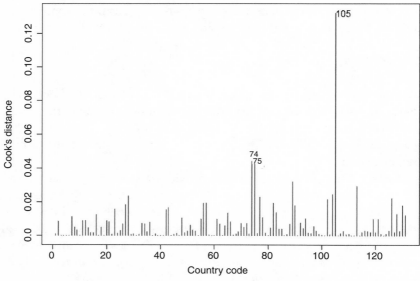

FIGURE 5.6. Potential influential cases. The Cook's distance scores for an OLS regression of democracy on logged per capita GDP. The three numbered cases have high Cook's distance scores.

quite low scores. The three most serious exceptions to this generalization are the numbered lines in the figure: Jamaica (74), Japan (75), and Nepal (105). Of these three, Nepal is clearly the most influential by a wide margin. Hence, any study of influential cases would want to start with an in-depth consideration of Nepal.

Conclusion

The use of an influential-case strategy of case selection is limited to instances in which a researcher has reason to be concerned that her results are being driven by one or a few cases. This is most likely to be true in small to moderate-sized samples. Where N is very large – greater than 1,000, let us say – it is extremely unlikely that a small set of cases (much less an individual case) will play an "influential" role. Of course, there may be influential *sets* of cases – for example, countries within a particular continent or cultural region, or persons of Irish extraction. Sets of influential observations are often problematic in a time-series cross-section dataset where each unit (e.g., country) contains multiple observations (through time) and hence may have a strong influence on aggregate results. Still, the general rule is: the larger the sample, the less important individual cases are likely to be and, hence, the less likely a researcher is to use hat matrix and Cook's distance statistics for purposes of case selection. In these instances, it may not matter very much what values individual cases display. (It may of course matter for the purpose of investigating causal mechanisms. However, for this purpose one would not employ influential statistics to choose cases.)

Crucial Case

Of all the extant methods of case selection, perhaps the most storied – and certainly the most controversial – is the *crucial-case* method, introduced to the social science world several decades ago by Harry Eckstein. In his seminal essay, Eckstein describes the crucial case as one "that *must closely fit* a theory if one is to have confidence in the theory's validity, or, conversely, *must not fit* equally well any rule contrary to that proposed."[39] A case is "crucial" in a somewhat weaker – but much more common – sense when it is most, or least, likely to fulfill a theoretical prediction. A "most-likely" case is one that, on all dimensions *except* the dimension of theoretical interest, is predicted to achieve a certain outcome, and yet does not. It is therefore used to disconfirm a theory. A "least-likely" case is one that, on all dimensions *except* the dimension of theoretical interest, is predicted not to achieve a certain outcome, and yet does so. It is therefore used to confirm a theory. In all formulations, the crucial case offers a most-difficult test for an argument, and hence provides what is perhaps the strongest sort of evidence possible in a nonexperimental, single-case setting.

Since the publication of Eckstein's influential essay, the crucial-case approach has been claimed in a multitude of studies across several social science disciplines and has come to be recognized as a staple of the case study method.[40] Yet the idea of any single case playing a crucial (or "critical") role is not widely accepted among most methodologists.[41] (Even its progenitor seems to have had doubts.)

Unfortunately, discussion of this method has focused misleadingly on what are presumed to be largely inductive issues. Are there good crucial

---

[39] Eckstein (1975: 118).

[40] For examples of the crucial-case method, see Bennett, Lepgold, and Unger (1994); Desch (2002); Goodin and Smitsman (2000); Kemp (1986); and Reilly and Phillpot (2003). For general discussion, see George and Bennett (2005); Levy (2002a); and Stinchcombe (1968: 24–8).

[41] See, e.g., Sekhon (2004).

cases out there in the empirical world? Have social scientists done a good job in identifying them? Yet the practicability of this method rests on issues that are largely deductive in nature, as we shall see.

The Confirmatory (Least-Likely) Crucial Case

Let us begin with the confirmatory (a.k.a. least-likely) crucial case. The implicit logic of this research design may be summarized as follows. Given a set of facts, we are asked to contemplate the probability that a given theory is true. While the facts matter, to be sure, the effectiveness of this sort of research also rests upon the formal properties of the theory in question. Specifically, the degree to which a theory is amenable to confirmation is contingent upon how many predictions can be derived from the theory and on how "risky" each individual prediction is. In Popper's words,

Confirmations should count only if they are the result of *risky predictions*; that is to say, if, unenlightened by the theory in question, we should have expected an event which was incompatible with the theory – an event which would have refuted the theory. Every 'good' scientific theory is a prohibition; it forbids certain things to happen. The more a theory forbids, the better it is.[42]

A risky prediction is therefore one that is highly precise and determinate, and thus unlikely to be explainable by other causal factors (external to the theory of interest) or through stochastic processes. A theory produces many such predictions if it is fully elaborated, issuing predictions not only on the central outcome of interest but also on specific causal mechanisms, and if it is broad in purview. (The notion of riskiness may be conceptualized within the Popperian lexicon as *degrees of falsifiability*.)

These points can also be articulated in Bayesian terms. Colin Howson and Peter Urbach explain: "The degree to which h [a hypothesis] is confirmed by e [a set of evidence] depends... on the extent to which $P(e|h)$ exceeds $P(e)$, that is, on how much more probable e is relative to the hypothesis and background assumptions than it is relative just to background assumptions." Again, "confirmation is correlated with how much more probable the evidence is if the hypothesis is true than if it is false."[43] Thus, the stranger the prediction offered by a theory – relative to what we would normally expect – the greater the degree of confirmation that will be afforded by the evidence. As an intuitive example, Howson and Urbach offer the following:

---

[42] Popper (1963: 36). See also Popper (1934/1968).
[43] Howson and Urbach (1989: 86).

If a soothsayer predicts that you will meet a dark stranger sometime and you do in fact, your faith in his powers of precognition would not be much enhanced: you would probably continue to think his predictions were just the result of guesswork. However, if the prediction also gave the correct number of hairs on the head of that stranger, your previous scepticism would no doubt be severely shaken.[44]

While these Popperian/Bayesian insights[45] are relevant to all empirical research designs, they are especially relevant to case study research designs, for in these settings a single case (or, at most, a small number of cases) is required to bear a heavy burden of proof. It should be no surprise, therefore, that Popper's idea of "riskiness" was appropriated by case study researchers like Harry Eckstein to validate the enterprise of single-case analysis. (Although Eckstein does not cite Popper, the intellectual lineage is clear.) Riskiness, here, is analogous to what is usually referred to as a "most-difficult" research design, which in a case study research design would be understood as a least-likely case. Note also that the distinction between a must-fit case and a least-likely case – that, in the event, actually does fit the terms of a theory – is a matter of degree. Cases are more or less crucial for confirming theories. The point is that, in some circumstances, the riskiness of the theory may compensate for a paucity of empirical evidence.

The crucial-case research design is, perforce, a highly deductive enterprise; much depends on the quality of the theory under investigation. It follows that the theories most amenable to crucial-case analysis are those that are lawlike in their precision, degree of elaboration, consistency, and scope. The more a theory attains the status of a causal law, the easier it will be to confirm, or to disconfirm, with a single case.

Indeed, risky predictions are common in natural science fields such as physics, which in turn served as the template for the deductive-nomological ("covering-law") model of science that influenced Eckstein and others in the postwar decades.[46] A frequently cited example is the first important empirical demonstration of the theory of relativity, which took the form of a single-event prediction on the occasion of the May 29, 1919, solar eclipse. Stephen Van Evera describes the impact of this prediction on the validation of Einstein's theory.

---

[44] Ibid.

[45] A third position, which purports to be neither Popperian nor Bayesian, has been articulated by Mayo (1996: Chapter 6). From this perspective, the same idea is articulated as a matter of "severe tests."

[46] See, e.g., Hempel (1942).

Einstein's theory predicted that gravity would bend the path of light toward a gravity source by a specific amount. Hence it predicted that during a solar eclipse stars near the sun would appear displaced – stars actually behind the sun would appear next to it, and stars lying next to the sun would appear farther from it – and it predicted the amount of apparent displacement. No other theory made these predictions. The passage of this one single-case-study test brought the theory wide acceptance because the tested predictions were unique – there was no plausible competing explanation for the predicted result – hence the passed test was very strong.[47]

The strength of this test is the extraordinary fit between the theory and a set of facts found in a single case, and the corresponding lack of fit between all other theories and this set of facts. Einstein offered an explanation of a particular set of anomalous findings that no other existing theory could make sense of. Of course, one must assume that there was no – or limited – measurement error. And one must assume that the phenomenon of interest is largely invariant; light does not bend differently at different times and places (except in ways that can be understood through the theory of relativity). And one must assume, finally, that the theory itself makes sense on other grounds (other than the case of special interest); it is a plausible general theory. If one is willing to accept these a priori assumptions, then the 1919 "case study" provides a very strong confirmation of the theory. It is difficult to imagine a stronger proof of the theory from within an observational (nonexperimental) setting.

In social science settings, by contrast, one does not commonly find single-case studies offering knock-out evidence for a theory. This is, in my view, largely a product of the looseness (the underspecification) of most social science theories. George and Bennett point out that while the thesis of the democratic peace is as close to a "law" as social science has yet seen, it cannot be confirmed (or refuted) by looking at specific causal mechanisms because the causal pathways mandated by the theory are multiple and diverse. Under the circumstances, no single-case test can offer strong confirmation of the theory (though, as we shall discuss, the theory may be *dis*confirmed with a single case).[48]

However, if one adopts a softer version of the crucial-case method – the least-likely (most difficult) case – then possibilities abound. Lily Tsai's investigation of governance at the village level in China employs several in-depth case studies of villages that are chosen (in part) because of their

---

[47] Van Evera (1997: 66–7). See also Eckstein (1975) and Popper (1963).
[48] George and Bennett (2005: 209).

least-likely status relative to the theory of interest. Tsai's hypothesis is that villages with greater social solidarity (based on preexisting religious or familial networks) will develop a higher level of social trust and mutual obligation and, as a result, will experience better governance. Crucial cases, therefore, are villages that evidence a high level of social solidarity but that, along other dimensions, would be judged least-likely to develop good governance – that is, they are poor, isolated, and lack democratic institutions or accountability mechanisms from above. "Li Settlement," in Fujian province, is such a case. The fact that this impoverished village nonetheless boasts an impressive set of infrastructural accomplishments such as paved roads with drainage ditches (a rarity in rural China) suggests that something rather unusual is going on here. Because her case is carefully chosen to eliminate rival explanations, Tsai's conclusions about the special role of social solidarity are difficult to gainsay. How else would one explain this otherwise anomalous result? This is the strength of the least-likely case, where all other plausible explanations for an outcome have been mitigated.[49]

Jack Levy refers to this, evocatively, as a "Sinatra inference": if it can make it here, it can make it anywhere.[50] Thus, if social solidarity has the hypothesized effect in Li Settlement, it should have the same effect in more propitious settings (e.g., where there is greater economic surplus). The same implicit logic informs many case study analyses where the intent of the study is to confirm a hypothesis on the basis of a single case (without extensive cross-case analysis). Indeed, I suspect that, *implicitly*, most case study work that focuses on a single case and is not nested within a cross-case analysis relies largely on the logic of the least-likely case. Rarely is this logic made explicit, except perhaps in a passing phrase or two. Yet the deductive logic of the "risky" prediction may in fact be central to the case study enterprise. Whether a case study is convincing or not often rests on the reader's evaluation of how strong the evidence for an argument might be, and this in turn – wherever cross-case evidence is limited and no manipulated treatment can be devised – rests upon an estimation of the degree of "fit" between a theory and the evidence at hand, as discussed.

---

[49] Tsai (2007). It should be noted that Tsai's conclusions do not rest solely on this crucial case. Indeed, she employs a broad range of methodological tools, encompassing case study and cross-case methods.

[50] Levy (2002a: 144). See also Khong (1992: 49); Sagan (1995: 49); and Shafer (1988: 14–6).

The Disconfirmatory (Most-Likely) Crucial Case

A central Popperian insight is that it is easier to disconfirm an inference than to confirm that same inference. (Indeed, Popper doubted that any inference could be fully confirmed, and for this reason preferred the term "corroborate.") This is particularly true of case study research designs, where evidence is limited to one or several cases. The key proviso is that the theory under investigation must take a consistent (a.k.a. invariant, deterministic) form, even if its predictions are not terrifically precise, well elaborated, or broad.

As it happens, there are a fair number of invariant propositions floating around the social science disciplines.[51] In Chapter Three, we discussed an older theory that stipulated that political stability would occur only in countries that are relatively homogeneous, or where existing heterogeneities are mitigated by cross-cutting cleavages.[52] Arend Lijphart's study of the Netherlands, a peaceful country with reinforcing social cleavages, is commonly viewed as refuting this theory on the basis of a single in-depth case analysis.[53]

Heretofore, I have treated causal factors as dichotomous. Countries have either reinforcing or cross-cutting cleavages, and they have regimes that are either peaceful or conflictual. Evidently, these sorts of parameters are often matters of degree. In this reading of the theory, cases are *more or less* crucial. Accordingly, the most useful – that is, most crucial – case for Lijphart's purpose is one that has the most segregated social groups and the most peaceful and democratic track record. In these respects, the Netherlands was a very good choice. Indeed, the degree of disconfirmation offered by this case study is probably greater than the degree of disconfirmation that might have been provided by another case, such as India or Papua New Guinea – countries where social peace has not always been secure. The point is that where variables are continuous rather than dichotomous, it is possible to evaluate potential cases in terms of their *degree of crucialness.*

Note that when *dis*confirming a causal argument, background causal factors are irrelevant (except as they might affect the classification of the case within the population of an inference). It does not matter how the

---

[51] Goertz and Levy (forthcoming); Goertz and Starr (2003).

[52] Almond (1956); Bentley (1908/1967); Lipset (1960/1963); Truman (1951).

[53] Lijphart (1968). See also discussions in Eckstein (1975) and Lijphart (1969). For additional examples of case studies disconfirming general propositions of a deterministic nature, see Allen (1965); Lipset, Trow, and Coleman (1956); Njolstad (1990); Reilly (2000/2001); and the discussions in Dion (1998) and Rogowski (1995).

Netherlands, India, and Papua New Guinea score on *other* factors that affect democracy and social peace.

Granted, it may be questioned whether presumed invariant theories are *really* invariant; perhaps they are better understood as probabilistic. Perhaps, that is, the theory of cross-cutting cleavages is still true, probabilistically, despite the apparent Dutch exception. Or perhaps the theory is still true, deterministically, within a subset of cases that does not include the Netherlands. (This sort of claim seems unlikely in this particular instance, but it is quite plausible in many others.) Or perhaps the theory is in need of reframing; it is true, deterministically, but applies only to cross-cutting ethnic/racial cleavages, not to cleavages that are primarily religious. One may quibble over what it means to "disconfirm" a theory. The point is that the crucial case has, in all these circumstances, provided important updating of a theoretical prior.

Conclusion

In this section, I have argued that the degree to which crucial cases can provide decisive confirmation or disconfirmation of a theory is in large part a product of the structure of the theory to be tested. It is a deductive matter rather than an inductive matter, strictly speaking. In this respect, a "positivist" orientation toward the work of social science may lead to a greater appreciation of the case study format – not a denigration of that format, as is usually supposed. Those who, with Eckstein, embrace the notion of covering laws are likely to be attracted to the idea of cases that are crucial. By the same token, those who are impressed by the irregularity and complexity of social behavior are unlikely to be persuaded by crucial-case studies, except as a method of *dis*confirming absurdly rigid causal laws.

I have shown, relatedly, that it is almost always easier to disconfirm a theory than to confirm it with a single case. Thus, a theory that is understood to be deterministic may be disconfirmed by a case study, properly chosen. This is the most common employment of the crucial-case method in social science settings.

Note that the crucial-case method of case selection *cannot* be employed in a large-N context. This is because the method of selection would render the case study redundant. Once one identifies the relevant parameters and the scores of all cases on those parameters, one has in effect constructed a cross-case model that will, by itself, confirm or disconfirm the theory in question. The case study is thenceforth irrelevant, at least as a means of confirmation or disconfirmation. It remains highly relevant as a means of exploring causal mechanisms, of course. However, because this objective is quite different from that which is usually associated with the term, I enlist a new term for this technique.

Pathway Case

One of the most important functions of case study research is the elucidation of causal mechanisms. This is well established (see Chapter Three). But what sort of case is most useful for this purpose? Although all case studies presumably shed light on causal mechanisms, not all cases are equally transparent. In situations where a causal hypothesis is clear and has already been confirmed by cross-case analysis, researchers are well advised to focus on a case where the causal effect of one factor can be isolated from other potentially confounding factors. I shall call this a *pathway case* to indicate its uniquely penetrating insight into causal mechanisms.

To clarify, the pathway case exists only in circumstances where cross-case covariational patterns are well studied but where the mechanism linking X_1 and Y remains dim. Because the pathway case builds on prior cross-case analysis, the problem of case selection must be situated within that sample. There is no stand-alone pathway case. Thus, the following discussion focuses on how to select one (or a few) cases from a cross-case sample.

Cross-Case Technique with Binary Variables

The logic of the pathway case is clearest in situations of causal sufficiency – where a causal factor of interest, X_1, is sufficient by itself (though perhaps not necessary) to cause a particular outcome, Y, understood as a unidirectional or asymmetric casual relationship. The other causes of Y, about which we need make no assumptions, are designated as a vector, X_2.

Note that wherever various causal factors are deemed to be substitutable for one another, each factor is conceptualized (individually) as sufficient.[54] Situations of causal equifinality presume causal sufficiency on the part of each factor or set of conjoint factors. The QCA technique, for example, presumes causal sufficiency for each of the designated causal paths.

---

[54] Braumoeller (2003).

Consider the following examples culled by Bear Braumoeller and drawn from diverse fields of political science.[55] The decision to seek an alliance is motivated by the search for either autonomy or security.[56] Conquest is prevented by either deterrence or defense.[57] Civilian intervention in military affairs is caused by either political isolation or geographical encirclement.[58] War is the product of miscalculation or loss of control.[59] Nonvoting is caused by ignorance, indifference, dissatisfaction, or inactivity.[60] Voting decisions are influenced either by high levels of information or by the use of candidate gender as a proxy for social information.[61] Democratization comes about through leadership-initiated reform, a controlled opening to opposition, or the collapse of an authoritarian regime.[62] These, and many other, social science arguments take the form of causal substitutability – multiple paths to a given outcome.

For heuristic purposes, it will be helpful to pursue one of these examples in greater detail. For consistency, I focus on the last of the exemplars – democratization. The literature, according to Braumoeller, identifies three main avenues of democratization (there may be more, but for present purposes let us assume that the universe is limited to three). The case study format constrains us to analyze one at a time, so let us limit our scope to the first one – leadership-initiated reform. So considered, a causal-pathway case would be one with the following features: (a) democratization, (b) leadership-initiated reform, (c) no controlled opening to the opposition, (d) no collapse of the previous authoritarian regime, and (e) no other extraneous factors that might affect the process of democratization. In a case of this type, the causal mechanisms by which leadership-initiated reform may lead to democratization will be easiest to study. Note that it is not necessary to assume that leadership-initiated reform *always* leads to democratization; it may or may not be a deterministic cause. But it is necessary to assume that leadership-initiated reform can *sometimes* lead to democratization. This covariational assumption about the relationship

---

[55] Ibid. My chosen examples are limited to those that might plausibly be modeled with dichotomous variables. For further discussion and additional examples, see Most and Starr (1984) and Cioffi-Revilla and Starr (1995).

[56] Morrow (1991: 905).

[57] Schelling (1966: 78).

[58] Posen (1984: 79).

[59] Levy (1983: 86).

[60] Ragsdale and Rusk (1993: 723–4).

[61] McDermott (1997).

[62] Colomer (1991).

TABLE 5.2. *Pathway case with dichotomous causal factors*

		X_1	X_2	Y
	A	1	1	1
	B	0	0	0
	C	0	1	1
Case	D	0	0	1
types	E	1	0	0
	F	1	1	0
	G	0	1	0
	H	1	0	1

X_1 = the variable of theoretical interest. X_2 = a vector of controls (a score of zero indicates that all control variables have a score of zero, while a score of one indicates that all control variables have a score of one). Y = the outcome of interest. $A–H$ = case types (the N for each case type is indeterminate). H = pathway case. Sample size = indeterminate.

Assumptions: (a) all variables can be coded dichotomously; (b) all independent variables are positively correlated with Y in the general case; (c) X_1 is (at least sometimes) a sufficient cause of Y.

between X_1 and Y is presumably sustained by the cross-case evidence (if it is not, there is no justification for a pathway case study).

Now let us move from these examples to a general-purpose model. For heuristic purposes, let us presume that all variables in that model are dichotomous (coded as zero or one) and that the model is complete (all causes of Y are included). All causal relationships will be coded so as to be positive: X_1 and Y covary as do X_2 and Y. This allows us to visualize a range of possible combinations at a glance.

Recall that the pathway case is always focused, by definition, on a single causal factor, denoted X_1. (The researcher's focus may shift to other causal factors, but may focus only on one causal factor at a time.) In this scenario, and regardless of how many additional causes of Y there might be (denoted X_2, a vector of controls), there are only eight relevant case types, as illustrated in Table 5.2. Identifying these case types is a relatively simple matter, and can be accomplished in a small-N sample by the construction of a truth table (modeled after Table 5.2) or in a large-N sample by the use of cross-tabs.

Note that the total number of combinations of values depends on the number of control variables, which we have represented with a single vector, X_2. If this vector consists of a single variable, then there are only eight case types. If this vector consists of two variables (X_{2a}, X_{2b}), then the total number of possible combinations increases from eight (2^3) to sixteen (2^4), and so forth. However, none of these combinations is relevant for present purposes except those where X_{2a} and X_{2b} have the *same value* (zero or one). "Mixed" cases are not causal pathway cases, for reasons that should become clear.

The pathway case, following the logic of the crucial case, is one where the causal factor of interest, X_1, correctly predicts Y's positive value (Y = 1) while all other possible causes of Y (represented by the vector, X_2) make "wrong" predictions. If X_1 is – at least in some circumstances – a sufficient cause of Y, then it is these sorts of cases that should be most useful for tracing causal mechanisms. There is only one such case in Table 5.2 – H. In all other cases, the mechanism running from X_1 to Y would be difficult to discern, because the outcome to be explained does not occur (Y = 0), because X_1 and Y are not correlated in the usual way (violating the terms of our hypothesis), or because other confounding factors (X_2) intrude. In case A, for example, the positive value on Y could be a product of X_1 or X_2. Consequently, an in-depth examination of cases A–G is not likely to be very revealing.

Keep in mind that because we already know from our cross-case examination what the general causal relationships are, we know (prior to the case study investigation) what constitutes a correct or incorrect prediction. In the crucial-case method, by contrast, these expectations are deductive rather than empirical. This is what differentiates the two methods. And this is why the causal-pathway case is useful principally for elucidating causal mechanisms rather than for verifying or falsifying general propositions (which are already apparent from the cross-case evidence).[63]

Now let us complicate matters a bit by imagining a scenario in which at least some of these substitutable causes are conjoint (a.k.a. conjunctural). That is, several combinations of factors – $X_a + X_b$ *or* $X_c + X_d$ – are sufficient to produce the outcome, Y. This is known in philosophical circles as an INUS condition,[64] and it is the pattern of causation assumed in most

---

[63] Of course, we should leave open the possibility that an investigation of causal mechanisms might invalidate a general claim, if that claim is utterly contingent upon a specific set of causal mechanisms and the case study shows that no such mechanisms are present. However, this is rather unlikely in most social science settings. Usually, the result of such a finding will be a reformulation of the causal processes by which X_1 causes Y – or, alternatively, a realization that the case under investigation is aberrant (atypical of the general population of cases).

[64] An INUS condition refers to an Insufficient but Necessary part of a condition which is itself Unnecessary but Sufficient for a particular result. Thus, when one identifies a short circuit as the "cause" of a fire, one is saying, in effect, that the fire was caused by a short

QCA (Qualitative Comparative Analysis) models.[65] Here, everything that has been said so far must be adjusted so that X_1 refers to a *set* of causes (e.g., $X_a + X_b$) and X_2 refers to a vector of sets (e.g., $X_c + X_d$, $X_e + X_f$, $X_g + X_h$, ...). The scoring of all these variables makes matters more difficult than in the previous set of examples. However, the logical task is identical, and can be accomplished in a similar fashion, that is, in small-N datasets with truth tables and in large-N datasets with cross-tabs. Case H now refers to a conjunction of causes, but it is still the only possible pathway case.

Cross-Case Technique with Continuous Variables

Finally, we must tackle the most complicated scenario – when all (or most) variables of concern to the model are continuous, rather than dichotomous. Here, the job of case selection is considerably more complex, for causal "sufficiency" (in the usual sense) cannot be invoked. It is no longer plausible to assume that a given cause can be entirely partitioned, that is, that all rival factors can be eliminated. Even so, the search for a pathway case may be viable.

What we are looking for in this scenario is a case that satisfies two criteria: (1) it is not an outlier (or at least not an extreme outlier) in the general model, and (2) its score on the outcome (Y) is strongly influenced by the theoretical variable of interest (X_1), taking all other factors into account (X_2). In this sort of case it should be easiest to identify the causal mechanisms that lie between X_1 and Y.

In a large-N sample, these two desiderata may be judged by a careful attention to the residuals attached to each case. Recall that the question of deviance, which we have discussed in previous sections, is a matter of degree. Cases are more or less typical/deviant relative to a general model, as judged by the size of their residuals. It is easy enough to exclude cases with very high residuals (e.g., standardized residual $> |2|$). For cases that lie closer to their predicted value, small differences in the size of residuals may not matter so much. But, ceteris paribus, one would prefer a case that lies closer to the regression line.

circuit in conjunction with some other background factors (e.g., oxygen) that were also necessary to that outcome. But one is not implying that a short circuit was necessary to that fire, which might have been (under different circumstances) caused by other factors. See Mackie (1965/1993).

[65] Ragin (2000).

Achieving the second desideratum requires a bit of manipulation. In order to determine which (non-outlier) cases are most strongly affected by X_1, given all the other parameters in the model, one must compare the size of the residuals (their absolute value) for each case in a reduced-form model, $Y = \text{Constant} + X_2 + \text{Res}_{\text{reduced}}$, to the size of the residuals for each case in a full model, $Y = \text{Constant} + X_2 + X_1 + \text{Res}_{\text{full}}$. The pathway case is that case, or set of cases, that shows the greatest difference between the residuals for the reduced-form model and the full model (ΔResidual). Thus,

$$\text{Pathway} = |\text{Res}_{\text{reduced}} - \text{Res}_{\text{full}}|, \text{ if } |\text{Res}_{\text{reduced}}| > |\text{Res}_{\text{full}}| \qquad (5.10)$$

Note that the residual for a case must be smaller in the full model than in the reduced-form model; otherwise, the addition of the variable of interest (X_1) pulls the case *away* from the regression line. We want to find a case where the addition of X_1 pushes the case toward the regression line, that is, it helps to "explain" the case.

As an example, let us suppose that we are interested in exploring the effect of mineral wealth on the prospects for democracy in a society. According to a good deal of work on this subject, countries with a bounty of natural resources – particularly oil – are less likely to democratize (or, once having undergone a democratic transition, are more likely to revert to authoritarian rule).[66] The cross-country evidence is robust. Yet, as is often the case, causal mechanisms remain rather obscure. Consider the following list of possible causal pathways, summarized by Michael Ross:

A 'rentier effect'...suggests that resources rich governments use low tax rates and patronage to relieve pressures for greater accountability; a 'repression effect'...argues that resource wealth retards democratization by enabling governments to boost their funding for internal security; and a 'modernization effect'...holds that growth based on the export of oil and minerals fails to bring about the social and cultural changes that tend to produce democratic government.[67]

Are all three causal mechanisms at work? Although Ross attempts to test these factors in a large-N cross-country setting, his answers remain rather

---

[66] Barro (1999), Humphreys (2005); Ross (2001).
[67] Ross (2001: 327–8).

speculative.[68] Let us see how this might be handled by a pathway-case approach.

The factor of theoretical interest, oil wealth, may be operationalized as per capita oil production (barrels of oil produced, divided by the total population of a country).[69] As previously, we measure democracy with a continuous variable coded from −10 (most authoritarian) to +10 (most democratic). Additional factors in the model include GDP per capita (logged), Muslims (as percent of the population), European language (percent speaking a European language), and ethnic fractionalization (1 − likelihood of two randomly chosen individuals belonging to the same ethnic group).[70] These are regarded as background variables (X_2) that may affect a country's propensity to democratize. The full model, limited to 1995 (as in previous analyses), is as follows:

$$\text{Democracy} = {}^{-}3.71 \text{ Constant} + 1.258 \text{ GDP} \tag{5.11}$$
$$+{}^{-}.075 \text{ Muslim} + 1.843 \text{ European}$$
$$+{}^{-}2.093 \text{ Ethnic fract} +{}^{-} 7.662 \text{ Oil}$$
$$R2_{adj} = .450 \quad (N = 149)$$

The reduced-form model is identical except that the variable of theoretical interest, Oil, is removed.

$$\text{Democracy} = {}^{-}.831 \text{ Constant} + .909 \text{ GDP} \tag{5.12}$$
$$+{}^{-}.086 \text{ Muslim} + 2.242 \text{ European}$$
$$+{}^{-}3.023 \text{ Ethnic fract}$$
$$R2_{adj} = .428 \ (N = 149)$$

What does a comparison of the residuals across equations 5.11 and 5.12 reveal? Table 5.3 displays the highest ΔResidual cases. Several of

---

[68] Ross tests these various causal mechanisms with cross-country data, employing various proxies for these concepts in the benchmark model and observing the effect of these – presumably intermediary – effects on the main variable of interest (oil resources). This is a good example of how cross-case evidence can be mustered to shed light on causal mechanisms; one is not limited to case study formats, as discussed in Chapter Three. Still, as Ross notes (2001: 356), these tests are by no means definitive. Indeed, the coefficient on the key oil variable remains fairly constant, except in circumstances where the sample is severely constrained.

[69] Derived from Humphreys (2005).

[70] GDPpc data are from World Bank (2003). Muslims and European language are coded by the author. Ethnic fractionalization is drawn from Alesina et al. (2003).

TABLE 5.3. *Possible pathway cases where variables are scalar and assumptions probabilistic*

Country	$Res_{reduced}$	Res_{full}	$\Delta Residual$
Iran	−.282	−.456	.175
Turkmenistan	−1.220	−1.398	.178
Mauritania	−.076	−.255	.179
Turkey	2.261	2.069	.192
Switzerland	.177	−.028	.205
Venezuela	.148	.355	−.207
Belgium	.518	.310	.208
Morocco	−.540	−.776	.236
Jordan	.382	.142	.240
Djibouti	−.451	−.696	.245
Bahrain	−1.411	−1.673	.262
Luxembourg	.559	.291	.269
Singapore	−1.593	−1.864	.271
Oman	−1.270	−.981	−.289
Gabon	−1.743	−1.418	−.325
Saudi Arabia	−1.681	−1.253	−.428
Norway	.315	1.285	−.971
United Arab Emirates	−1.256	−.081	−1.175
Kuwait	−1.007	.925	−1.932

$Res_{reduced}$ = the standardized residual for a case obtained from the reduced model (without Oil) – equation 5.12.
Res_{full} = the standardized residual for a case obtained from the full model (with Oil) – equation 5.11.
$\Delta Residual = Res_{reduced} − Res_{full}$. Listed in order of absolute value.

these may be summarily removed from consideration by virtue of the fact that $|Res_{reduced}| < |Res_{full}|$. Thus, we see that the inclusion of Oil increases the residual for Norway; this case is apparently better explained *without* the inclusion of the variable of theoretical interest. Needless to say, this is not a good case to explore if we wish to examine the causal mechanisms that lie between natural resource wealth and democracy. (It might, however, be a good case for model diagnostics, as discussed in the previous section on influential cases.)

Among cases where the residual declines from the reduced to the full model, several are clear-cut favorites as pathway cases. The United Arab Emirates and Kuwait have the highest $\Delta Residual$ values and also have fairly modest residuals in the full model (Res_{full}), signifying that these cases are not extreme outliers; indeed, according to the parameters of this model, the United Arab Emirates would be regarded as a typical case. The analysis suggests, therefore, that researchers seeking to explore the effect of oil wealth on regime type might do well to focus on these two cases, since their patterns of democracy cannot be well explained by other factors such as, economic development, religion, European influence, or ethnic fractionalization. The presence of oil wealth in these countries would appear to have a strong *independent* effect on the prospects for democratization in these countries, an effect that is well modeled by our general theory and by the available cross-case evidence. And this effect should be interpretable in a case-study format – more interpretable, at any rate, than it would be in other cases.

Conclusion

The logic of causal "elimination" is much more compelling where variables are dichotomous and where causal sufficiency can be assumed (X_1 is sufficient by itself, at least in some circumstances, to cause Y). Where variables are continuous the strategy of the pathway case is more dubious, for potentially confounding causal factors (X_2) cannot be neatly partitioned. Even so, this discussion has shown why the selection of a pathway case is a logical approach to case study analysis in many circumstances.

The exceptions may be briefly noted. Sometimes, where all variables in a model are dichotomous, there are no pathway cases, that is, no cases of type H (in Table 5.2). This is known as the "empty cell" problem, or a problem of severe causal multicollinearity. The universe of observational data does not always oblige us with cases that allow us to test a given hypothesis independently of all others.

Where variables are continuous, the analogous problem is that of a causal variable of interest (X_1) that has only minimal effects on the outcome of interest. That is, its role in the general model is quite minor (as judged by its standardized coefficient or by F-tests comparing the reduced-form model and the full model). In these situations, the only cases that are strongly affected by X_1 – if there are any at all – may be extreme outliers, and these sorts of cases are not properly regarded as providing confirmatory evidence for a proposition, for reasons that are abundantly clear by now.

Finally, it must be underlined that the identification of a causal-pathway case does not obviate the utility of exploring other cases. However, this sort of multicase investigation moves beyond the logic of the causal pathway case, underlining a point that we shall return to in the concluding section of the chapter: case-selection procedures often combine different logics.

Despite the technical nature of this discussion, it should be noted that when researchers refer to a particular case as an "example" of a broader phenomenon, they are often referring to a pathway case. This sort of case illustrates the causal relationship of interest in a particularly vivid manner, and therefore may be regarded as a common trope among case study researchers.

Most-Similar Case

The most-similar method, unlike the previous methods, employs a minimum of two cases.[71] In its purest form, the chosen pair of cases is similar in all respects *except* the variable(s) of interest.

If the study is *exploratory* (i.e., hypothesis-generating), the researcher looks for cases that differ on the outcome of theoretical interest but are similar on various factors that might have contributed to that outcome, as illustrated in Table 5.4 (A). This is a common form of case selection at the initial stage of research. Often, fruitful analysis begins with an apparent anomaly: two cases are apparently quite similar, and yet demonstrate surprisingly different outcomes. The hope is that intensive study of these cases will reveal one – or at most several – factors that differ across these cases. These differing factors (X_1) are the putative causes.

Sometimes, a researcher begins with a strong hypothesis, in which case her research design is confirmatory (hypothesis-testing) from the get-go. That is, she strives to identify cases that exhibit different scores on the factor of interest and similar scores on all other possible causal factors, as illustrated in the second (hypothesis-testing) diagram in Table 5.4 (B). If she discovers such a case, it is regarded as providing confirmatory evidence for the proposition, as well as fodder for an exploration of causal mechanisms.

The point is that the purpose of a most-similar research design, and hence its basic set-up, may change as a researcher moves from an exploratory to a confirmatory mode of analysis. However, regardless of

---

[71] Sometimes the most-similar method is known as the "method of difference," after its inventor (Mill 1843/1872). For later treatments see Cohen and Nagel (1934); Eggan (1954); Gerring (2001: Chapter 9); Lijphart (1971, 1975); Meckstroth (1975); Przeworski and Teune (1970); and Skocpol and Somers (1980).

TABLE 5.4. *Most-similar analysis with two case types*

(A) Hypothesis-generating (Y-centered):

		X_1	X_2	Y
Case	A	?	0	1
types	B	?	0	0

(B) Hypothesis-testing (X_1/Y-centered):

		X_1	X_2	Y
Case	A	1	0	?
types	B	0	0	?

X_1 = the variable of theoretical interest. X_2 = a vector of controls. Y = the outcome of interest.

where one begins, the results, when published, look like a hypothesis-testing research design. Question marks have been removed: (A) becomes (B) in Table 5.4. Consequently, the notion of a "most-similar" analysis is usually understood as a tool for understanding a specific X_1/Y relationship.

As an example, let us consider Leon Epstein's classic study of party cohesion, which focuses on two similar countries, the United States and Canada. Canada has highly disciplined parties whose members vote together on the floor of the House of Commons, while the United States has weak, undisciplined parties whose members often defect on floor votes in Congress. In explaining these divergent outcomes, persistent over many years, Epstein first discusses possible causal factors that are held more or less constant across the two cases. Both the United States and Canada inherited English political cultures; both have large territories and heterogeneous populations; both are federal; and both have a fairly loose party structures with strong regional bases and a weak center. These are the "control" variables (X_2). Where they differ is in one constitutional feature: Canada is parliamentary, while the United States is presidential. And it is this institutional difference that Epstein identifies as the differentiating cause (X_1).[72]

Several caveats apply to any most-similar analysis (in addition to the usual set of assumptions applying to all case study analysis). First,

---

[72] For further examples of the most-similar method, see Brenner (1976); Hamilton (1977); Lipset (1968); Miguel (2004); Moulder (1977); and Posner (2004).

one must code cases dichotomously (high/low, present/absent). This is straightforward if the underlying variables are also dichotomous (e.g., federal/unitary). However, it is often the case that variables of concern in the model are continuous (e.g., party cohesion). In this setting, the researcher must "dichotomize" the scoring of cases so as to simplify the two-case analysis. This is relatively unproblematic if the actual scores on this dimension are quite different (on X_1 and Y) or virtually identical (on X_2). Unfortunately, the empirical universe does not always oblige the requirements of Millean-style analysis, and in these instances the logic of most-similar comparison becomes questionable.

Some flexibility is admissible on the vector of controls (X_2) that are "held constant" across the cases. Nonidentity is tolerable if the deviation runs counter to the predicted hypothesis. For example, Epstein describes both the United States and Canada as having strong regional bases of power, a factor that is probably more significant in recent Canadian history than in recent American history. However, because regional bases of power should lead to weaker parties, rather than to stronger parties, this element of nonidentity does not challenge Epstein's conclusions. Indeed, it sets up a most-difficult research scenario, as discussed earlier. At the same time, Epstein's description of Canadian and American parties as "loose" might be questioned. Arguably, American parties, dominated in the latter twentieth century by direct primaries (open to all who declare themselves a member of a party and, in some states, even to those who are members of the opposing party), are considerably more diffuse than Canadian parties. The problem of coding continuous variables in a dichotomous manner is threatening to any most-similar analysis.

In one respect, however, the requirements for case control are not so stringent. Specifically, it is not usually necessary to *measure* control variables (at least not with a high degree of precision) in order to control for them. If two countries can be assumed to have similar cultural heritages, one needn't worry about constructing variables to measure that heritage. One can simply assert that, whatever they are, they are more or less constant across the two cases. This is similar to the technique employed in a randomized experiment, where the researcher typically does not attempt to measure all the factors that might affect the causal relationship of interest. She assumes, rather, that these unknown factors have been neutralized across the treatment and control groups by randomization. This can be a huge advantage over large-N cross-case methods, where each case must be assigned a specific score on all relevant control variables – often a highly questionable procedure, and one that must impose strong assumptions about the shape of the underlying causal relationship (usually presumed to be linear).

Cross-Case Technique

The most useful statistical tool for identifying cases for in-depth analysis in a most-similar setting is some variety of "matching" strategy.[73] Statistical estimates of causal effects based on matching techniques have been a major topic in quantitative methodology over the last twenty-five years, first in statistics[74] and subsequently in econometrics[75] and political science.[76]

Matching techniques are based on an extension of experimental logic. In a randomized experiment, elaborate statistical models are unnecessary for causal inference because, for a large enough selection of cases, the treatment group and the control group have a high probability of being similar in their background characteristics (X_2). Hence, a simple difference-of-means test is often sufficient to analyze the effects of a treatment variable (X_1) across groups.

In observational studies where the hypothesized causal factor (X_1) is dichotomous, the situation is superficially the same. For purposes of discussion, we shall refer to cases with a "high" score on X_1 as members of the treatment group, and to cases with "low" scores as members of the control group. Thus are observational studies translated into the lexicon of experimental analysis.

However, in observational studies it is unusual to find cases that differ on X_1 but not on various background characteristics (X_2) that might affect the outcome of interest. For example, countries that are strongly democratic (or strongly authoritarian) are likely to be similar in more than one respect. This greatly complicates the analysis of X_1's independent effect on the outcome.

The traditional approach to this problem is to introduce a variable for each potential confounder in a regression model of causal relationships. But this standard-issue technique requires a strong set of assumptions about the behavior of the various factors introduced into the model. Matching techniques have been developed as an explicit alternative to

---

[73] For good introductions, see Ho et al. (2004); Morgan and Harding (2005); Rosenbaum (2004); and Rosenbaum and Silber (2001). For a discussion of matching procedures in Stata, see Abadie et al. (2001).

[74] Rosenbaum and Rubin (1985); Rosenbaum (2004).

[75] Hahn (1998).

[76] Ho et al. (2004); Imai (2005).

the control-variable approach. This alternative begins by identifying a set of variables (other than the dependent variable or the main independent variable) on which the cases are to be matched. Then, for each case in the treatment group, the researcher identifies as many cases as possible from the control group with the exact same scores on the matching variables (the covariates). Finally, the researcher looks at the difference on the dependent variable between the cases in the treatment group and the matching cases in the control group. If the set of matching variables is broad enough to include all confounders, the average difference between the treatment-group and the matching control-group cases should provide a good estimate of the causal effect. Even in a situation in which the set of matching variables includes some, but not all, confounders, matching may produce better causal inferences than regression models because cases that match on a set of explicitly selected variables are also more likely to be similar on unmeasured confounders.[77]

Unfortunately, the relatively simple matching procedure just described, known as *exact matching*, is often impossible. This procedure typically fails for continuous variables such as wealth, age, and distance, since there may be no two cases with the same score on a continuous variable. For example, there is no undemocratic country with the exact same per capita GDP as the United States. Note that the larger the number of covariates, the lower the likelihood of finding exact matches.

In situations where exact matching is infeasible, researchers may instead employ *approximate matching*, where cases from the control group that are close enough to matching cases from the treatment group are accepted as matches. Major weaknesses of this approach include the fact that the definition of "close enough" is inevitably arbitrary, as well as the fact that, for large sets of matching variables, few treatment cases are likely to have even approximate matches.

To deal with situations in which exact matching is impossible, methodologists have developed an alternative procedure known as *propensity-score matching*. This approach suggests a somewhat different definition of similarity than the previous two. Rather than focusing on sharing scores on the matching variables, propensity-score matching focuses on sharing a similar estimated probability of having been in the treatment group,

---

[77] However, matching is clearly inferior to a well-designed and well-executed randomized experiment. The benefits of matching extend only so far as equivalence on the variables explicitly included and any unmeasured variables that fortuitously happen to be similar across the cases. By contrast, proper randomization handles all unmeasured variables.

conditional on the matching variables. In other words, when looking for a match for a specific case in the treatment group, researchers look for cases in the control group that – before the score on the independent variable is known – would have been as likely to be in the treatment group as actually chosen cases. This is accomplished by a two-stage analysis, the first stage of which approaches the key independent variable, X_1, as a dependent variable and the matching variables as independent variables. (This is similar in spirit to *selection models*, where a two-stage approach to causal inference is adopted.) Once this model has been estimated, the coefficient estimates are disregarded. Instead, the second stage of the analysis employs the fitted values for each case, which tell us the probability of that case being assigned to the treatment group, conditional on its scores on the matching variables. These fitted values are referred to as propensity scores. The final step in the process is to choose matches for each case in the treatment group. This is accomplished by selecting cases from the control group with similar propensity scores.

The end result of this procedure is a set of matched cases that can be compared in whatever way the researcher deems appropriate. These are the "most-similar" cases, returning to the qualitative terminology. Rosenbaum and Silber summarize the results of recent medical studies:

Unlike model-based adjustments, where patients vanish and are replaced by the coefficients of a model, in matching, ostensibly comparable patterns are compared directly, one by one. Modern matching methods involve statistical modeling and combinatorial algorithms, but the end result is a collection of pairs or sets of people who look comparable, at least on average. In matching, people retain their integrity as people, so they can be examined and their stories can be told individually.[78]

Matching, conclude the authors, "facilitates, rather than inhibits, thick description."[79]

Indeed, the same matching techniques that have been used successfully in observational studies of medical treatments might also be adapted to the study of nation-states, political parties, cities, or indeed any paired cases in the social sciences. Suppose that, in order to study the relationship between wealth and democracy, the researcher wishes to select a case that is as similar as possible to Costa Rica in background variables, while being as different as possible on per capita GDP, the variable of theoretical interest, and the outcome of interest, democracy.

[78] Rosenbaum and Silber (2001: 223).
[79] Ibid.

In order to select most-similar cases for the study of the relationship between wealth and democracy, one must arrive at a statistical model of the causes of a country's wealth. Obviously, such a proposition is complex. Since this is an illustrative example, we shall be satisfied with a cartoon model that includes only a few independent variables. A country's wealth will be assumed to be a function of the origin of its legal system (measured by dummy variables for English legal heritage, French legal heritage, socialist legal heritage, German legal heritage, and Scandinavian legal heritage) and its geographic endowments (measured by the distance of each country's capital city from the equator).

The first step in selecting most-similar cases is to run a nonparametric regression with these independent variables and logged per capita GDP (the independent variable of theoretical interest) as the dependent variable. The fitted values from this regression serve as propensity scores, and cases with similar propensity scores are interpreted as matching. The propensity score for our focus case, Costa Rica, is 7.63. Examining the propensity-score data, one sees that Benin has a propensity score of 7.58 – quite similar to Costa Rica's. At the same time, Benin's per capita GDP of $1,163 is substantially different from Costa Rica's per capita GDP of $5,486, as are their democracy scores in 1995 (Benin is much less democratic than Costa Rica). Hence, Costa Rica and Benin may be viewed as most-similar cases for testing the relationship between wealth and democracy, as illustrated in Table 5.5. An in-depth analysis of these two cases may shed light on the causal pathways between economic development and democracy. Indeed, these two cases are probably more informative than other two-case comparisons precisely because the case-selection procedure has identified countries whose *other* attributes are roughly equal in their propensity to democracy/authoritarianism. This means that the differences on the variable of theoretical interest (GDP per capita) and the outcome (democracy) can be given a causal interpretation – an interpretation that would probably not be suggested by a qualitative assessment of these two countries (which are quite different in culture, region, and historical experience).

It is important to keep in mind that the quality of the "match" depends entirely on the quality of the statistical model used to generate the propensity scores. A superficial model like the one used here may produce rather superficial matches. Yet, in a large-N context – where dozens, if not thousands of cases vie for inclusion – a formal approach to case selection offers significant advantages. At the very least, one's assumptions are rendered transparent.

TABLE 5.5. *Paired cases resulting from matching procedure*

		GDP per capita (X_1)	Propensity score (X_2)	Democracy (Y)
Cases	Benin	$1,163	7.58	6
	Costa Rica	$5,486	7.63	10

Conclusion

The most-similar method is one of the oldest recognized techniques of qualitative analysis, harking back to J. S. Mill's classic study, *System of Logic* (first published in 1834). By contrast, matching statistics are a relatively new technique in the arsenal of the social sciences, and have rarely been employed for the purpose of selecting cases for in-depth analysis. Yet, as suggested in the foregoing discussion, there may be a fruitful interchange between the two approaches. Indeed, the current popularity of matching among statisticians – relative, that is, to garden-variety regression models – rests upon what qualitative researchers would recognize as a "case-based" approach to causal analysis. If Rosenbaum and Silber are correct, it may be perfectly reasonable to appropriate this large-N method of analysis for case study purposes.

To be sure, the purpose of a case study is somewhat different in situations where a large-N cross-case analysis has already been conducted. Here, the general causal relationship is usually clear. We know from our cross-case study that GDP per capita is strongly associated with democracy; there is a strong presumption of causality. Of course, the case study analysis may give us reasons to doubt. Perhaps the causal pathways from economic development to regime type are difficult to identify. Perhaps the presumed causal pathways, as identified by previous research or theoretical hunch, are simply not in evidence. Even so, the usual purpose of a case study analysis in this setting is to corroborate an initial cross-case finding.

By contrast, if there is no prior cross-case investigation – at least none of a formal nature – the case study performs a somewhat different role. Here, we will be more interested in the covariational patterns that are discovered between X_1 and Y. Thus, Epstein's study of American and Canadian political parties is notable for its principal finding: that the underlying cause of party cohesion is to be found in the structure of the executive (parliamentary/presidential). Indeed, Epstein spends relatively little time in this article discussing possible causal mechanisms; his principal focus is on "scoring" the relevant variables, as discussed. By the same token, if Epstein had already conducted a large-N cross-case analysis prior to his case study, and if this cross-case analysis had revealed a strong pattern between executive type and party cohesion, his two-case analysis of the United States and Canada (cases that we presume would have very similar propensity scores) would now serve a rather different purpose. Evidently, the function of the most-similar case study shifts subtly but importantly when the case-selection procedure is, itself, a mode of analysis, offering strong prima facie evidence of a causal relationship.

As with other methods of case selection, the most-similar method is prone to problems of non-representativeness. If this technique is employed in a qualitative fashion (without a systematic cross-case selection strategy), potential biases in the chosen cases must be addressed in a speculative way. If the researcher employs a matching technique of case selection within a large-N sample, the problem of potential bias can be addressed by assuring a choice of cases that are not extreme outliers, as judged by their residuals in the full model. Most-similar cases should also be "typical" cases, though some scope for deviance around the regression line may be acceptable for purposes of finding a good fit among cases.

Most-Different Cases

A final case-selection method is the reverse image of the previous method. Here, variation on independent variables is prized, while variation on the outcome is eschewed. Rather than looking for cases that are most-similar, one looks for cases that are *most-different*. Specifically, the researcher tries to identify cases where just one independent variable (X_1), as well as the dependent variable (Y), covary, while all other plausible factors (X_{2a-d}) show different values.[80]

---

[80] The most-different method is sometimes referred to as the "method of agreement," following its inventor, J. S. Mill (1843/1872). See also DeFelice (1986); Gerring (2001: 212–14); Lijphart (1971, 1975); Meckstroth (1975); Przeworski and Teune (1970); and Skocpol and Somers (1980). For examples of this method, see Collier and Collier (1991/2002); Converse and Dupeux (1962); Karl (1997); Moore (1966); Skocpol (1979); and Yashar (2005: 23). However, most of these studies are described as *combining* most-similar and most-different methods.

TABLE 5.6. *Most-different analysis with two cases*

		X_1	X_{2a}	X_{2b}	X_{2c}	X_{2d}	Y
Case	A	1	1	0	1	0	1
types	B	1	0	1	0	1	1

X_1 = the variable of theoretical interest. X_{2a-d} = a vector
of controls. Y = the outcome of interest.

The simplest form of this two-case comparison is illustrated in Table 5.6. Cases A and B are deemed "most-different," though they are similar in two essential respects – the causal variable of interest and the outcome.

As an example, I follow Marc Howard's recent work, which explores the enduring impact of communism on civil society.[81] Cross-national surveys show a strong correlation between former communist regimes and low social capital, controlling for a variety of possible confounders. It is a strong result. Howard wonders why this relationship is so strong and why it persists, and perhaps even strengthens, in countries that are no longer socialist or authoritarian. In order to answer this question, he focuses on two most-different cases, Russia and East Germany. These two countries were quite different – in all ways *other than* their communist experience – prior to the Soviet era, during the Soviet era, and in the post-Soviet era, as East Germany was absorbed into West Germany. Yet they both score near the bottom of various cross-national indices intended to measure the prevalence of civic engagement in the current era. Thus, Howard's case selection procedure meets the requirements of the most-different research design: variance is found on all (or most) dimensions aside from the key factor of interest (communism) and the outcome (civic engagement).[82]

What leverage is brought to the analysis by this approach? Howard's case studies combine evidence drawn from mass surveys and from in-depth interviews of small, stratified samples of Russians and East Germans. (This is a good illustration, incidentally, of how quantitative and qualitative evidence can be fruitfully combined in the intensive study of several cases.) The product of this analysis is the identification of three causal pathways that, Howard claims, help to explain the laggard status of civil society in post-communist polities: "the mistrust of communist

[81] Howard (2003). In the following discussion I treat the terms "social capital," "civil society," and "civic engagement" interchangeably.
[82] Howard (2003: 6–9).

organizations, the persistence of friendship networks, and the disappoint-ment with post-communism."[83] Simply put, Howard concludes, "a great number of citizens in Russia and Eastern Germany feel a strong and lin-gering sense of distrust of any kind of public organization, a general sat-isfaction with their own personal networks (accompanied by a sense of deteriorating relations within society overall), and disappointment in the developments of post-communism."[84]

Results obtained from the analysis of East Germany and Russia are pre-sumed to apply in other post-communist polities (e.g., Lithuania, Poland, Bulgaria, Albania). Indeed, by choosing a heterogenous sample, Howard solves potential problems of representativeness in his restricted sample. However, this sample is *not* representative across the entire population of the inference, which is intended to cover all countries, not just commu-nist ones. (To argue that communism impedes the development of civil society is to imply that noncommunism stimulates the development of civil society. The chosen sample is truncated [censored] on the dependent variable).

Equally problematic is the lack of variation on key causal factors of interest – communism and its putative causal pathways. For this reason, it is generally difficult to reach conclusions about the causal status of these factors on the basis of the most-different analysis alone. It is possible, that is, that the three causal pathways identified by Howard also operate within polities that have never experienced communist rule. If so, they are not properly regarded as causal.

Nor does it seem possible to conclusively eliminate rival hypotheses on the basis of this most-different analysis. Indeed, this is not Howard's intention. He wishes merely to show that whatever influence on civil soci-ety might be attributed to economic, cultural, and other factors does not exhaust this subject.

My considered judgment, based on the foregoing methodological dilemmas, is that the most-different research design provides only minimal insight into the problem of why communist systems appear to suppress civic engagement, years after their disappearance. Fortunately, this is not the only research design employed by Howard in his admirable study. Indeed, the author employs two other small-N cross-case methods, as well as a large-N cross-country statistical analysis. In my opinion, these methods do most of the analytic work. East Germany may be regarded

---

[83] Ibid., 122.
[84] Ibid., 145.

as a causal-pathway case (as discussed earlier). It has all the attributes normally assumed to foster civic engagement (e.g., a growing economy, multiparty competition, civil liberties, a free press, close association with Western European culture and politics), but nonetheless shows little or no improvement on this dimension during the post-transition era.[85] It is plausible to attribute this lack of change to its communist past, as Howard does. The contrast between East and West Germany provides a most-similar analysis, since the two polities share virtually everything except a communist past. This variation is also deftly exploited by Howard. In short, Howard's conclusions are justifiable, but not on the basis of most-different analysis.

I do not wish to dismiss the most-different research method entirely. Surely, Howard's findings are stronger with the intensive analysis of Russia than they would be without. Yet if one strips away the pathway case (East Germany) and the most-similar analysis (East/West Germany), there is little left upon which to base an analysis of causal relations (aside from the large-N cross-national analysis). Indeed, most scholars who employ the most-different method do so in conjunction with other methods.[86] It is rarely, if ever, a stand-alone method.[87]

Conclusion

Generalizing from this discussion of Marc Howard's work, I offer the following summary remarks on the most-different method of case analysis. (I leave aside issues faced by *all* case study analyses, issues that formed the basis of Chapter Three.)

---

[85] Ibid., 8.

[86] See, e.g., Collier and Collier (1991/2002); Karl (1997); Moore (1966); Skocpol (1979); and Yashar (2005: 23). Karl (1997), which affects to be a most-different system analysis (20), is a particularly clear example of this. Her study, focused ostensibly on petro-states (states with large oil reserves), makes two sorts of inferences. The first concerns the (usually) obstructive role of oil in political and economic development. The second sort of inference concerns variation *within* the population of petro-states, showing that some countries (e.g., Norway, Indonesia) manage to avoid the pathologies brought on elsewhere by oil resources. When attempting to explain the constraining role of oil on petro-states, Karl usually relies on contrasts between petro-states and non-petro-states (e.g., Chapter 10). Only when attempting to explain differences among petro-states does she restrict her sample to petro-states. In my opinion, very little use is made of the most-different research design.

[87] This was recognized, at least implicitly, by Mill (1843/1872: 258–9). Skepticism has been echoed by methodologists in the intervening years (e.g., Cohen and Nagel 1934: 251–6; Gerring 2001; Skocpol and Somers 1980). Indeed, explicit defenses of the most-different method are rare (but see DeFelice 1986).

Let us begin with a methodological obstacle that is faced by both Millean styles of analysis – the necessity of dichotomizing every variable in the analysis. Recall that, as with most-similar analysis, differences across cases must be sizeable enough to be interpretable in an essentially dichotomous fashion (e.g., high/low, present/absent), and similarities must be close enough to be understood as essentially identical (e.g., high/high, present/present). Otherwise the results of a Millean-style analysis are not interpretable. The problem of "degrees" is deadly if the variables under consideration are by nature continuous (e.g., GDP). This is a particular concern in Howard's analysis, where East Germany scores somewhat higher than Russia in civic engagement; they are both low, though Russia is considerably lower. Howard assumes that this divergence is minimal enough to be understood as a difference of degree rather than of kind, a judgment that might be questioned. In these respects, most-different analysis is no more secure – but also no less – than most-similar analysis.

In one respect, most-different analysis is superior to most-similar analysis. If the coding assumptions are sound, the most-different research design may be useful for *eliminating necessary causes*. Causal factors that do not appear across the chosen cases – e.g., X_{2a-d} in Table 5.6 – are evidently unnecessary for the production of Y. However, it does not follow that the most-different method is the *best* method for eliminating necessary causes. Note that the defining feature of this method is the shared element across cases – X_1 in Table 5.6. This feature does not help one to eliminate necessary causes. Indeed, if one were focused solely on eliminating necessary causes, one would presumably seek out cases that register the same outcomes and have maximum diversity on other attributes. In Table 5.6, this would be a set of cases that satisfy conditions X_{2a-d}, but not X_1. Thus, even the presumed strength of the most-different analysis is not so strong.

Usually, case study analysis is focused on the identification (or clarification) of causal relations, not on the elimination of possible causes. In this setting, the most-different technique is useful, but only if assumptions of "causal uniqueness" hold. By this I mean a situation in which a given outcome is the product of only one cause: Y cannot occur except in the presence of X_1. X_1 is necessary, and in some situations (given certain background conditions) sufficient, to cause Y.[88]

Consider the following hypothetical example. Suppose that a new disease, about which little is known, has appeared in Country A. There are

---

[88] Another way of stating this is to say that X is a "nontrivial necessary condition" of Y.

hundreds of infected persons across dozens of affected communities in that country. In Country B, located at the other end of the world, several new cases of the disease surface in a single community. In this setting, we can imagine two sorts of Millean analyses. The first examines two similar communities within Country A, one of which has developed the disease and the other of which has not. This is the most-similar style of case comparison, and focuses accordingly on the identification of a difference between the two cases that might account for variation across the sample. A second approach focuses on (highly dissimilar) communities where the disease has appeared across the two countries and searches for any similarities that might account for these similar outcomes. This is the most-different research design.

Both are plausible approaches to this particular problem, and we can imagine epidemiologists employing them simultaneously. However, the most-different design demands stronger assumptions about the underlying factors at work. It supposes that the disease arises from the *same cause* in any setting. This may be a reasonable operating assumption when one is dealing with certain natural phenomena like diseases. Even so, there are many exceptions. Death, for example, has many causes. For this reason, it would not occur to us to look for most-different cases of high mortality around the world. In order for the most-different research design to effectively identify a causal factor at work in a given outcome, the researcher must assume that X_1 – the factor held constant across the diverse cases – is the only possible cause of Y (see Table 5.6). This assumption rarely holds in social scientific settings, for most outcomes of interest to anthropologists, economists, political scientists, and sociologists have *multiple* causes. There are many ways to win an election, to build a welfare state, to get into a war, to overthrow a government, or – returning to Marc Howard's work – to build a strong civil society. And it is for this reason that most-different analysis is rarely applied in social science work and, where applied, is rarely convincing.

If this seems a tad severe, there is a more charitable way of approaching the most-different method. Arguably, this is not a pure "method" at all but merely a supplement, a way of incorporating diversity in the subsample of cases that provide the unusual outcome of interest. If the unusual outcome is revolution, one might wish to encompass a wide variety of revolutions in one's analysis. If the unusual outcome is post-communist civil society, it seems appropriate to include a diverse set of post-communist polities in one's sample of case studies, as Marc Howard does. From this perspective, the most-different method (so-called) might be better labeled a *diverse-case* method, as explored earlier.

Conclusion

In order to be a case of something broader than itself, the chosen case must be representative (in some respects) of a larger population. Otherwise – if it is purely idiosyncratic ("unique") – it is uninformative about anything other than itself. A study based on a nonrepresentative sample has no (or very little) external validity. To be sure, no phenomenon is purely idiosyncratic; the notion of a unique case is a matter that would be difficult to define. One is concerned, as always, with matters of degree. Cases are *more or less* representative of some broader phenomenon and, on that score, may be considered better or worse subjects for intensive analysis. (The one exception, as noted, is the influential case.)

Of all the problems besetting case study analysis, perhaps the most persistent – and the most persistently bemoaned – is the problem of sample bias.[89] Lisa Martin finds that the overemphasis of international relations scholars on a few well-known cases of economic sanctions – most of which failed to elicit any change in the sanctioned country – "has distorted analysts' view of the dynamics and characteristics of economic sanctions."[90] Barbara Geddes charges that many analyses of industrial policy have focused exclusively on the most successful cases – primarily the East Asian NICs – leading to biased inferences.[91] Anna Breman and Carolyn Shelton show that case study work on the question of structural adjustment is systematically biased insofar as researchers tend to focus on disaster cases – those where structural adjustment is associated with very poor health and human development outcomes. These cases, often located in sub-Saharan Africa, are by no means representative of the entire population. Consequently, scholarship on the question of structural adjustment is highly skewed in a particular ideological direction (against neoliberalism).[92]

---

[89] Achen and Snidal (1989); Collier and Mahoney (1996); Geddes (1990); King, Keohane and Verba (1994); Rohlfing (2004); Sekhon (2004). Some case study researchers appear to denigrate the importance of case representativeness. George and Bennett (2005: 30) write emphatically, "Case researchers do *not* aspire to select cases that are directly 'representative' of diverse populations and they usually do not and should not make claims that their findings are applicable to such populations except in contingent ways." However, it becomes clear that what the authors are inveighing against is not the goal of representativeness per se but rather the problem of a case study researcher who claims an inappropriately broad extension for her findings. "To the extent that there is a representativeness problem or a selection bias problem in a particular case study, it is often better described as the problem of 'overgeneralizing' findings to types or subclasses of cases unlike those actually studied" (ibid., 32).

[90] Martin (1992: 5).

[91] Geddes (1990).

[92] Breman and Shelton (2001). See also Gerring, Thacker, and Moreno (2005).

These examples might be multiplied many times. Indeed, for many topics the most-studied cases are acknowledged to be less than representative. It is worth reflecting upon the fact that our knowledge of the world is heavily colored by a few "big" (populous, rich, powerful) countries, and that a good portion of the disciplines of economics, political science, and sociology are built upon scholars' familiarity with the economics, political science, and sociology of one country, the United States.[93] Case study work is particularly prone to problems of investigator bias because so much rides on the researcher's selection of one case (or a few cases). Even if the investigator is unbiased, her sample may still be biased simply by virtue of "random" error (which may be understood as measurement error, error in the data-generation process, or an underlying causal feature of the universe).

There are only two situations in which a case study researcher need not be concerned with the representativeness of her chosen case. The first is the influential-case research design, where a case is chosen because of its possible influence on a cross-case model, and hence is not expected to be representative of a larger sample. The second is the deviant-case method, where the chosen case is employed to confirm a broader cross-case argument to which the case stands as an apparent exception. Yet in the latter instance, the chosen case is expected to be representative of a broader set of cases – those, in particular, that are poorly explained by the extant model.

In all other circumstances, cases must be representative of the population of interest in whatever ways might be relevant to the proposition in question. Note that where a researcher is attempting to disconfirm a deterministic proposition, the question of representativeness is perhaps more appropriately understood as a question of classification: is the chosen case appropriately classified as a member of the designated population? If so, then it is fodder for a disconfirming case study.

If the researcher is attempting to confirm a deterministic proposition, or to make probabilistic arguments about a causal relationship, then the problem of representativeness is of the more usual sort: is Case A unit-homogenous relative to other cases in the population? This is not an easy matter to test. However, in a large-N context the residual for that

---

[93] Wahlke (1979: 13) writes of the failings of the "behavioralist" mode of political science analysis. "It rarely aims at generalization; research efforts have been confined essentially to case studies of single political systems, most of them dealing ... with the American system."

case (in whatever model the researcher has greatest confidence in) is a reasonable place to start. Of course, this test is only as good as the model at hand. Any incorrect specifications or incorrect modeling procedures will likely bias the results and give an incorrect assessment of each case's "typicality." In addition, there is the possibility of stochastic error, errors that cannot be modeled in a general framework. Given the explanatory weight that individual cases are asked to bear in a case study analysis, it is wise to consider more than just the residual test of representativeness. Deductive logic and an in-depth knowledge of the case in question are often more reliable tools than the results of a rather superficial cross-case model.

In any case, there is no dispensing with the question. Case studies (with the two exceptions already noted) rest upon an assumed synecdoche: the case should stand for a population. If this is not true, or if there is reason to doubt this assumption, then the utility of the case study is brought severely into question.

Fortunately, there is some safety in numbers. Insofar as case study evidence is combined with cross-case evidence, the issue of sample bias is mitigated. Indeed, the skepticism about case study work that one commonly encounters in the social sciences today is, in my view, a product of a too-literal interpretation of the case study method. A case study *tout court* is thought to mean a case study *tout seul*. Insofar as case studies and cross-case studies can be enlisted within the same investigation (either in the same study or by reference to other studies of the same subject), problems of representativeness are less worrisome. This is the virtue of cross-level work, a.k.a. "triangulation."

Ambiguities

Before concluding, I wish to draw attention to two ambiguities in case-selection strategies for case study research. The first concerns the admixture of several case-selection strategies. The second concerns the changing status of a case as a study proceeds.

Some case studies follow only one strategy of case selection. They are *typical, diverse, extreme, deviant, influential, crucial, pathway, most-similar*, or *most-different* research designs, as discussed. However, many case studies mix and match among these case-selection strategies. Indeed, insofar as all case studies seek representative samples, they are all in search of "typical" cases. Thus, it is common for writers to declare that their case is, for example, both extreme and typical; it has an extreme value on X_1 or Y but is not, in other respects, idiosyncratic. There is not much that one can say about these combinations of strategies except that, where the cases allow for a variety of empirical strategies, there is no reason not to pursue them. And where the same case legitimately serves several functions at once (without further effort on the researcher's part), there is little cost to a multipronged approach to case analysis.

The second issue that deserves emphasis is the changing status of a case during the course of a researcher's investigation – which may last for years, if not decades. The problem is particularly acute when a researcher begins in an exploratory mode and then proceeds to hypothesis testing (that is, she develops a specific X_1/Y proposition), or when the operative hypothesis or key control variable changes (a new causal factor is discovered or another outcome becomes the focus of analysis). Things change. And it is the mark of a good researcher to keep her mind open to new evidence and new insights. Too often, methodological discussions give the misleading impression that hypotheses are clear and remain fixed over the course of a study's development. Nothing could be further from the truth. The unofficial transcripts of academia – accessible in informal settings, where researchers let their guards down (particularly if inebriated) – are filled with stories about dead ends, unexpected findings, and drastically revised theory chapters. It would be interesting, in this vein, to compare published work with dissertation prospectuses and fellowship applications. I doubt that the correlation between these two stages of research is particularly strong.

Research, after all, is about discovery, not simply the verification or falsification of existing hypotheses. That said, it is also true that research on a particular topic should move from hypothesis generating to hypothesis testing. This marks the progress of a field, and of a scholar's own work. As a rule, research that begins with an open-ended (X- or Y-centered) analysis should conclude with a determinate X_1/Y hypothesis.

The problem is that research strategies that are ideal for exploration are not always ideal for confirmation. I discussed this trade-off in Chapter Three as it pertains to the cross-case/case study dilemma. It also applies to various methods of case study analysis, as presented in this chapter. The extreme-case method is inherently exploratory, since there is no clear causal hypothesis; the researcher is concerned merely to explore variation on a single dimension (X_1 or Y). Other methods can be employed in either an open-ended (exploratory) or a hypothesis-testing (confirmatory/disconfirmatory) mode. The difficulty is that once the researcher has arrived at a determinate hypothesis, the originally chosen research design may no longer be so well constructed.

This is unfortunate, but inevitable. One cannot construct the perfect research design until (a) one has a specific hypothesis and (b) one is reasonably certain about what one is going to find "out there" in the empirical world. This is particularly true of observational research designs, but it also applies to many experimental research designs: usually, there is a "good" (informative) finding, and a finding that is less insightful. In short, the perfect case study research design is usually apparent only ex post facto.

There are three ways to handle this. One can explain, straightforwardly, that the initial research was undertaken in an exploratory fashion, and therefore not constructed to test the specific hypothesis that is – now – the primary argument. Alternatively, one can try to redesign the study after the new (or revised) hypothesis has been formulated. This may require additional field research or perhaps the integration of additional cases or variables that can be obtained through secondary sources or consultation of experts. A final approach is to simply jettison, or deemphasize, that portion of the research that no longer addresses the (revised) key hypothesis. A three-case study may become a two-case study, and so forth. Lost time and effort are the costs of this downsizing.

In the event, practical considerations will probably determine which of these three strategies, or combinations of strategies, is to be followed. The point to remember is that revision of one's cross-case research design is *normal* and to be expected. Not all twists and turns on the meandering trail of truth can be anticipated.

Are There Other Methods of Case Selection?

At the outset of this chapter, I summarized the task of case selection as a matter of achieving two objectives: representativeness (typicality) and variation (causal leverage). Evidently, there are other objectives as well. For example, one wishes to identify cases that are *independent* of each other. If chosen cases are affected by each other, the problem (sometimes known as Galton's problem or a problem of diffusion) must be corrected before analysis can take place. I have neglected this issue because it is usually apparent to the researcher and, in any case, there are no easy techniques that might be utilized to correct for such biases.[94]

I have also disregarded *pragmatic/logistical* issues that might affect case selection. Evidently, case selection is often influenced by a researcher's

---

[94] For further discussion of this and other factors impinging upon case selection, see Gerring (2001: 178–81).

familiarity with the language of a country, a personal entrée into that locale, special access to important data, or funding that covers one archive rather than another. Pragmatic considerations are often – and quite rightly – decisive in the case-selection process.

A final consideration concerns the *theoretical prominence* of a particular case within the literature on a subject. Researchers are sometimes obliged to study cases that have received extensive attention in previous studies. These are sometimes referred to as "paradigmatic" cases or "exemplars."[95]

However, neither pragmatic/logistical utility nor theoretical prominence qualifies as a *methodological* factor in case selection. That is, these features of a case have no bearing on the validity of the findings stemming from a study. As such, it is appropriate to grant these issues a peripheral status in this chapter, as I have elsewhere in the book.

One final caveat must be issued. While it is traditional to make a distinction between the tasks of case selection and case analysis, a close look at these processes reveals them to be indistinct and overlapping. One cannot choose a case without considering the sort of analysis that it might be subjected to, and vice versa. Thus, the reader should consider choosing cases by employing the nine techniques laid out in this chapter *along with* any considerations that might be introduced by virtue of a case's quasi-experimental qualities (Chapter Six) and its potential for process tracing (Chapter Seven), subjects to which we now turn.

---

[95] Flyvbjerg (2004: 427).

6

Internal Validity

An Experimental Template

Let us suppose that one has chosen one's case (or cases) according to one of the techniques (or some combination of techniques) described in the previous chapter. And let us further suppose that one has refined one's research question into a specific (X_1/Y) hypothesis. One then faces a problem of internal validity. How does one construct a research design that might illuminate the causal relationship of interest?

The fundamental problem of causal inference is that one cannot rerun history to see what effects X_1 actually had on Y in a particular case. At an ontological level, this problem is unsolvable. There are no time machines. However, there are various ways of reducing uncertainty so that causal inference is possible, and indeed quite plausible. The argument of this chapter is that the various methods of doing so are all quasi-experimental in nature. This is because the true experiment is the closest approximation we have at our disposal to a time machine. Through this technique, and others modeled on it, one can imagine what it would be like to go back in time, alter a "treatment," and observe its true causal effect.

This chapter thus calls into question some of the usual assumptions applied to case study research. Most case study researchers perceive only a distant and tenuous connection between their work and the laboratory experiment, with a manipulated treatment and randomized control. They are inclined to the view that experimental and observational work inhabit different worlds, perhaps even employ different logics of inquiry. Granted, case study researchers working with observational data occasionally refer to their work as "quasi-experiments," "natural experiments," "thought experiments," "crucial experiments," or "counterfactual thought experiments." However, these designations are often loose and ambiguous.

Arguably, they obscure more than they clarify. What does it *mean* for a case study to be quasi-experimental, and how might case study research be reconstructed through the lens of the experimental method?

I believe that, in those instances where case study research is warranted, the strongest methodological defense for this research design often derives from its quasi-experimental qualities. All case study research is quasi-experimental. But some case studies are more experimental than others.

An Experimental Template

Broadly speaking, there are two dimensions upon which any causal effect may be observed – temporal and spatial. Temporal effects may be observed directly when an intervention occurs: X_1 intervenes upon Y, and we observe any change in Y that may follow. Here, the "control" is the pre-intervention state of Y; what Y was prior to the intervention (a state that we presume would remain the same, or whose trend would remain constant, in the absence of intervention). Spatial effects may be observed directly when two phenomena are similar enough to be understood as examples (cases) of the same thing. Ideally, they are similar in all respects but one – the causal factor of interest. In this situation, the "control" is the case without the intervention.

Classic experimental research designs achieve variation through time and across space, thus maximizing leverage into the fundamental problem of causal inference. Here, we apply the same dimensions to all research, whether or not the treatment is manipulated. This produces a matrix with four cells, as illustrated in Figure 6.1. Cell 1, understood as a Dynamic Comparison, mirrors the paradigmatic laboratory experiment, since it exploits temporal and spatial variation. Cell 2, labeled a Longitudinal Comparison, employs only temporal variation and is similar in design to an experiment without control. Cell 3, dubbed a Spatial Comparison, employs only spatial variation; it purports to measure the outcome of an intervention that occurred at some point in the past but is not directly observable. Cell 4, a Counterfactual Comparison, relies on variation (temporal and/or spatial) that is imaginary, that is, where the researcher seeks to replicate the circumstances of an experiment in her head or with the aid of some mathematical (perhaps computer-generated) model.[1]

---

[1] One always hesitates to introduce new terms to an already confusing semantic field. However, there are good reasons to shy away from the traditional lexicon. To begin with, most of the terms associated with case study research have nothing to do with the empirical

		Spatial variation: Yes	*Spatial variation:* No
Temporal variation:	Yes	1. Dynamic comparison	2. Longitudinal comparison
	No	3. Spatial comparison	4. Counterfactual comparison

FIGURE 6.1. Matrix of case study research designs.

In order to familiarize ourselves with the differences among these four paradigmatic research designs, it may be useful to begin with a series of scenarios built around a central (hypothetical) research question: does the change from a first-past-the-post (FPP) electoral system to a list-proportional (list-PR) electoral system moderate interethnic attitudinal hostility in a polity with high levels of ethnic conflict? Let us assume that one can effectively measure interethnic hostility through a series of polls administered to a random sample (or panel) of respondents at regular intervals throughout the research period. This registers the outcome of the study, the propensity for people to hold hostile attitudes toward other ethnic groups.[2] With this setup, how might one apply the four foregoing designs?

A Dynamic Comparison would proceed by the selection of two communities that are similar in all respects, including the employment of a majoritarian electoral system and relatively high levels of interethnic hostility. The researcher would then either administer an electoral system change,

variation embodied in the case chosen for intensive analysis. As such, they focus attention on how a case is situated within a broader population of cases (e.g., "extreme," "deviant," "typical," "nested") or on the perceived function of that case within some field of study (e.g., "exploratory," "heuristic," "confirmatory"). These issues, while important, do not speak to the causal leverage that might be provided by a chosen case(s). Mill's suggestion of a "most-similar" research design (a.k.a. the Method of Difference) is directly relevant to the covariational properties of chosen cases. However, it is strikingly ambiguous, since it may refer to a set of cases where there is an intervention (a change on the key variable of theoretical interest) or where there is no intervention. These are quite different kinds of comparisons, as signaled by the typology (the first is much more informative than the second), and deserve to be called by different names. Thus, in the interests of clarity, a new set of categories is amply justified.

2 I recognize that the attitudes do not directly link to behavior, and thus measuring attitudinal hostility will not directly translate into the manifestation of interethnic behavioral hostility.

or hope for a naturally occurring electoral system reform in one of these communities, holding the other constant. The final step would be to compare the results to see if there is a difference over time between treatment and control groups.

A Longitudinal Comparison would follow the same procedure, but without the control group. Consequently, the researcher's judgment of results rests solely on a before/after comparison of interethnic conflict in the community that undergoes a change in its electoral system.

A Spatial Comparison is identical to the Dynamic Comparison except that in this instance there is no observable intervention. Here, the researcher again searches for two communities similar in various respects that might affect interethnic hostility. One happens to employ a majoritarian electoral system, while the other has a proportional electoral system. This spatial variation on the key independent variable forms the crux of causal inference, but is not observable through time. The research question, based upon a survey of attitudes in the two communities, is whether interethnic hostility is lower in the community using PR electoral rules.

In a Counterfactual Comparison, finally, the researcher observes a community with a majoritarian electoral system and high levels of interethnic hostility that does *not* undergo an electoral system change to PR. Since there is no observable change over time in the key variable of interest, her only leverage on this question is the counterfactual: what would have happened, in all likelihood, if this country had reformed its electoral system?

The essential properties of these four research designs are illustrated in Table 6.1, where Y refers to the outcome of concern, X_1 marks the independent variable of interest, and X_2 represents a vector of controls (other exogenous factors that might influence the outcome). These controls may be directly measured or simply assumed (as they often are in randomized experiments). The initial value of X_1 is denoted as "$-$" and a change of status as "$+$." The vector of controls, by definition, remains constant. A question mark indicates that the value of the dependent variable is the major objective of the analysis. Observations are taken before (t_1) and after (t_2) an intervention and thus comprise pre- and post-tests.

In these examples, an intervention (a change in X_1) may be manipulated or natural, sudden or slow, major or minuscule, dichotomous or continuous, and causal effects may be immediate or lagged. For ease of discussion, I shall speak of interventions as dichotomous (present/absent, high/low, on/off), but the reader should keep in mind that the actual research situation may be more variegated (though this inevitably complicates the

TABLE 6.1. *An experimental template for case study research designs*

EXAMPLE

Hypothesis: A change from FPP to list-PR mitigates ethnic hostility.

1. Dynamic Comparison

Treatment
```
       t₁   t₂
Y    -  |  ?
X₁   -  |  +
X₂   -  |  -
```
Control
```
Y    -     ?
X₁   -     -
X₂   -     -
```

Two similar communities with FPP electoral systems and high ethnic hostility, one of which changes from FPP to list-PR. Ethnic hostility is compared in both communities before and after the intervention.

2. Longitudinal Comparison

Treatment
```
       t₁   t₂
Y    -  |  ?
X₁   -  |  +
X₂   -  |  -
```

A community with an FPP electoral system and high ethnic hostility changes to list-PR. Ethnic hostility is compared before and after the intervention.

3. Spatial Comparison

Treatment
```
       t₁
Y    ?
X₁   +
X₂   -
```
Control
```
Y    ?
X₁   -
X₂   -
```

Two similar communities, one of which has FPP and the other list-PR. Ethnic hostility is compared in both communities.

4. Counterfactual Comparison

Treatment
```
       t₁   [t₂]
Y    -  |  ?
X₁   -  |  +
X₂   -  |  -
```

A community with an FPP electoral system and high ethnic hostility is considered, by a counterfactual thought experiment, to undergo a change to list-PR. (t_2 is hypothetical.)

Cases:
  Treatment = with intervention
  Control = without intervention
Variables:
  Y = outcome
  X_1 = independent variable of interest
  X_2 = a vector of controls

Observations:
  t_1 = pre-test (before intervention)
  t_2 = post-test (after intervention)
Cells:
  | = intervention
  − = stasis (no change in status of variable)
  + = change (variable changes value or trend alters)
  ? = the main empirical finding: Y changes (+) or does not (−)

interpretation of a causal effect). Thus, I use the term intervention (a.k.a. "event" or "stimulus") in the broadest possible sense, indicating any sort of change in trend in the key independent variable, X_1. It should be underlined that the absence of an intervention does not mean that a case does not change over time; it means simply that it does not experience a change of *trend*. Any evaluation of an intervention involves an estimate of the baseline – what value a case would have had without the intervention. A "+" therefore indicates a change in this baseline trend.

A key point, and one liable to misunderstanding, is that an intervention (a change in X_1) refers to a change in the independent variable of theoretical interest, not to changes in other variables. By contrast, an "exogenous shock" research design, as that term is sometimes employed, is one where a peripheral variable intervenes upon a set of cases and the researcher observes the results across some set of outcomes. For example, Robert Putnam's study of social capital in Italy makes use of the fact that the country experienced a far-reaching decentralization of power in 1970.[3] Consequently, it was possible to observe institutional divergence across regions during the subsequent period; regions became a viable unit of analysis. Italy's constitutional reform thus serves the function of an exogenous shock because it is unaffected by any of the factors Putnam wishes to study. However, the shock is *not* quasi-experimental, in the sense in which we have been using the term, precisely because the intervention is unrelated to the causal factor of theoretical interest. For an intervention to be experimental, it must embody the treatment of theoretical interest. In this instance, an experimental treatment would presumably involve a change in levels of social capital (it is not clear how this treatment would be administered), thus allowing for pre- and post-tests that would measure the causal impact of the intervention. Thus, Putnam's study, as constructed, is properly classified as a Spatial Comparison among regions.

Because interventions may be multiple or continuous within a single case, it follows that the number of temporal observations within a given case may also be extended indefinitely. This might involve a very long period of time (e.g., centuries) or multiple observations taken over a short period of time (e.g., an hour). Observations are thus understood to occur temporally within each case (t_1, t_2, t_3, ... t_n).

Although the number of cases in the following examples varies, and is sometimes limited to one or two, research designs may – in principle – incorporate any number of cases. Thus, the designations "treatment" and "control" in Table 6.1 may be understood to refer to individual cases *or* to groups of cases. (In this chapter, "case" and "group" are used interchangeably.) The caveat is that, at a certain point, it is no longer possible to conduct an in-depth analysis of a case (because there are so many), and thus the research loses its case study designation.

In numbering these research designs (1–4), I intend to indicate a gradual falling away from the experimental ideal. However, it would be incorrect to assume that a higher number necessarily indicates an inferior research design. To begin with, my discussion in this chapter focuses on issues of

[3] Putnam et al. (1993). For other examples of exogenous-shock research designs, see MacIntyre (2003) and Lieberman (2005b).

internal validity. Sometimes the need for greater external validity prompts a research design that is less "experimental." Equally important is the ubiquitous ceteris paribus assumption – that all peripheral factors that might affect the X_1/Y relationship of interest are held constant, before and after the intervention and/or across treatment and control groups. Usually, ceteris paribus assumptions are more secure in experimental contexts, but not always. This issue is taken up in the final section of the chapter.

Dynamic Comparison

The classic experiment involves one or more cases observed through time where the key independent variable undergoes a manipulated change. One or more additional cases (the control group), usually chosen randomly, are not subject to treatment. Consequently, the analyst observes both temporal and spatial variation.

Experimental research designs have long served as the staple method of psychology and are increasingly common in other social sciences.[4] For practical reasons, experiments are usually easiest to conduct where the units of analysis are comprised of individuals or small groups. Thus, experimental work in political science most commonly concerns the explanation of vote choice, political attitudes, party identification, and other topics grouped together under the rubric of "political behavior." An analogous subfield has developed in economics, where it is known as "behavioral (or experimental) economics."

Experiments may be conducted in laboratory settings or in natural settings. One innovative natural-setting approach employs a standard mass survey with a split-question format.[5] Randomly chosen respondents are divided into several groups (which may be denoted as "treatment" or "control" groups), each of which is administered a slightly different survey. Since the intervention (the setup, the question, or the question ordering) is different, the results are interpretable in the same way that alterations might be in the case of a laboratory intervention.

---

[4] Admonitions to social scientists to adopt experimental methods can be found in Mill (1843/1872), and much later in Fisher (1935); Gosnell (1926); and Stouffer (1950). For general discussion, see Achen (1986); Campbell (1988); Campbell and Stanley (1963); Kagel and Roth (1997); Kinder and Palfrey (1993); McDermott (2002); Shadish, Cook, and Campbell (2002); *Political Analysis* 10:4 (Autumn 2002); *American Behavioral Scientist* 48:1 (January 2004); and the "ExperimentCentral" website.

[5] Glaser (2003); Schuman and Bobo (1988).

More realistic settings are adopted by *field experiments*.[6] One such experiment was conducted by Leonard Wantchekon in Benin in order to discover whether clientelistic electoral appeals were superior to programmatic appeals in a country where clientelism had been the acknowledged behavioral norm since the inauguration of electoral politics. Wantchekon selected eight electoral districts, similar to each other in all relevant respects. Within each district, three villages were randomly identified. In one, clientelistic appeals for support were issued by the candidate. In a second, programmatic (national) appeals were issued by the same candidate. And in a third, both sorts of appeals were employed. Wantchekon found that the clientelist approach did indeed attract more votes than the programmatic alternative.[7]

Regrettably, experimentation on large organizations or entire societies is usually impossible – by reason of cost, lack of consent by relevant authorities, or ethical concerns. Experimentation directed at elite actors is equally difficult, for elites are busy, well remunerated (and hence unresponsive to material incentives), and loathe to speak freely, for obvious reasons. However, researchers occasionally encounter situations in which a nonmanipulated treatment and control approximates the circumstances of a true experiment with randomized controls.[8]

Svante Cornell's study of ethnic integration/disintegration offers a good example. Cornell is interested in the question of whether granting regional autonomy fosters (a) ethnic assimilation within a larger national grouping or (b) a greater propensity for ethnic groups to resist central directives and demand formal separation from the state. He hypothesizes the latter. His study focuses on the USSR/Russia and on regional variation within this heterogeneous country. Cases consist of regionally concentrated ethnic groups (N = 9), some of which were granted formal autonomy within the USSR and others of which were not. This is the quasi-experimental intervention. Cornell must assume that these nine territories are equivalent in all respects that might be relevant to the proposition, or that any remaining differences do not bias results in favor of his hypothesis.[9] The transition from autocracy to democracy (from the USSR to Russia) provides an external shock that sets the stage for the subsequent analysis.

[6] Cook and Campbell (1979); Gerber and Green (2000); McDermott (2002).
[7] Wantchekon (2003).
[8] See, e.g., Brady and McNulty (2004) and Card and Krueger (1994).
[9] Whether this is really true need not concern us; it is Cornell's claim, and it is a plausible one.

Cornell's hypothesis is confirmed: patterns of ethnic mobilization (the dependent variable) are consistent with his hypothesis in eight of the nine cases. Note that variation is available both spatially (across ethnic groups) and temporally.[10]

Another sort of Dynamic Comparison involves a *synthetic* (or composite) match. This is a relatively new approach to case comparison, so I follow Alberto Abadie and Javier Gardeazabal's example closely. The authors are interested in understanding the effect of violent political conflict on economic growth. The problem is that political conflicts are extraordinarily diverse (e.g., in scope, endurance, intensity, and with respect to various other factors that might impact growth performance), as are various background factors that characterize nation-states. Thus, the usual approach taken to this problem – the global cross-national regression – provides a rather "noisy" picture of causal relationships.[11] Abadie and Gardeazabal define their cases as subnational regions within a single country, Spain, where each unit has a fairly high degree of autonomy (and hence satisfies the condition of case independence). Their primary interest is in a single case, the Basque country, where conflict has been severe over the past several decades. (While moderate political conflict between center and periphery is ubiquitous, it has not devolved into violence in other regions.) The authors note that a simple time-series analysis could reveal the economic performance of the Basque region after the onset of ETA-sponsored terrorism. However, this "intervention" began slowly in the 1960s and 1970s (there was no well-defined point of onset) and was coincident with a general economic downturn in Spain. Thus, temporal patterns are difficult to interpret.

As with traditional matching methods, Abadie and Gardeazabal identify a series of covariates that might help to identify a territory or territories in Spain that is most similar to the Basque region with respect to various factors that might affect growth performance and yet has not experienced violent conflict. These covariates include real per capita GDP, investment, population density, the shape of the economy (e.g., agriculture, industry, and other sectors), as well as various measures of human capital. However, there is no perfect match for the Basque country among the sixteen other

---

[10] Cornell (2002). Because there are nine cases, rather than just two, it is possible for Cornell to analyze covariational patterns in a probabilistic fashion. Thus, although one region does not conform to theoretical expectation, this exception does not jeopardize his overall findings.

[11] Alesina et al. (1996).

Spanish regions. Rather than consigning themselves to a less-than-perfect comparison, the authors instead construct a hypothetical case from the two cases that match relatively well with the Basque region, Madrid and Catalonia. Each is weighted according to the strength of the match (with the Basque region) along the various dimensions noted earlier; the two are then combined into a single case. This composite case is looked upon as providing a best "control" case for the treatment case, the Basque region. "Our goal," the authors explain, "is to approximate the per capita GDP path that the Basque Country would have experienced in the absence of terrorism. This counterfactual per capita GDP path is calculated as the per capita GDP of the synthetic Basque Country."[12] Based on this synthetic counterfactual, the authors conclude that the Basque region experienced a 10 percent loss in per capita GDP due to terrorist violence over the course of two decades (the 1980s and 1990s). This is the economic effect of terrorism. One may question the generalizability of this result. Indeed, the authors tread lightly on this matter, since their study is narrowly focused on a single region. (Arguably, it is better classified as a single-outcome study, as discussed in the epilogue.) Even so, the technique is innovative and is potentially applicable to many research contexts.

Because the classic experiment is indistinguishable in its essentials from a natural experiment (so long as there is a suitable control), I employ the term Dynamic Comparison for this set of experimental and quasi-experimental designs. Granted, observational settings that offer variation through time and through space are relatively rare. Where they exist, however, they possess the same attributes as the classic experiment and are rightly accorded pride of place among case study research designs.

Longitudinal Comparison

Occasionally, manipulated treatment groups are *not* accompanied by controls (untreated groups), a research design that I call Longitudinal Comparison.[13] This is so for three possible reasons. Sometimes, the effects of a treatment are so immediate and obvious that the existence of a control

---

[12] Abadie and Gardeazabal (2003: 117).

[13] Franklin, Allison, and Gorman (1997: 1); Gibson, Caldeira, and Spence (2002: 364); Kinder and Palfrey (1993: 7); McDermott (2002: 33). This is sometimes referred to as a "within-subjects" research design. For additional examples in the area of medical research, see Franklin, Allison, and Gorman (1997: 2); in psychology, see Davidson and Costello (1969).

is redundant. Consider a simple experiment in which participants are asked their opinions on a subject, then told a relevant piece of information about that subject (the treatment), and then asked again for their opinions. The question of interest in this research design is whether the treatment has any effect on the participants' views, as measured by pre- and post-tests (the same question asked twice about their opinions). Evidently, one *could* construct a control group of respondents who are not given the treatment; they are not told the relevant bit of information and are simply re-polled for their opinion several minutes later. But it seems unlikely that anything will be learned from the treatment/control comparison, for opinions are likely to remain constant over the course of several minutes in the absence of any intervention. In this circumstance, which is not at all rare in experiments focused on individual respondents, the control group is extraneous.

Another reason for dispensing with a control group is pragmatic. In many circumstances it simply is not feasible for the researcher to enlist subjects to complement a treatment group. Recall that in order to serve as a useful control, untreated individuals must be similar in all relevant respects to the treatment group. Consider the situation of the clinical researcher (e.g., a therapist) who "treats" a group or an individual. She can, within limits, manipulate the treatment and observe the response for this group or individual. But she probably will not be able to enlist the services of a control group that is similar in all respects to the treatment group. In such circumstances, causal leverage comes from observing changes (or lack of change) in the subject under study, as revealed by pre- and post-tests. This provides much more reliable evidence of a treatment's true effect than a rather artificial comparison to some stipulated control group that is quite different from the group that has been treated.[14]

Many experiments are time-consuming, intensive, expensive, and/or intrusive. Where the researcher's objective is to analyze the effect of a lengthy therapeutic treatment, for example, it may be difficult to monitor a large panel of subjects, and it may be virtually impossible to do so in

---

[14] Lundervold and Belwood (2000). Granted, if there is a group that has applied for treatment but has been denied (by reason of short capacity), then this group may be enlisted as a control. This is often found in studies focused on drug users, where a large wait-listed group is considered as a formal control for the treated group. However, most research situations are not so fortunate as to have a "wait-listed" group available for analysis.

an intensive fashion (e.g., with daily or weekly sessions between investigator and patient). It is not surprising that the field of psychology began with the experimental analysis of individual cases or small numbers of cases – either humans or animals. Single-case research designs occupied most of the founding fathers of the discipline, including Wilhelm Wundt (1832–1920), Ivan Pavlov (1849–1936), and B. F. Skinner (1904–1990). Indeed, Wundt's work on "hard introspection" dictated that his most common research subject remained himself.[15] Skinner once commented that "instead of studying a thousand rats for one hour each, or a hundred rats for ten hours each, the investigator is likely to study one rat for a thousand hours."[16] Early psychologists were avid proponents of the experimental method, but their employment of this method often did not include a randomized control group, a relatively recent invention.[17]

A final reason for neglecting a formal control in experimental research designs is that it may violate ethical principles. Consider the case of a promising medical treatment that investigators are attempting to study. If there is good reason to suppose, ex ante, that the treatment will save lives, or if this becomes apparent at a certain point in the course of an experiment, it may be unethical to maintain a control group – for, in not treating them, one may be putting their lives at risk.

Regrettably, in most social science research situations the absence of a formal control introduces serious problems into the analysis. This is a particular danger where human decision-making behavior is concerned, since the very act of studying an individual may affect her behavior. The subject of our hypothetical treatment may exhibit a response simply because she is aware of being treated (e.g., "placebo" or "Hawthorne" effects). In this sort of situation, there is virtually no way to identify causal effects unless the researcher can compare treatment and control groups. This is why, incidentally, single-case experimental studies are more common in natural science settings (including cognitive psychology), where the researcher is concerned with the behavior of inanimate objects or with biologically induced behavior.

In observational work (where there is no manipulated treatment), by contrast, the Longitudinal Comparison is quite common. Indeed, most

---

[15] Heidbreder (1933).

[16] Quoted in Hersen and Barlow (1976: 29). See also Franklin, Allison, and Gorman (1997: 23); Kazdin (1982: 5–6).

[17] Kinder and Palfrey (1993: 9).

case studies probably take this form. Wherever the researcher concentrates on a single case and that case undergoes a change in the theoretical variable of interest, a Longitudinal Comparison is in play.

Consider the introduction of compulsory voting laws in the Netherlands just prior to the 1970 general election.[18] If one is interested in the effect of compulsory voting on turnout, this statutory change offers a useful quasi-experimental intervention. One has only to compare turnout rates in 1970 with turnout rates in the previous election in order to determine the causal effect of the law (turnout increased dramatically). One assumes, of course, that nothing else that might influence turnout rates occurred during this period and that the two elections are similar enough – in all ways that might affect turnout – that they can be meaningfully compared. One also assumes more or less complete voter knowledge of the statutory change; otherwise there is, effectively, no treatment. But these assumptions, at least in this instance, seem relatively secure. Under the circumstances, it is fair to regard such a study as a natural experiment, for the intervention of policy makers resembles the sort of intervention that might have been undertaken by investigators, if they had the opportunity.

Another example, somewhat more technical in nature, concerns the interrelationship of monetary policy and economic fluctuations. This topic is undertaken by Milton Friedman and Anna Schwartz in their *Monetary History of the United States*, a classic work in monetarist theory, recently reviewed by Jeffrey Miron, whose account I follow.[19] The empirical heft of the book rests on four historical occasions on which the stock of money changed due to policy choices largely unrelated to the behavior of the economy (and hence exogenous to the research question). These four interventions were "the increase in the discount rate in the first half of 1920, the increase in the discount rate in October 1931, the increase in reserve requirements in 1936–1937, and the failure of the Federal Reserve to stem the tide of falling money in 1929–1931."[20] Each was followed by a substantial change in the behavior of the stock of money, thus validating a central pillar of monetarist theory.

Frequently, a study will incorporate several cases, each of which incorporates a Longitudinal Comparison. This may be referred to as a series of case studies or, more extravagantly, as an "iterated natural

---

[18] Jackman (1985: 173–5).
[19] Friedman and Schwartz (1963); Miron (1994).
[20] Miron (1994: 19).

experiment."[21] The key point is that the primary focus of comparison in this type of research design is temporal, rather than spatial. Do not be misled by the fact that there is more than one case; these cases are properly regarded simply as multiple instances of the same intervention. If there is an explicit spatial component to the comparison, then it is properly classified as a Dynamic Comparison (as already discussed) or a Spatial Comparison, to which we now turn.

Spatial Comparison

A third archetypal research design involves a comparison between two cases (or groups of cases), neither of which experiences an observable change on the variable of theoretical interest. I call this a Spatial Comparison, since the causal comparison is spatial rather than temporal. To be sure, there is an assumption that spatial differences between the two cases are the product of antecedent changes in one (or both) of the cases. However, because these changes are not observable – we can observe only their outcome – the research takes on a different, and necessarily more ambivalent, form. One cannot "see" X_1 and Y interact; one can only observe residues of their prior interaction. Evidently, where there is no variation in the theoretical variable of interest, no experimental intervention can have taken place, so this research design is limited to observational settings.

One interesting example of this sort of work focuses on intracountry differences in electoral system type. Here, researchers exploit the fact that in some countries, such as Germany, different electoral systems are employed simultaneously. These are known as "mixed" electoral systems, since they employ both proportional and first-past-the-post (single-member district) designs in a parallel fashion.[22] In this setting, it is possible for researchers to observe differences in legislator behavior between these two groups – those chosen by PR rules and those chosen by majoritarian rules – in order to discover clues about the conditioning role of electoral system design.[23] Are members chosen from PR districts less susceptible to pork barrel legislating? less sensitive to district preferences? less inclined to district-level campaigning? more sensitive to cues from party leaders?

---

[21] Gerring et al. (2005).

[22] Sometimes, the PR seats are employed to compensate for disproportional results at the district level (e.g., in Germany); in other cases (e.g., Japan), the two systems operate independently (Shugart and Wattenberg 2001).

[23] Lancaster and Patterson (1990); Patzelt (2000); Stratmann and Baur (2002).

Another sort of comparison rests upon spatial comparisons across regions within a single country. Abhijit Banerjee and Lakshmi Iyer investigate the long-term consequences of different property rights regimes across various regions of India. The authors explain:

The British made different arrangements for the collection of [land] revenue in different areas, leading to different distributions of ownership rights. The different systems fall into three main groups: in landlord-based systems, the revenue collection responsibilities for a number of villages was vested in a landlord who was allowed to retain a part of the revenue he collected; in individual-based systems the British government officers collected revenue directly from the actual cultivators without the intermediation of a landlord; in village-based systems, a village community body bore the revenue responsibility.[24]

The main finding is that these property rights systems have strong effects on post-independence investments in agriculture and on measures of agricultural productivity in these areas. Varying patterns of colonial rule instituted varying patterns of land tenure, leading to varying patterns of agricultural modernization.

In these two examples, one focused on contemporary electoral systems and the other on secular-historical patterns of development, it is difficult to observe the effect of the intervention directly. It is not useful, that is, to look at Germany before and after the installation of a mixed electoral system, because the situation prior to this electoral institution was not democratic. In the case of India, it would be very useful to observe how different areas evolved before and after the British instituted different property rights systems; however, we lack the historical materials to do so. Thus, in both situations the primary leverage scholars have on the causal problem is spatial rather than temporal. Even so, variations across space (i.e., across different types of legislators or across different regions) provide ample ground for reaching conclusions about probable causes.

Counterfactual Comparison

A final research design available to case study researchers involves the use of a case (or cases) where there is no variation at all – either temporal or spatial – in the variable of interest. Instead, the intervention is imagined.

[24] Banerjee and Iyer (2002: 5).

I call this a Counterfactual Comparison, since the thought experiment provides all the covariational evidence that is available.[25]

Regrettably, there are quite a few instances in which a key variable of theoretical interest does not change appreciably within the scope of any possible research design. This is the classic instance of the dog that refuses to bark, and is often the only recourse for studies focused on "structural" variables – geographic, constitutional, sociological – which tend not to change very much over periods that might feasibly be observed. Even so, causal analysis is not precluded. It did not stop Sherlock Holmes, and it does not stop social scientists. But it does lend the resulting investigations the character of a detective story, for in this setting the researcher is constrained to adopt a research design in which the temporal variation is imaginary and there is no spatial control.

Although it sounds rather exotic, this species of temporal reconstruction is so common as to be second nature. Consider the following remarks of a journalist seeking to explain the rise of a Maoist insurgency in Nepal in the 1990s.

By 1994, Nepal's Communists had split. One faction, led by Prachanda – what would become the Communist Party of Nepal (Maoist) – was kept out of the elections. Many Nepalis regard that as the crucial moment in the political history of Communism in Nepal. Had the C.P.N. (M) been allowed to contest for power, it might never have resorted to war. By the time this was clear, however, it was too late.[26]

Although the writer follows journalistic standards by couching all analysis in terms of expressed views ("many Nepalis regard..."), the counterfactual claim is clear. And it is plausible. Indeed, the elimination of such claims would make much case-based social science – not to mention journalism and history – impossible, for without such counterfactual thought experiments writers would be constrained to analyze only

[25] This definition of "counterfactual analysis" amplifies on Fearon (1991) and is narrower than others (e.g., Brown 1991), where the term is employed quasi-synonymously with "thinking." This section thus argues against the contention of King, Keohane, and Verba (1994: 129) that "nothing whatsoever can be learned about the causes of the dependent variable without taking into account other instances when the dependent variable takes on other values." For additional work on counterfactual thought experiments in the humanities and social sciences, see Cowley (2001); Elster (1978); Lebow (2000); and Tetlock and Belkin (1996).

[26] Sengupta (2005: 2).

situations where there was a change in the independent variable of interest (a Longitudinal Comparison), relevant variation across cases (a Spatial Comparison), or both (a Dynamic Comparison).

One of the most famous observational studies without control or intervention was conducted by Jeffrey Pressman and Aaron Wildavsky on the general topic of policy implementation. The authors follow the implementation of a federal bill, passed in 1966, to construct an airport hangar, a marine terminal, a thirty-acre industrial park, and an access road to a major coliseum in the city of Oakland, California. The authors point out that this represented free money for a depressed urban region. There was every reason to assume that these projects would benefit the community, and every reason – at least from an abstract public interest perspective – to suppose that the programs would be speedily implemented. Yet, three years later, progress was agonizingly slow, and few projects had actually been completed. The explanation provided by the authors rests upon the bureaucratic complexities of the American polity. Pressman and Wildavsky show that the small and relatively specific tasks undertaken by the federal government necessitated the cooperation of seven federal agencies (the Economic Development Administration [EDA] of the Department of Commerce, the Seattle Regional Office of the EDA, the Oakland Office of the EDA, the General Accounting Office, the Department of Health, Education, and Welfare [HEW], the Department of Labor, and the Navy), three local agencies (the mayor of Oakland, the city council, and the port of Oakland), and four private groups (World Airways Company, Oakland business leaders, Oakland black leaders, and conservation and environmental groups). These fourteen governmental and private entities had to agree on at least seventy important decisions in order to implement a law initially passed in Washington.[27] James Q. Wilson observes, "It is rarely possible to get independent organizations to agree by 'issuing orders'; it is never possible to do so when they belong to legally distinct levels of government."[28] The plausible counterfactual is that with a unitary system of government, these tasks would have been accomplished in a more efficient and expeditious fashion.

If one is willing to accept this conclusion, based upon the evidence presented in Pressman and Wildavsky's study, then one has made a causal

---

[27] Pressman and Wildavsky (1973), summarized in Wilson (1992: 68).

[28] Wilson (1992: 69). For further discussion of methodological issues in implementation research, see Goggin (1986).

inference based (primarily) on observational evidence drawn from cases without variation in the hypothesis of interest (the United States remains federal throughout the period under study, and there is no difference in the "degree of federalism" pertaining to the various projects under study).

This style of causal analysis may strike the reader as highly tenuous, on general methodological grounds. Indeed, it deviates from the experimental paradigm in virtually every respect. However, before dismissing this research design one must consider the available alternatives. One could discuss lots of hypothetical research designs, but the only one that seems relatively practicable in this instance is the Spatial Comparison. That is, Pressman and Wildavsky might have elected to compare the United States to a similar country that does not have a federal system, but does grapple with a similar set of policies. Unfortunately, there is no really good paired case available for such a comparison. Countries that are unitary and democratic tend to be quite different from the United States, and differ in ways that might affect their policy-making processes. Britain is unitary and democratic, but also quite a bit smaller in size than the United States. More importantly, it possesses a parliamentary executive, and this factor is difficult to disentangle from the policy process, posing serious issues of spurious causality.[29] At the end of the day, Pressman and Wildavsky's choice of research methodology may have been the best of all available alternatives. This is the pragmatic standard to which we rightly hold all scholars.

Ceteris Paribus

Thus far, I have set forth a typology intended to capture the covariational properties of case study research designs. The typology answers the question: what sort of variation is being exploited for the purpose of drawing causal conclusions from a small number of cases? I have shown that such variation may be temporal and/or spatial, thus providing four archetypal research designs: Dynamic Comparison, Longitudinal Comparison, Spatial Comparison, and Counterfactual Comparison (see Table 6.1).

I have also shown that these four research designs can be profitably understood as deviations from the classic experiment. The Dynamic

---

[29] For further examples and discussion of this sort of research design, see Weaver and Rockman (1993).

Comparison exploits both spatial and temporal variation, and may be manipulated (in which case it *is* a classic experiment) or nonmanipulated (observational). The Longitudinal Comparison exploits only temporal variation, along the lines of an experiment without controls – though the intervention may be manipulated or natural. The Spatial Comparison exploits variation across cases observed cross-sectionally. The Counterfactual Comparison, finally, employs evidence that is nonempirical (imaginary), but nonetheless aspires to the experimental ideal. This typology, while it does not exhaust the features of a good case study research design, summarizes the most important of these features in a compact form and may serve as a useful template for the construction – and critique – of case study research.

Largely ignored in the previous discussion has been the ceteris paribus caveat that undergirds all causal analysis. To say that X_1 is a cause of Y is to say that X_1 causes Y, all other things being equal. The ceteris paribus clause may be defined in many different ways; that is, the context of a causal argument may be bounded, qualified. But within those stipulated boundaries, the assumption must hold; otherwise, causal argument is impossible. All of this is well established, indeed definitional. Where it enters the realm of empirical testing is in the construction of research designs that maintain ceteris paribus conditions along the two possible dimensions of analysis. This means that any temporal variation in Y observable from t_1 to t_2 should be the product of X_1 (the causal factor of interest), rather than of any other confounding causal factor (designated as X_2 in the previous discussion). Similarly, any spatial variation in Y observable across the treatment and control cases should be the product of X_1, not X_2. (The latter issue is sometimes referred to as "pre-treatment equivalence.") These are the temporal and spatial components of the ceteris paribus assumption. Needless to say, they are not easily satisfied.

It is here that the principal difference between experimental and nonexperimental research is located. Donald Campbell's cautionary tale of the state of Connecticut's crackdown on speeding (a nonmanipulated Longitudinal Comparison) serves as a reminder of how short-term trends may arise for reasons having nothing to do with the quasi-experimental treatment in question, leading to spurious conclusions. The story may be briefly retold.[30] Connecticut's imposition of a harsh antispeeding law in

---

[30] I offer here a highly abbreviated, selective account of Campbell's well-known article (1968/1988).

1955 was followed by a dramatic fall in traffic fatalities in the following year, leading the governor (Ribicoff) to declare the law a success. Campbell shows, however, that this apparent decline could have been the product of several other factors having nothing to do with the change in state policy. These include (a) regression to the mean (1955 was an exceptionally bad year for traffic fatalities, so it is no surprise that 1956 would be an improvement); (b) long-term trends (traffic fatalities appear to have been declining for some time, nationally and in the state of Connecticut); and (c) a change in the baseline (an increasing number of cars on the road).

Whether the research is experimental or not may make considerable difference in the degree to which a given research design satisfies the ceteris paribus assumption of causal analysis. First, where an intervention is manipulated by the researcher it is unlikely to be correlated with other things that might influence the outcome of interest. Thus, any changes in Y may be interpreted as the product of X_1 and only X_1, other factors being held constant. Second, where the selection of treatment and control cases is randomized, they are more likely to be identical in all respects that might affect the causal inference in question. Finally, in an experimental format the treatment and control groups are effectively isolated from each other, preventing spatial contamination. This means that the ceteris paribus assumption inherent in all causal inference is usually relatively safe in an experimental study. The control may be understood as reflecting a vision of reality as it would have been without the specified intervention.

All of these ceteris paribus assumptions are considerably more difficult to achieve in observational settings, as a close look at the foregoing examples will attest.[31] However, the point remains that they can be achieved in observational settings, and they can also be violated in experimental settings. As J. S. Mill observed, "we may either *find* an instance in nature suited to our purposes, or, by an artificial arrangement of circumstances, *make* one. The value of the instance depends on what it is in itself, not on the mode in which it is obtained.... There is, in short, no difference in kind, no real logical distinction, between the two processes of investigation."[32]

---

[31] See Campbell (1968/1988); Shadish, Cook, and Campbell (2002).
[32] Mill (1843/1872: 249).

It is the satisfaction of ceteris paribus assumptions, not the use of a manipulated treatment or a randomized control group, that rightly qualifies a research product as methodologically sound. Accordingly, the methodological issues of case study research may be conceptualized as a product of four paradigmatic styles of evidence, each of which calls forth a set of extremely important ceteris paribus assumptions.

7

Internal Validity: Process Tracing

In the previous chapter, the problem of internal validity was discussed from an experimental perspective. That is, the case study method was understood as an attempt to satisfy the methodological criteria that define a well-designed experiment. To the extent that a single case, or a small number of cases, exemplify a quasi-experimental design, the case study method is vindicated.

However, few case studies are truly experimental, in the sense of having a manipulated treatment. This is because a manipulable treatment is usually easy to replicate across multiple cases, thus providing a large-N cross-case research design. Moreover, among observational case studies, perfect "natural experiments" are rare. The observational world does not usually provide cases with both temporal variation (making possible "pre" and "post" tests) and spatial variation ("treatment" and "control" cases) across variables of theoretical interest, while holding all else constant. Usually, there are important violations of the ceteris paribus assumption.

What this means is that case study research usually relies heavily on contextual evidence and deductive logic to reconstruct causality within a single case. It is not sufficient simply to examine the covariation of X_1 and Y, because there are too many confounding causal factors and because the latter cannot usually be eliminated by the purity of the research design or by clever quantitative techniques (control variables, instrumental variables, matching estimators, and the like).[1] Thus, a "covariational" style of research is usually insufficient to prove causation in a case study format.

---

[1] Statistical techniques may be employed in the analysis of within-case evidence but not at the level of across-case evidence, because the sample is too small (by definition).

Lest there be any confusion about this, it is important to emphasize that the pattern of covariation found between X_1 (the causal variable of interest) and Y (the outcome of interest) is always central to case study analysis. (How could it be otherwise?) All causal analyses are covariational in this obvious way. The point is that in case study research evidence pertaining to X_1 and Y is often opaque, and must therefore be supplemented by another form of analysis that has come to be known as *process tracing*.[2]

The hallmark of process tracing, in my view, is that multiple types of evidence are employed for the verification of a single inference – bits and pieces of evidence that embody different units of analysis (they are each drawn from unique populations). Individual observations are therefore noncomparable. Additionally, process tracing usually involves long causal chains. Rather than multiple instances of $X_1 \rightarrow Y$ (the large-N cross-case style of research), one examines a single instance of $X_1 \rightarrow X_2 \rightarrow X_3 \rightarrow X_4 \rightarrow Y$. (Of course, this causal path may be much longer and more circuitous, with multiple switches and feedback loops.)

In these respects, process tracing is akin to detective work. The maid said this; the butler said that; and the suspect was seen at the scene of the crime on Tuesday, just prior to the murder. Each of these facts is relevant to the central hypothesis – that Jones killed Smith – but they are not directly comparable to one another. And because they cannot be directly compared, they cannot be analyzed in a unified sample. The maid's testimony is empirical, and it is certainly relevant, but it cannot be reduced to standard dataset observations, and it is not meaningfully understood within a formal research design.

Because this is a difficult "method" to wrap one's mind around, we begin this chapter with a series of examples – diverse instances of process tracing at work in social science explanation. I then expatiate on the general features of this form of analysis. In the conclusion, I try to address the knotty question of what characterizes a *good* (convincing) process-tracing analysis.

---

[2] A number of vaguely synonymous terms might also be invoked, including causal-process observations, pattern matching, causal-chain explanation, colligation, congruence method, genetic explanation, interpretive method, narrative explanation, and sequential explanation. See Brady and Collier (2004); Danto (1985); George and Bennett (2005: Chapters 9–10); Goldstone (1991: 50–62); Hall (2003); Little (1995: 43–4); Roberts (1996); Scriven (1976); and Tarrow (1995: 472). Readers should be warned that my understanding of process tracing varies somewhat from that found elsewhere in the field, where it is sometimes equated with any investigation into causal mechanisms (George and Bennett 2005).

Examples

Theda Skocpol's renowned study of social revolution rests centrally on an in-depth examination of three key cases – Russia, China, and France.[3] With respect to France, Skocpol identifies three general causal factors leading to the breakdown of state authority in the eighteenth century: agrarian backwardness, international pressure, and state autonomy. These factors, in turn, may be disaggregated into thirty-seven discrete steps that connect structural causes to the outcome of interest in this particular country-case. The entire argument is carefully mapped by James Mahoney in a causal diagram, reproduced in Figure 7.1. Notice that each stage of the case study is qualitatively distinct, creating a series of nested research designs. Thus, evidence for one link in the chain has no bearing on the next (or previous) link.

As a second example, consider Pressman and Wildavsky's study of implementation procedures, first introduced in the previous chapter. This study rests largely upon a demonstration of proximal relationships between key actors. The authors show, for example, that there is resistance to federal directives on the part of local political leaders who have their own agendas and who often do not see eye to eye with the Washington bureaucrats assigned to implement the construction of public works projects in Oakland. Interviews with these actors, as well as their own public statements, bolster the counterfactual reasoning of the book. These local actors have different perspectives because they have different constituencies, different organizational norms, and consequently different incentive structures. All of this, including the ability of the local actors to resist federal directives, may be considered as a product of the constitutional and statutory structure of the American polity. Without federalism, and without the local bureaucratic independence and multiplication of agencies with overlapping jurisdictions that stems from a federal constitution, things would have been very different. Again, a series of one-shot observations is enlisted to demonstrate a macro-causal claim applying not just to the United States at large but to democratic polities everywhere.

As a third example, consider Henry Brady's reflections on his study of the Florida election results in the 2000 presidential election.[4] In the wake of this close election, at least one commentator – John Lott, an

---

[3] Skocpol (1979). My account draws on Mahoney (1999).
[4] Brady (2004: 269–70).

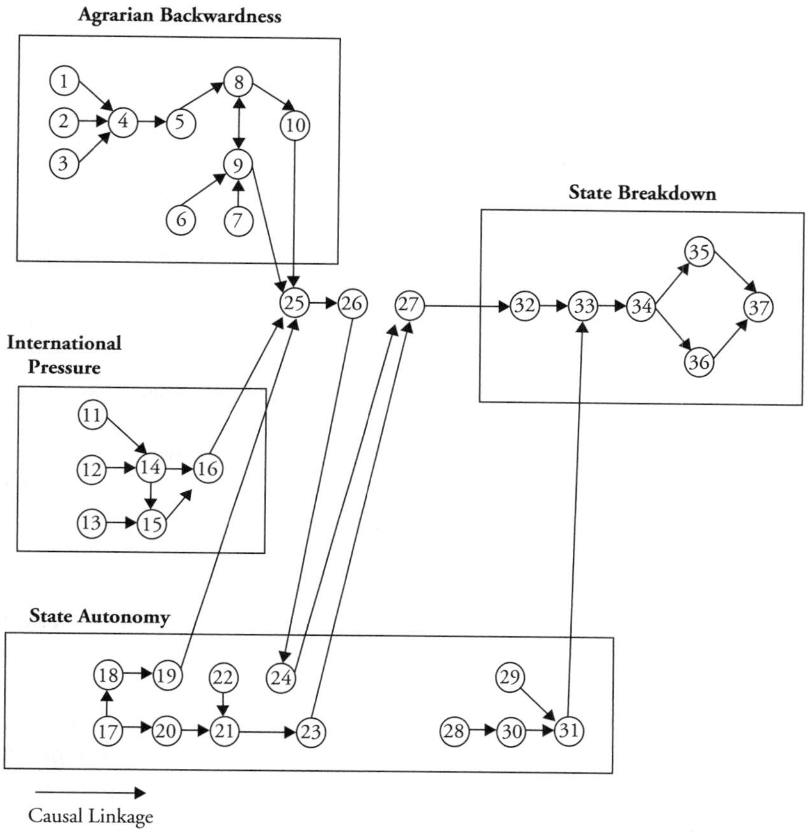

Agrarian Backwardness

International Pressure

State Breakdown

State Autonomy

Causal Linkage

FIGURE 7.1. Skocpol's explanation of the breakdown of the French state (1789). 1. Property relations prevent introduction of new agricultural techniques. 2. Tax system discourages agricultural innovation. 3. Sustained growth discourages agricultural innovation. 4. Backwardness of French agriculture. 5. Weak domestic market for industrial goods. 6. Internal transportation problems. 7. Population growth. 8. Failure to achieve industrial breakthrough. 9. Failure to sustain economic growth. 10. Inability to successfully compete with England. 11. Initial military successes under Louis XIV. 12. Expansionist ambitions of state. 13. French geographical location vis-à-vis England. 14. Sustained warfare. 15. State needs to devote resources to both army and navy. 16. Repeated defeats in war. 17. Creation of absolutist monarchy; decentralized medieval institutions persist. 18. Dominant class often exempted from taxes. 19. State faces obstacles generating loans. 20. Socially cohesive dominant class based on proprietary wealth. 21. Dominant class possesses legal right to delay royal legislation. 22. Dominant class exercises firm control over offices. 23. Dominant class is capable of blocking state reforms. 24. Dominant class resists financial reforms. 25. Major financial problems of state. 26. State attempts tax/financial reforms. 27. Financial reforms fail. 28. Recruitment of military officers from privileged classes. 29. Military officers hold grievances against the crown. 30. Military officers identify with the dominant class. 31. Military is unwilling to repress dominant class resistance. 32. Financial crisis deepens. 33. Pressures for creation of the Estates-General. 34. King summons the Estates-General. 35. Popular protests spread. 36. Conflict among dominant class members in the Estates-General; paralysis of old regime. 37. Municipal revolution; the old state collapses. Adapted from Mahoney (1999: 1166) after Skocpol (1979).

175

economist – suggested that because several networks had called the state for Gore prior to a closing of the polls in the panhandle section of the state, Republican voters may have been discouraged from going to the polls, and this in turn might have affected the margin (which was razor-thin and bitterly contested in the several months following the election). Lott reaches his conclusions on the basis of a regression analysis of turnout in all sixty-seven Florida counties over the course of four presidential elections, with a collection of controls (including fixed-year and county effects).[5]

Brady is unconvinced by the method, and by the results. Instead, he stitches together isolated pieces of evidence in an "ad hoc" fashion. He begins with the timing of the media calls – ten minutes before the closing of the polls in the panhandle. "If we assume that voters go to the polls at an even rate throughout the day," Brady continues, "then only $1/72^{nd}$ (ten minutes over twelve hours) of the [379,000 eligible voters in the panhandle] had not yet voted when the media call was made." This is probably a reasonable assumption. ("Interviews with Florida election officials and a review of media reports suggest that, typically, no rush to the polls occurs at the end of the day in the panhandle.") This means that "only 4,200 people could have been swayed by the media call of the election, if they heard it." He then proceeds to estimate how many of these 4,200 might have heard the media call, how many of these who heard it were inclined to vote for Bush, and how many of these might have been swayed, by the announcement, to go to the polls in the closing minutes of the day. Brady concludes: "the approximate upper bound for Bush's vote loss was 224 and . . . the actual vote loss was probably closer to somewhere between 28 and 56 votes."[6]

Brady's conclusions rest not on a formal research design but rather on isolated observations (both qualitative and quantitative) combined with deductive inferences. How many voters "had not yet voted when the media called the election for Gore? How many of these voters heard the call? Of these, how many decided not to vote? And of those who decided not to vote, how many would have voted for Bush?"[7] These questions are very different from those encountered in the foregoing studies of social revolution and policy implementation. Yet the approach has certain similarities insofar as Brady and colleagues enlist a set of observations that do not fall neatly into a standard research design and rely heavily on

---

[5] Lott (2000).
[6] Brady (2004: 269–70).
[7] Ibid., 269.

inferential reasoning, rather than on the sheer weight of the data, to reach their conclusions.

Often, process tracing is employed *in conjunction with* a standard research design – that is, as a supplementary tool. A good example is provided by a recent paper that examines the behavior of the U.S. Federal Reserve during the Great Depression. The central question is whether the Fed was constrained to adopt tight monetary policies because any deviation from this standard would have led to a loss of confidence in the nation's commitment to the gold standard (i.e., an expectation of a general devaluation), and hence to a general panic.[8] To test this proposition, Chang-Tai Hsieh and Christina Romer examine an incident in monetary policy during the spring of 1932, when the Federal Reserve embarked on a brief program of rapid monetary expansion. "In just fourteen weeks," the authors note, "the Federal Reserve purchased $936 million worth of U.S. government securities, more than doubling its holdings of government debt."[9] To determine whether the Fed's actions fostered investor insecurity, Hsieh and Romer track the forward dollar exchange rate during the spring of 1932, which is then compared to the spot rate, using "a measure of expected dollar devaluation relative to the currencies of four countries widely thought to have been firmly attached to gold during this period."[10] Finding no such devaluation, they conclude that the standard account is false – investor confidence could not have constrained the Fed's actions during the Great Depression. This is the sort of empirical evidence that we are accustomed to, and it fits neatly into the Dynamic Comparison research design introduced in Chapter Six (the treatment case, the United States, is compared to several control cases during the same period).

However, this conclusion would be questionable were it not bolstered by additional evidence bearing on the probable motivations of the officials of the Federal Reserve at the time. In order to shed light on this matter, the authors survey the *Commercial and Financial Chronicle* (a widely read professional journal, presumably representative of the banking community) and other documentary evidence. They find that "the leaders of the Federal Reserve ... expressed little concern about a loss of credibility. Indeed, they took gold outflows to be a sign that expansionary open market operations were needed, not as a sign of trouble."[11] The adjunct

---

[8] This line of argumentation is pursued by Eichengreen (1992).
[9] Hsieh and Romer (2001: 2).
[10] Ibid., 4.
[11] Ibid., 2.

evidence is instrumental in helping the authors to disconfirm a reigning theory. Moreover, this evidence sheds light on a new theory about Fed behavior during this critical era.

Our reading of the Federal Reserve records suggests that a misguided model of the economy, together with infighting among the twelve Federal Reserve banks, accounts for the end of concerted action. The Federal Reserve stopped largely because it thought it had accomplished its goal and because it was difficult to achieve consensus among the twelve Federal Reserve banks.[12]

This interpretation would not be possible (or at least would be highly suspect) without the adjunct evidence provided by process tracing.

The Nature of Process-Tracing Evidence

These varied examples illustrate the most distinctive feature of process-tracing styles of research, namely, the noncomparability of adjacent pieces of evidence. All pieces of evidence are relevant to the central argument (they are not "random"), but they do not comprise observations in a larger sample. They are more correctly understood as a series of $N = 1$ (one-shot) observations. Brady's observation about the timing of the media call – ten minutes before the closing of the polls – is followed by a second piece of evidence, the total number of people who voted on that day, and a third and a fourth. Although the procedure seems messy, we are often convinced by its conclusions. It seems reasonable to suppose that, at least in some circumstances, inferences based on noncomparable observations are more scientific than sample-based inferences, even though the method borders on the ineffable. Our confidence rests on specific propositions and specific observations; it is, in this sense, ad hoc. Indeed, there appears to be little one can say, *in general*, about the research designs employed by Skocpol, Pressman and Wildavsky, Brady, and Hsieh and Romer. While other methods can be understood according to their quasi-experimental properties, process tracing invokes a more complex logic, one analogous to detective work, legal briefs, journalism, and traditional historical accounts. The analyst seeks to make sense of a congeries of disparate evidence, each of which sheds light on a single outcome or set of related outcomes.

Note that although process tracing is always based on the analysis of a single case, the ramifications of that case study may be generalizable, and

[12] Ibid., 3.

indeed may be quite broad in scope. Skocpol's explanatory sketch enlists the minutiae of French history to demonstrate a macro-theoretical account pertaining to all countries that are wealthy and independent (noncolonies) in the modern era.

Note also that process-tracing evidence may be either qualitative or quantitative. Indeed, many of the examples just discussed involve evidence that takes a predominantly quantitative form. However, because each quantitative observation is quite different from the rest, they do not collectively constitute a sample. Each observation is sampled from a different population. This means that each quantitative observation is qualitatively different. It is thus the *noncomparability* of adjacent observations, not the nature of individual observations, that differentiates the process-tracing method from standard research designs.

Note, thirdly, that because each observation is qualitatively different from the next, the total number of observations in a study is usually indeterminate. While the cumulative number of process-tracing observations may be quite large, because these observations are not well defined it is difficult to say exactly how many there are. Noncomparable observations are, by definition, difficult to count. In an effort to count, one may resort to lists of what appear to be discrete pieces of evidence. This approximates the numbering systems employed in legal briefs. ("There are fifteen reasons why X is unlikely to have killed Y.") But lists can always be composed in multiple ways, and each piece of evidence carries a different weight in the researcher's overall assessment. So the total number of observations remains an open question. We do not know, and by the nature of the analysis cannot know, precisely how many observations are present in the studies by Skocpol, Pressman and Wildavsky, Brady, and Hsieh and Romer, or in other accounts such as Richard Fenno's *Homestyle* and Herbert Kaufman's *The Forest Ranger*.[13]

Process-tracing observations are not different examples of the same thing; they are *different things* ("apples and oranges"). Consequently, it is not clear where one observation ends and another begins. They flow seamlessly together. We cannot reread the foregoing studies with the aid of a calculator and hope to discover their true N; nor would we gain any analytic leverage by so doing.

Quantitative researchers are inclined to assume that if observations cannot be counted, they must not be there, or – more charitably – that

---

[13] Fenno (1978); Kaufman (1960).

there must be very few of them. Qualitative researchers may insist that they have many "rich" observations at their disposal, which provide them with the opportunity for thick description. But they are unable to say, precisely, how many observations they have, or where these observations are, or how many observations are needed for thick analysis. Indeed, the observations themselves remain undefined.

This ambiguity is not necessarily troublesome, for the number of observations in a process-tracing study does not bear directly on the usefulness or truthfulness of that study. While the number of observations in a sample drawn from a well-defined population contains information directly relevant to any inferences that might be based on that sample, the number of observations in a non-sample-based study (assuming one could estimate the N) has no obvious relevance to the validity of those inferences. Consider that if it were merely quantity that mattered, we might conclude that longer studies, which presumably contain more observations, are more valid than shorter studies. Yet it is laughable to assert that long narratives are more convincing than short narratives. It is the quality of the observations and how they are analyzed, not the quantity of observations, that is relevant in evaluating the truth claims of a process-tracing study. Indeed, the various noncomparable observations drawn upon in a given study are quite unlikely to be of equal importance, so merely counting them gives no indication of their overall significance.

This brings us to a final characteristic of process tracing: it leans heavily on general assumptions about the world, which may be highly theoretical (nomothetic "laws") or pre-theoretical ("common sense"). Precisely because of the absence of a formal research design, the researcher must assume a great deal about how the world works. The process-tracing observation makes sense only if it fits snugly within a comprehensible universe of causal relations. I do not wish to imply that process-tracing evidence is "shaky"; indeed, much of it is quite matter-of-fact and close to the ground. My point is simply that these facts are comprehensible only when they can be ordered, categorized, "narrativized," and this in turn rests upon a broad set of assumptions about the world.

The contrast with an ideal-typical experiment is revelatory. Where there is a manipulated treatment and a control, a priori assumptions about the world are minimized. There is not much to intuit in reaching conclusions about whether X_1 causes Y (though the question of *why* X_1 causes Y – the question of causal mechanisms – is often more complex). However, as one moves away from the experimental ideal, one perforce leans more heavily on background assumptions about the way the world works.

Insofar as these assumptions provide "priors" against which subsequent pieces of evidence can be evaluated, the analysis of noncomparable observations takes on a Bayesian flavor.[14] But the importance of contextual knowledge about the world also extends to other features of the analysis – the identification of viable alternatives (what, under the circumstances, were the options?), the playing out of various scenarios (counterfactual logic), and so forth. The insufficiencies of the formal research design must be compensated for by natural wisdom – an intuitive "feel" for a situation, usually gained through many years' experience in that area, be it a foreign country, a historical era, or a medical specialty.

Thus, although background knowledge informs *all* causal analysis, it is more prominently on display in case studies where some portion of the evidence derives from process-tracing observations, for each observation must be separately evaluated. Indeed, each noncomparable observation may be considered to constitute a separate research design, requiring a different set of background assumptions.

The Usefulness of Process Tracing

Having defined the characteristic features of process tracing, we may now inquire into its utility. What is it that makes a process tracing study (or portion of a study) useful and convincing? What is it that makes one process tracing study better than another?

Let us say that process tracing is convincing insofar as the multiple links in a causal chain can be formalized, that is, diagrammed in an explicit way (as a visual depiction and/or a mathematical model), and insofar as each micro-mechanism can be proven.

The first step seems fairly easy. If a causal relationship can be described in prose, then it ought to be diagrammable, even if it cannot be captured in a precise mathematical model. Mahoney's exegesis of Skocpol's analysis of the French Revolution ought to be replicable for any similar account, that is, for any account that aims to explain a chain of causation within a single case. Granted, the identification of a discrete "step" in a causal chain is always a matter of judgment. The same causal process might be diagrammed in different ways, and there is no end, in principle, to the infinite regress of causal mechanisms. And, to be sure, the act of formalizing a long set of concatenated inferences is apt to lead to some

---

[14] George and Bennett (2005); Gill, Sabin, and Schmid (2005).

scary-looking diagrams. Robert Fogel's causal diagram of the political realignment occurring in mid-nineteenth-century America involves over *fifty* discrete steps and many more causal arrows (often bidirectional).[15] Not a pretty picture. However, if this is Fogel's best estimation of the causal mechanisms, one can hardly deride the effort.

I do not mean to suggest that a formal diagram should replace a description in prose. Indeed, one can scarcely imagine one without the other. What I mean to suggest is that the formal diagram is a useful heuristic, forcing the author to make a precise and explicit statement of her argument.

The second admonition is more complicated. Could all thirty-seven steps in Skocpol's argument about France (and about Russia and China) be *tested*? What would this mean? Note that if we isolate a single step in this long argument, the nature of the causal analysis is now simplified. There is a single X_1 and Y lying at the same level of analysis, which means that we can understand that link within the rubric of a quasi-experimental framework, as discussed in the previous chapter. In principle, a researcher engaged in a process-tracing analysis could propose a unique research design for each step at each stage of the analysis. Thirty-six research designs for thirty-seven steps, if they are all arrayed in a single chain; many more if they are variously interconnected, as in Mahoney's diagram.

However, it is typical of case study research that these multiple links cannot be tested in a rigorous fashion. Usually, the author is forced to reconstruct a plausible account on the basis of what I have called Counterfactual Comparison (what would have happened if X_1 were different?). The reader will note a counterfactual style of analysis underlying each of the foregoing examples. This is what gives process tracing its highly deductive quality. Typically, one finds oneself comparing states of affairs as they exist to states of affairs as they might have existed. Upon the soundness of each link, and the wealth of assumptions that inform each link, the soundness of the entire enterprise rests. And because these assumptions are often assumptions about a particular context – the context in which the case is situated – it is very difficult to assign a level of uncertainty to that conclusion. A fortiori, it is difficult to arrive at a summary estimate of uncertainty for the entire analysis (based upon a long chain of causal mechanisms).

---

[15] Fogel (1992: 233).

Granted, one need not remain within a counterfactual mode of analysis. Sometimes, there is natural variation (temporal and/or spatial) in X_1 and Y that comes closer to the experimental ideal. And sometimes it is possible to convert noncomparable observations into large-N research designs. Noncomparable bits of evidence can be transformed into comparable bits of evidence – that is, standardized "observations" – simply by getting more bits of evidence and coding them according to type. Thus, the noncomparable observations enlisted by Hsieh and Romer might have been converted into standardized (comparable) observations. For example, the authors might have conducted a content analysis of the *Commercial and Financial Chronicle* and/or of the Federal Reserve records. This would have required coding sentences (or some other linguistic unit) according to whether they registered anxiety about a loss of credibility. Here, the sentence becomes the unit of analysis, and the number of sentences comprises the total "N" in a quantitative research design.

In many instances, however, there is no suitable temporal and/or spatial variation that approximates the experimental ideal, and/ or it is not possible to convert noncomparable observations into comparable observations so as to increase the sample size. It is difficult to see, for example, how Henry Brady's research question could be generalized across additional (comparable) observations, given the absence of suitable surveys on election day 2000. In other circumstances, there may be little advantage to be gained from the conversion of noncomparable to comparable observations. In the Hsieh/Romer study, for example, it is not clear what would be realized from this sort of formalization. If there is no evidence whatsoever of credibility anxiety in the documentary record, then the reader is not likely to be more convinced by an elaborate counting exercise (coded as 0, 0, 0, 0, 0, ...). More useful, I would think, are specific examples of what the leaders of the Fed actually said, as provided by the authors of this study. Sometimes formalization is useful, and sometimes it is not.

We have already noted that a large number of standardized observations are not always superior to a single noncomparable observation. Indeed, one of the foregoing examples, which pits Henry Brady's process tracing against the large-N statistical analysis conducted by John Lott, is a good case for the superiority of an informal method over a formal one. The reader can probably think of many others. Thus, the $N = 1$ designation that I have attached to process tracing should not be understood as pejorative. In some circumstances, one lonely observation (qualitative or quantitative) is sufficient to prove an inference. This is quite common, for example, when the author is attempting to reject a necessary or sufficient condition. If we are inquiring into the cause of Joe's demise, and we know that he was shot at close range, we can eliminate suspects who were not in the general vicinity. One observation – say, a videotape from a surveillance camera – is sufficient to provide conclusive proof that a suspect was not, in fact, the killer, even though the evidence is neither quantitative nor comparable to other pieces of evidence.

Recall, as well, that although many causal claims are typically nested within a single process tracing account, not all of these are equally suspect or equally important (for the overall argument). Two factors – theoretical importance and generally recognized priors – should determine the energy with which each claim is pursued. As a general rule, the need for a formally designated "research design" ends at the point where a causal conclusion becomes obvious, as judged by the contextual evidence at hand or our commonsense knowledge of the world. Or, to put the matter differently, since the motivating goal of causal research is to determine the relationship between X_1 and Y, and since all such conclusions rest delicately upon a skein of assumptions about how the world works, the purpose of a research design – a formal investigation into causes – is to supplement that everyday knowledge wherever it appears weak. There is no point in investigating the obvious. This greatly simplifies the task of the process tracer. The researcher rightly focuses her attention on those links in the causal chain that are (a) weakest and (b) most crucial for the overall argument.

Conclusion

To reiterate, our query regarding the validity of process tracing research has two very general answers: (1) clarify the argument, with all its attendant twists and turns (preferably with the aid of a visual diagram or formal model) and (2) verify each stage of this model, along with an estimate of relative uncertainty (for each stage and for the model as a whole). Simple though it sounds, these two desiderata (and particularly the latter) are not always easy to accomplish. Process tracing evidence is, almost by definition, difficult to verify, for it extends to evidence that is nonexperimental and cannot be analyzed in a sample-based format (by virtue of the incommensurability of individual bits of evidence).

Fortunately, there are several mitigating features of process tracing that may give us greater confidence in results that are based, at least in part, on this unorthodox style of evidence. First, process tracing is often employed as an adjunct form of analysis – a complement to a formal research design (experimental or observational). Indeed, one way to think about process tracing is as a cross-check, a triangulation, that can be – and ought to be – applied to all results gained through formal methods. Studies based on a formal research design will sometimes note parenthetically that the account is consistent with "anecdotal" or "narrative" evidence, that is, with evidence that falls outside the formal research design. It makes sense of the statements made by the actors, of their plausible motives, and so forth. This is often extremely important evidence and deserves a more respectful label than "anecdotal" and a more revealing label than "narrative." (What is the evidentiary status of a narrative?) In any case, process tracing, when employed in an adjunct fashion, is not intended to bear the entire burden of an empirical study. It offers supporting evidence.

Second, process tracing rests upon contextual assumptions and assumptions about how the world works. Insofar as there is a comfortable fit between the evidence and the assumptions of a process tracing account, that account should pass muster. Granted, the reader of a process tracing account may not be in a position to judge the veracity of an author's conclusions that rest on the specific circumstances of a highly particular context. Even so, these conclusions may be vetted by those intimately familiar with that region, policy area, or historical era. So long as sufficient documentation is included in the account, the verification of a process tracing study is eminently achievable. Therefore, even though it may be impossible to arrive at a set of standardized methodological rules – thus depriving process tracing of the status of a "method" – we may have confidence in process tracing accounts once they have been vetted by suitably trained experts.

In sum, despite its apparently mysterious qualities, process tracing has an important role to play in case-based social science. Whether it is employed in an adjunct capacity or whether the author's conclusions rest primarily on the analysis of noncomparable observations, it deserves an honored place in the tool kit of social science.

Epilogue

Single-Outcome Studies

This book has understood case studies as a method for generalizing across populations (see Chapter Two). The population may be small or large, but the analysis is synecdochic. It infers a larger whole from a smaller part. (Occasionally, where there is a very small population, the researcher may be able to study every case in the population intensively. In this rare circumstance there is no inferential leap from sample to population.)

At times, however, the term "case study" may also refer to a piece of research whose inference is limited to the case under study. This sort of case study may be characterized (loosely) as "idiographic" rather than "nomothetic" insofar as the objective of analysis is narrowly scoped to one particular (relatively bounded) unit. Arguably, this is not a case study at all, since it is not a case of something broader than the case itself. Thus, I enlist a slightly different concept – the *single-outcome study* – as my topic in this epilogue.

Formally, a single-outcome study refers to a situation in which the researcher seeks to explain a single outcome for a single case. This outcome may register a change on Y – something happens. Or it may reflect stasis on Y – something might have happened but, in the event, does not. That is, the outcome may be "positive" or "negative." The actual duration of the outcome may be short (eventful) or long. A revolution (e.g., the American Revolution) and a political culture (e.g., American political culture) are both understood as outcomes, since they register distinct values for a single case.

For the statistically minded, the single-outcome study may be understood as a study oriented toward explaining the point score for a single case rather than a range of values across a population of cases, or a range of values occurring within a single case. One might also describe this as a "single-observation study," for an outcome may be recorded on a single line of a rectangular dataset, registering only one value for each of the relevant variables. However, the term is awkward and also somewhat misleading, since it implies that there are other comparable observations adjacent to the observation of interest, which may or may not be true. Alternatively, one might refer to this format as an idiographic case study. However, this would imply the opposite – that the outcome under analysis is unique – which may or may not be true. Happily, the concept of an outcome makes no a priori assumptions about neighboring phenomena; the outcome of interest may be routine or idiosyncratic.

By way of illustration, consider the following research questions focused on the contemporary welfare state (as measured by revenue or expenditure levels as a share of total GDP):

(1) What explains the relatively weak American welfare state?
(2) What explains welfare state development within the OECD?
(3) What explains variation in U.S. welfare spending over time?
(4) What explains variation in U.S. welfare spending across states?

Of these, only the first would be correctly classified as a study of a single outcome. Question #1 pertains to a single outcome because the case (the United States) is understood to have achieved a single, relatively stable value on this dimension. There is implied variation on the dependent variable (welfare state spending) across cases; indeed, the research question implicitly compares the United States to other countries. However, the researcher is not interested in explaining that variation; she is, instead, motivated to explain the point score of the United States.

By contrast, question #2 envisions the study of a population because it establishes a range of variation – at least one differentiable outcome for each OECD country; more if each case is observed over time. Question #3 recasts the first question from a single outcome to a population; it is focused on a range of comparable outcomes within a single case (the United States), defined temporally. Question #4 defines cases spatially rather than temporally; this is also a population.

It will be seen that a study focused on a single outcome must, of necessity, interrogate within-case evidence, and may therefore construct comparable observations within the case of primary interest. Thus, in answering question #1, a researcher might employ strategies #3 and #4. Similarly, a single-outcome study might incorporate evidence drawn from adjacent cases (at the same level of analysis), that is, strategy #2. However, if the purpose of this within-case and across-case evidence is to illuminate a single outcome within a single case it is still appropriately classified as a single-outcome study.

With these definitional matters under our belts, we may now proceed. What difference does it make whether an author is studying a case of something broader than itself or a single outcome?[1] What is the difference between studying the U.S. welfare state (a) as an example of welfare state development more generally and (b) as a topic in its own right? In philosophical circles, this may be understood as a distinction between a cause (in general) and a cause in fact.[2] In the one instance, the American experience is enlisted to help explain something about welfare state development everywhere (or at least within the OECD). In the other instance, what we know about welfare states in general is enlisted to help explain one particular case. Virtually everything is identical about these two topics except that the theoretical objective has shifted from macro to micro.

Another example would be the distinction between crime (in general) and a particular crime. We might study a particular crime in order to elucidate some more general feature of crime in a society. This would be a case study. Or we might study the details of a particular crime – as well as more general features of crime – in order to understand who shot Joe, and why. This would be a single-outcome study. It is one thing to explain a rise in crime, and quite another to explain why Joe was killed. In this chapter, we shift gears from the first sort of explanation to the second.

I begin by discussing the utility of single-outcome studies and the different types of argumentation and causal logic that they embrace. I proceed to discuss the methodological components of the single-outcome study, which may be reduced to three angles: nested analysis (large-N cross-case analysis), most-similar analysis (small-N cross-case analysis), and within-case analysis (evidence drawn from the case of special interest). The chapter concludes with a discussion of a common difficulty encountered by single-outcome analysis – reconciling cross-case and within-case evidence, both of which purport to explain the outcome of interest.

It is important to bear in mind that this chapter focuses on the distinctive methodological features of single-outcome studies. I leave aside, or treat lightly, issues that are equally relevant to case studies. Thus, wherever

---

[1] For discussions of the methodological issues arising from the attempt to explain a single event, see Goertz and Levy (forthcoming) and Levy (2001).
[2] Hart and Honore (1959).

I choose *not* to expatiate on a point, the reader may assume that what I have said in previous chapters of this book also applies to the single-outcome study.

Why Study Single Outcomes?

Methodologists have traditionally taken a dim view of single-outcome studies. Case studies are bad enough (as reviewed in Chapter One). Single-outcome studies are, by implication, even worse. Arguably, we are better off focusing our efforts on things in general rather than on highly specific things. Nomothetic research is more profitable, theoretically speaking, and also – usually – more falsifiable.[3] (The reader will note that on an imagined idiographic-nomothetic scale, single-outcome studies lie at one end and cross-case studies at the other extreme, with case studies – the primary focus of this book – in the middle.)

Even so, there are many situations in which one might wish to understand specific circumstances, rather than circumstances in general. Pauline Young clarifies that the term "social case work" often refers to specific contexts.

In social case work we do not gather data in order to compare, classify, and analyze with a view to formulating general principles. We gather the data case by case in order to make a separate, differential diagnosis, with little or no regard for comparison, classification, and scientific generalization. The diagnosis is made with a view to putting treatment into operation in this particular case.[4]

While scholars of international relations have an interest in wars, they are also interested in the causal factors that led to specific wars, particularly big wars with large consequences.[5] Every country, every region, every business, every era, every event, every individual – for that matter, every phenomenon that a substantial number of people care about – inspires its own single-outcome research agenda. Citizens of Denmark wonder why Denmark has turned out the way it has. Chinese-American immigrants wonder why this group exhibits certain sociological and political patterns. Every public figure of note or notoriety sooner or later becomes the subject of a biography or autobiography. Indeed, the vast majority of the books and articles published in a given year are single-outcome analyses.

---

[3] Goldthorpe (1997); King, Keohane, and Verba (1994); Lieberson (1985, 1992).
[4] Young (1939: 235–6).
[5] Levy (2002b).

Social scientists, like lay citizens, are often interested in how their chosen subject plays out in their country of origin. Thus, American economists study the American economy; American sociologists study American society; and American political scientists study American politics. Of course, they may study particular aspects of these broad subjects; the point is that their concern in this genre of work is not a class of outcomes but rather a particular outcome or a set of outcomes pertaining to a particular country. It is not merely idle curiosity that fuels this sort of research. Understanding who we are – as individuals and as communities – rests, in part, on an understanding of what factors have made us who we are.

Why is the United States a welfare state laggard?[6] What caused World War One?[7] Why did the U.S. Federal Reserve not pursue a more expansionary monetary policy during the Great Depression?[8] What accounts for the rise of the West?[9] Why have growth rates in Botswana been so extraordinary over the past four decades?[10] How can the inception and growth of the European Union be explained?[11] Why did President Truman choose to employ nuclear weapons against Japan?[12] What are the causes of the terrorist attack on the World Trade Center that occurred on September 11, 2001?[13] Questions of this kind are not at all unusual in the social sciences.

Moreover, there are circumstances in which we can explain a particular outcome more easily than we can a class of outcomes. This is apt to be true when the cross-case evidence available on a topic is scarce and heterogeneous. Consider the following two questions: (1) why do social movements happen? and (2) why did the American civil rights movement happen? The first question is general, but its potential cases are few and extremely heterogeneous. Indeed, it is not even clear how one would construct a universe of comparable cases. The second question is narrow, but – I think – answerable. I hasten to add that quite a number of factors may provide plausible explanations for the American civil rights movement, and the methodological grounds for distinguishing good from

---

[6] Alesina and Glaeser (2004).
[7] Goertz and Levy (forthcoming).
[8] Hsieh and Romer (2001).
[9] McNeill (1991); North and Thomas (1973).
[10] Acemoglu, Johnson, and Robinson (2003).
[11] Moravcsik (1998).
[12] Alperovitz (1996).
[13] 9/11 Commission Report (2003).

bad answers is not entirely clear. Even so, I find work on this idiographic question more convincing than work on the nomothetic question of what causes social movements.[14]

Return for a moment to questions raised in our previous discussion: (1) what causes crime? and (2) who killed Joe? One can easily imagine propositions about the latter that are more secure than propositions about the former. Arguably, criminal justice verdicts are more dependable than criminal justice studies. We are able to convict or acquit in most cases with a high degree of certainty, while we are often unable to dispense with general questions about crime.

In sum, single-outcome analysis is both intrinsically valuable (because we wish to know about such occurrences) and, at least in some circumstances, methodologically tractable. There must, then, be some general principles upon which single-outcome analysis rests.

The Argument

As with case study research, it is essential for the researcher to specify a clear hypothesis, or at least a relatively clear research question. This point deserves special attention in light of the seeming obviousness of research connected with a particular event. If one is studying World War One, it seems self-evident that the researcher will be attempting to explain this historical fact. The problem is that this is a very immense fact, and consequently can be seen from many angles. "Explaining World War One" could mean explaining (a) why the war occured (at all); (b) why it broke out in 1914; (c) why it broke out on June 28, 1914; (d) why it broke out in the precise way that it did (i.e., shortly after the assassination of Archduke Ferdinand); (e) why it was prosecuted in the manner that it was, and so forth. Option (a) suggests – but does not mandate – a focus on antecedent (structural, distal) causes, while the other options suggest a focus on proximate causes (of many different kinds). Evidently, the way the research question is posed is likely to have an enormous impact on the chosen research design, not to mention the sort of conclusion that the author reaches. While this is true of any study – cross-case, case study, or single-outcome – it is particularly true for studies that focus on individual outcomes. Thus, single-outcome analysis requires the author to work hard to define and operationalize what it is that she is trying to explain.

---

[14] Contrast McAdam (1988) with McAdam, Tarrow, and Tilly (2001). On this general point, see Davidson (1963).

Andrew Bennett begins his book-length study by outlining a general quest: "to explain the rise of Soviet military interventionism in the 1970s, its fall in the 1980s, and its reprise in the form of Russia's interventions in the former Soviet republics and Chechnya in the 1990s."[15] Subsequently, Bennett lays out more nuanced indicators of interventionism. This escalation ladder includes the following steps: "a) shipment of arms to the client regime; b) transport of non-Soviet troops to or in the client regime; c) direct supply of non-Soviet troops on the front; d) deployment of Soviet military advisers in the war zone; e) military aid to allied troops in 'proxy' interventions; f) use of Soviet troops in combat roles; g) massive scale in the above activities; h) use of Soviet commanders to direct the military campaign; and i) use of Soviet ground troops."[16] This is a good example of how a general topic can be operationalized in a clear and falsifiable manner.

Granted, many single-outcome studies do *not* have clearly defined outcomes. A general history of World War One may be about many things related to World War One. A general history of Denmark is likely to focus on many things related to Denmark. A biography of Stalin is about many things related to Josef. There is nothing wrong with this traditional variety of historical, ethnographic, or journalistic narrative. Indeed, most of what we know about the world is drawn from this genre of work. (My bookshelves are filled with them.) However, we must also take note of the fact that this sort of study is essentially unfalsifiable. It cannot be proven or disproven, for there is no *argument* per se. It is causal analysis only in the loosest sense. My injunction for a clear hypothesis or research question is applicable only if the objective of the writer is causal-explanatory in a stricter, and more scientific, sense. It is this sort of work – a small minority of single-outcome studies – that I am concerned with.

Not only the outcome, but also the causal factor(s) of interest, must be clearly specified. Again, one finds that this is often more complicated in single-outcome analysis than it is in case study analysis, precisely because there is no larger field of cases to which the inference applies. Douglass

---

[15] Bennett (1999: 1). I shall assume that these are three discrete and relatively noncomparable outcomes, rather than a range of outcomes along a single dimension. If the latter, then Bennett's study would be more appropriately classified as the study of a population rather than of a series of single outcomes.

[16] Ibid., 15. The book focuses at the high end of this scale; the entire scale is reproduced here to illustrate how sensitive indicators may be developed in single-event contexts.

North and his colleagues take note of the following traditional arguments pertaining to U.S. economic history.

1. British policy was vindictive and injurious to the colonial economy after 1763.
2. The railroad was indispensable for American economic growth.
3. Speculators and railroads (through land grants) monopolized the best western lands in the nineteenth century, slowed down the westward movement, adversely affected the growth of the economy, and favored the rich over the poor.
4. In the era of the robber barons, farmers and workers were exploited.[17]

In looking closely at these arguments, North and colleagues observe that they are ambiguous because there is no clearly specified counterfactual. The authors therefore revise them as follows:

1. British policies were restrictive and injurious to the colonial economy after 1763, compared with what would have taken place had the colonies been independent during these years; or more precisely, income of the colonies under British rule after 1763 was less than it would have been had the colonists been free and independent.
2. Income in the United States would have been reduced by more than 10 percent had there been no railroads in 1890.
3. A different (but specified) land policy would have led to more rapid westward settlement in the nineteenth century, a higher rate of economic growth, and a more equal distribution of income.
4. In the absence of the monopolistic practices of the robber barons, farm income and real wages of manufacturing workers would have been significantly higher.[18]

Here is a set of falsifiable hypotheses. They specify an outcome, an alternative outcome, and a causal factor that is thought to be accountable for (imagined) variation across those outcomes.

Another point to be aware of is that the way in which an outcome is defined is likely to determine the extent to which it is comparable to other cases. Specifically, the more detailed the outcome – the more it is tailored to the circumstances of a specific country, group, or individual – the more difficult it will be to make reference to instances outside the area

---

[17] North, Anderson, and Hill (1983: 2–3).
[18] Ibid., 3.

of interest. If the case of special interest is defined too idiosyncratically it will no longer be a case of anything; that is, it will no longer be comparable (except in the most anodyne and unilluminating way) to other cases. Since one's objective is to explain *that* outcome, and not others, this is not necessarily problematic. However, it does mean that the author will be restricted to evidence drawn from that particular case. This is a serious restriction and limits the falsifiability of any such proposition, since it cannot be tested across other venues.

Causal Logic

Before going any further it is important to point out that the causal logic employed in case studies is often quite different from that of single-outcome studies, and this difference stems from their different objectives. Because the case study is focused on developing an explanation for some more general phenomenon it usually focuses on a particular causal factor, X_1, and its relationship to a class of outcomes, Y. It usually culminates in an X_1/Y–centered hypothesis which explains some amount of variation across instances of Y.

While it is a reasonable objective to seek to explain a small degree of variation across a wide range of cases, it is not a very reasonable objective to explain a small degree of variation across *one* outcome. Wherever a study focuses on a single outcome, the reader quite naturally wants to know everything, or almost everything, about the causes of that outcome (leaving aside the obvious background factors that every causal argument takes for granted). Thus, single-outcome studies usually seek to develop a more or less "complete" explanation of an outcome, including all causes that may have contributed to it, X_{1-N}.

Single-outcome studies make extensive use of necessary and sufficient conditions – deterministic ways of understanding causal relations. In case studies, by contrast, researchers usually assume probabilistic causal relations. The simple reason for this is that a general outcome encompassing multiple cases is less likely to conform to an invariant law. While there were undoubtedly necessary conditions for the occurrence of World War One, there is debate among scholars over the existence of necessary conditions pertaining to wars in general. (Only one such necessary condition has been proposed – nondemocracy – and it is hotly contested.)[19] As a rule, the larger the class of outcomes under investigation, the more likely

---

[19] Brown, Lynn-Jones, and Miller (1996).

it is that there will be exceptions, in which case the scholar rightly conceptualizes causes as probabilistic rather than necessary and/or sufficient.

Relatedly, because case studies seek general causes they tend to focus on structural causal factors. Because single-outcome studies seek the causes of specific outcomes, they often focus on contingent causal factors – for example, leadership, decisions, or other highly proximate factors. The assassination of Archduke Ferdinand is a plausible explanation of World War One, but not of wars in general.[20] It might of course be enlisted as an example of a more general explanation, but the author's emphasis would then shift to a more general factor (e.g., "triggering events"). Proper nouns are often embraced in the single-outcome study, while they must be regarded as examples of something else in the case study.

However, it would be wrong to conclude that because unique causes are admissible in single-outcome studies, they are also preferable. One does not imply the other. That is, an individual outcome may be the product of a very general cause (a "law"). Or it may not. There is no reason to presume that a case chosen for special study is different from a broader class of cases merely because it happens to form the topic of interest. A study of the American welfare state should not assume, as a point of departure, that the causal dynamics of welfare state development in the United States are fundamentally different from those unfolding in Europe and elsewhere in the world. An inquiry into a particular murder should not assume that the causes of this murder are any different from the causes of other murders, and so forth. The question of similarity and difference in causal analysis – the comparability of cases – is thus rightly left open, a matter for investigation.[21] To clarify, single-outcome research designs are open to idiographic explanation in a way that case study research is not. But single-outcome researchers should not assume, ex ante, that the truth about their case is contained in factors that are specific to that case.

Granted, there is an affinity between single-outcome analysis and idiographic explanations insofar as the outcomes that attract the most attention from social scientists are apt to be outcomes that are nonroutine – outcomes that don't fit into standard explanatory tropes. (I expatiate on this point in the conclusion). However, the "uniqueness" of a historian's (or

---

[20] Lebow (2000–01); Lebow and Stein (2004).
[21] Granted, some single-event analyses have as their primary objective a search for distinctiveness. Thus, the researcher's question might be "What is different about X (Denmark, the United States, etc.)?" However, this is an essentially descriptive question, while our concern in this chapter is with causal inference.

political scientist's or sociologist's) chosen topic is a poor point of departure, encouraging a prejudiced style of investigation into the actual causes of that outcome – which may be more routine than is generally realized.

Analysis

The analysis of a single outcome (a single outcome for a given case) may be approached from three different angles. The first, which I refer to (following Evan Lieberman) as *nested analysis*, employs cross-case analysis from a large sample in order to better understand the features of an individual outcome. The second, known most commonly as *most-similar analysis*, employs cross-case analysis within a small sample (e.g., two or three cases). The third, known generically as *within-case analysis*, draws on evidence from the case of special interest.[22]

The latter two methods are quintessentially case study methods, so my discussion of these topics builds on arguments from previous chapters. In particular, I draw on the experimental template of case study methods set forth in Chapter Six (see Table 6.1). There, I argued that all case studies could be understood as variants of four archetypal methods: the Dynamic Comparison, which mirrors the paradigmatic laboratory experiment (exploiting both temporal and spatial variation); the Longitudinal Comparison, which employs only temporal variation but is similar in design to the experiment without control; the Spatial Comparison, which employs only variation through space (purporting to measure the outcome of interventions that occurred at some point in the past, but that are not directly observable); and the Counterfactual Comparison, which relies on imaginary variation (i.e., where the researcher seeks to replicate the circumstances of an experiment in her head or with the aid of some formal model).

For purposes of discussion, I return to the question raised at the outset of this chapter: Why does the United States have a relatively small welfare state? This outcome is operationalized as aggregate central government revenue as a share of GDP. As previously, research on this topic may be either hypothesis-generating (Y-centered) or hypothesis-testing (where

---

[22] Note that the task of "case selection" in single event analysis is already partially accomplished: one has identified at least one of the cases that will be subjected to intensive study. It should also be noted that case analysis may be assisted by formal models (e.g., Bates et al. 1998) or statistical models (e.g., Houser and Freeman 2001). Here, I am concerned only with the evidentiary basis (the sorts of evidence that might be mustered) for such an analysis.

there is a specific X_1/Y proposition that the researcher is intending to prove or disprove). How, then, might (a) nested analysis, (b) most-similar analysis, and (c) within-case analysis be applied to this classic research question?

Nested Analysis

A nested analysis presumes that the researcher has at her disposal a large-N cross-case dataset containing variables that measure the outcome and at least some of the factors that might affect that outcome. With this information, the researcher attempts to construct a general model of the phenomenon that applies to the broader sample of cases. This model, which may be cross-sectional or time-series cross-sectional, is then employed to shed light on the case of special interest.[23]

Let us begin at the descriptive level. How exceptional (unique) is the American state? The first section in Table E.1 lists all minimally democratic countries for which central government expenditure data is available in 1995 (N = 77), along with their normalized – "Z" – scores (standard deviations from the mean). Here, it will be seen that the United States has a moderately low score – seventeenth out of seventy-seven – but not an extremely low score, relative to other democratic polities. So viewed, there is little to talk about; the American case is only moderately exceptional.

However, the traditional way of conceptualizing the question of American exceptionalism utilizes an economic baseline to measure the size of welfare states. The presumption is that richer, more developed societies are likely to tax and spend at higher rates ("Wagner's Law"). This way of viewing things may be tested by regressing government spending against GDP per capita (natural logarithm), as follows:

$$\text{Expenditure} = 4.89 + 3.10\text{GDPpc}$$
$$R2 = .1768 \quad N = 77 \tag{E.1}$$

The residuals produced by this analysis for all seventy-seven cases are listed in the second column of Table E.1. Here, it will be seen that the United States is indeed a highly exceptional case. Only four countries have higher negative residuals. Relative to its vast wealth, the United States is a very low spender.

---

[23] Lieberman (2005a). Coppedge (2002) employs the term "nested induction," but the gist of the method is quite similar.

TABLE E.1. *Three nested analyses of the U.S. welfare state*

Descriptive Analysis			Bivariate Analysis		Multivariate Analysis	
Country	Exp.	Z score	Country	Res. 1	Country	Res. 2
1. Colombia	13.37	(1.71)	1. South Korea	−17.15	1. South Korea	−18.39
2. India	14.84	(1.57)	2. Argentina	−16.73	2. Thailand	−16.71
3. Dominican Rep.	15.39	(1.51)	3. Colombia	−15.62	3. Bahamas	−15.97
4. Paraguay	15.41	(1.51)	4. Bahamas	−15.05	4. Turkey	−14.04
5. Argentina	15.75	(1.48)	5. **United States**	**−14.85**	5. Mauritius	−12.33
6. Thailand	15.78	(1.47)	6. Mexico	−13.90	6. Paraguay	−9.99
7. Mexico	15.92	(1.46)	7. Thailand	−13.75	7. Iceland	−8.98
8. South Korea	16.52	(1.40)	8. Paraguay	−12.81	8. Canada	−8.48
9. Nepal	16.54	(1.40)	9. Dominican Rep.	−12.25	9. Nepal	−8.25
10. Madagascar	17.39	(1.32)	10. Venezuela	−11.63	10. Argentina	−7.81
11. Philippines	17.93	(1.26)	11. Switzerland	−11.33	11. Costa Rica	−7.15
12. Venezuela	18.57	(1.20)	12. Chile	−11.14	12. Peru	−6.80
13. Bahamas	19.03	(1.16)	13. Canada	−10.49	13. New Zealand	−6.07
14. Peru	19.07	(1.15)	14. Australia	−10.32	14. Dominican Rep.	−5.70
15. Chile	19.85	(1.08)	15. Peru	−9.72	15. Madagascar	−5.47
16. Bolivia	21.10	(0.95)	16. Malaysia	−8.82	16. Lithuania	−5.12
17. **United States**	**21.72**	**(0.89)**	17. Philippines	−8.60	17. Malaysia	−5.04
18. Malaysia	21.98	(0.87)	18. India	−8.45	18. Colombia	−4.98
19. Turkey	22.23	(0.84)	19. Costa Rica	−7.66	19. Greece	−4.71
20. Costa Rica	22.43	(0.82)	20. Turkey	−7.23	20. St. Vincent/Grenada	−4.33
21. Pakistan	22.80	(0.79)	21. Mauritius	−6.82	21. Trinidad/Tobago	−4.15
22. Mauritius	23.26	(0.74)	22. Nepal	−4.99	22. India	−3.41
23. Mongolia	24.38	(0.63)	23. Panama	−4.98	23. Panama	−3.36

(continued)

TABLE E.1 *(continued)*

Descriptive Analysis			Bivariate Analysis		Multivariate Analysis	
Country	Exp.	Z score	Country	Res. 1	Country	Res. 2
24. Panama	24.71	−(0.60)	24. Bolivia	−4.87	24. Grenada	−3.25
25. Canada	25.04	−(0.57)	25. Madagascar	−4.44	25. Latvia	−3.17
26. Lithuania	25.22	−(0.55)	26. Iceland	−3.46	26. Australia	−2.99
27. Australia	25.33	−(0.54)	27. Russia	−3.44	27. Chile	−2.79
28. Russia	25.39	−(0.53)	28. Germany	−3.10	28. Fiji	−2.44
29. Switzerland	26.64	−(0.41)	29. Lithuania	−2.83	29. Ireland	−1.99
30. Grenada	28.11	−(0.27)	30. Uruguay	−2.78	30. Mexico	−1.64
31. Trinidad/Tobago	28.13	−(0.26)	31. New Zealand	−2.67	31. Denmark	−1.24
32. Fiji	28.61	−(0.22)	32. Trinidad/Tobago	−2.60	32. Luxembourg	−1.19
33. Uruguay	28.88	−(0.19)	33. Grenada	−1.49	33. Mongolia	−0.97
34. St. Vincent/Grenada	29.16	−(0.16)	34. Cyprus, Greek	−1.40	34. Norway	−0.95
35. Papua New Guinea	29.21	−(0.16)	35. Pakistan	−1.31	35. Albania	−0.80
36. Sri Lanka	29.33	−(0.15)	36. Greece	−1.07	36. Bolivia	−0.77
37. Vanuatu	29.34	−(0.15)	37. Fiji	−0.61	37. Venezuela	−0.48
38. South Africa	30.57	−(0.03)	38. South Africa	0.11	38. Cyprus, Greek	−0.17
39. Albania	31.01	(0.02)	39. St. Vincent/Grenada	0.20	39. United States	−0.14
40. Romania	31.78	(0.09)	40. Spain	0.58	40. Vanuatu	−0.07
41. Latvia	32.20	(0.13)	41. Mongolia	1.00	41. Estonia	−0.03
42. New Zealand	32.32	(0.15)	42. Ireland	1.36	42. Switzerland	0.04
43. Cyprus, Greek	32.60	(0.17)	43. Luxembourg	1.66	43. Spain	0.05
44. Greece	32.70	(0.18)	44. Norway	1.77	44. Uruguay	0.39
45. Congo, Rep.	32.82	(0.19)	45. Vanuatu	2.13	45. Papua New Guinea	0.50
46. Iceland	32.88	(0.20)	46. Papua New Guinea	2.87	46. Slovenia	0.59
47. Germany	33.72	(0.28)	47. Latvia	3.85	47. Czech Rep.	1.11
48. Nicaragua	34.09	(0.32)	48. Sri Lanka	3.93	48. Portugal	1.14
49. Lebanon	35.18	(0.43)	49. Denmark	4.12	49. South Africa	1.45
50. Spain	35.22	(0.43)	50. Romania	4.45	50. Philippines	1.58

Country	Exp		Country	Z score	Country	Res
51. Namibia	35.43	(0.45)	51. Czech Rep.	4.93	51. Botswana	1.74
52. Jamaica	35.44	(0.45)	52. Finland	4.97	52. Finland	1.80
53. Estonia	35.51	(0.46)	53. Austria	5.18	53. Germany	2.09
54. Moldova	35.72	(0.48)	54. Estonia	5.49	54. United Kingdom	2.25
55. Botswana	35.98	(0.50)	55. United Kingdom	5.57	55. Malta	2.33
56. Czech Rep.	36.21	(0.53)	56. Albania	5.57	56. Austria	2.38
57. Ireland	36.67	(0.57)	57. Lebanon	5.74	57. Namibia	3.35
58. Norway	38.93	(0.79)	58. Botswana	6.10	58. Romania	3.50
59. Malta	39.06	(0.81)	59. Malta	6.13	59. Jamaica	4.69
60. Luxembourg	39.67	(0.87)	60. Jamaica	6.59	60. Lebanon	4.89
61. Slovenia	39.92	(0.89)	61. Namibia	6.70	61. Sri Lanka	4.99
62. Poland	40.35	(0.93)	62. Slovenia	6.70	62. Russia	5.04
63. Portugal	40.81	(0.98)	63. Portugal	7.17	63. Sweden	5.54
64. Bulgaria	40.96	(0.99)	64. Congo, Rep.	7.18	64. Bulgaria	6.16
65. United Kingdom	41.04	(1.00)	65. France	9.51	65. Moldova	6.49
66. Finland	41.25	(1.02)	66. Moldova	10.49	66. Israel	6.53
67. Denmark	41.36	(1.03)	67. Nicaragua	10.54	67. Pakistan	7.48
68. Austria	41.91	(1.08)	68. Poland	10.81	68. Congo, Rep.	8.28
69. France	45.98	(1.48)	69. Sweden	11.04	69. Netherlands	9.15
70. Israel	47.18	(1.60)	70. Belgium	11.09	70. Nicaragua	9.83
71. Sweden	47.54	(1.64)	71. Netherlands	11.99	71. Poland	10.27
72. Belgium	47.61	(1.64)	72. Israel	12.34	72. France	12.64
73. Italy	48.13	(1.69)	73. Italy	12.70	73. Hungary	13.18
74. Netherlands	48.46	(1.73)	74. Bulgaria	13.31	74. Italy	13.50
75. Hungary	49.39	(1.82)	75. Hungary	18.55	75. Belgium	13.56
76. Lesotho	49.53	(1.83)	76. Seychelles	20.56	76. Lesotho	19.97
77. Seychelles	52.75	(2.15)	77. Lesotho	25.40	77. Seychelles	23.83

Exp. = central government expenditure/GDP. Z score = standard deviations from the mean. Res. = residuals from equations E.1 and E.2, respectively.

Why is the United States so poorly explained by this bivariate model? Why does this very rich country tax and spend at such low rates? While there are many hypotheses, drawn from a rich and storied research tradition,[24] I shall restrict myself here to the role of political institutions. Arguably, democratic institutions that centralize power, strengthen political parties, and condition an inclusive style of governance stimulate the growth of a welfare state.[25] Hence, one ought to find larger welfare states in countries with unitary (rather than federal) constitutions, list-proportional (rather than majoritarian or preferential-vote) electoral systems, and parliamentary (rather than presidential) executives. In order to test these propositions across country-cases, one must code extant countries on all three dimensions. Since these are complicated institutional features, with many admixtures, I employ the following three-point scales for each variable. UNITARISM: 1 = federal, 2 = semifederal, 3 = unitary. PR: 1 = majoritarian or preferential-vote, 2 = mixed electoral system, 3 = proportional. PARL: 1 = presidential, 2 = semipresidential, 3 = parliamentary.[26] With this information for each of the world's seventy-seven democracies, one may then regress expenditure levels on GDP per capita plus these additional factors:

$$\text{Expenditure} = -\ 3.92 + 2.52\text{GDPpc} + 2.66\text{Unitarism}$$
$$+\ 1.19\text{PR} + 3.60\text{Parl} \tag{E.2}$$
$$R2 = .445 \quad N = 77$$

Residuals from this equation are presented in the third column of Table E.1. The striking result is that the U.S. case has lost its outlier status. Indeed, it lies extremely close to the predicted value of the multivariate model.

One might conclude from this analysis that one has effectively "explained" the American case. Of course, any such conclusion rests on lots of assumptions pertaining to the veracity of the general model, the statistical technique, possible measurement error, the homogeneity of the population, and so forth. One can think of many different ways to model this problem, and one would probably want to make use of time-series data in doing so. I have kept things simple with the goal of illustrating the potential of nested analysis, when circumstances warrant.

Note that even if the model provides a good fit for the case of special interest, as in equation E.2, there still may be strong reasons for

[24] Marks and Lipset (2000).
[25] Huber and Stephens (2001); Huber, Ragin, and Stephens (1993); Swank (2002).
[26] Details on these coding procedures are explained in Gerring, Thacker, and Moreno (2005b) and in Gerring and Thacker (forthcoming).

supplementing nested analysis with a more intensive analysis of the case of special interest or of adjoining cases, as discussed in subsequent sections. However, in this circumstance the purpose of a researcher's case-based analysis is likely to shift from (a) exogenous causal factors to (b) causal mechanisms. How might American political institutions have contributed to the country's welfare state trajectory? Are these the critical causal variables that the general model supposes (or are there reasons to doubt)?

If, on the other hand, a case is poorly explained by a general model (i.e., when the residual is high), this also offers important clues for subsequent analysis. Specifically, one has strong reason to presume that additional factors are at work – or, alternatively, that the outcome is a product of pure chance (something that cannot be subjected to general explanation).

Regardless of how the evidence shakes out, one has presumably learned a good deal about the outcome of special interest – the American welfare state – by exploiting available evidence from a large sample of adjacent cases. This is the purpose of nested analysis.

Most-Similar Analysis

We have already discussed the most-similar method (see Chapter Five). It is no different in the context of a single-outcome analysis, with the exception that one of the most-similar cases is preselected. It follows that the chosen comparison case (or cases) should be that which is most similar to the case of special interest in all respects *except* the dimension(s) of interest to the researcher.

If the researcher has no hunch about the possible causes of American welfare state development, then the search for a most-similar case involves matching the United States to another case that has a higher level of government expenditures and is fairly similar on various dimensions that might affect this outcome. Britain or Canada might fit the bill, since both have similar political cultures and larger welfare states. The research then consists of examining these cases closely to try to identify some contrasting feature that might explain their different trajectories. This is most-similar analysis in an *exploratory* format.

If the researcher has a hunch about why the United States has low levels of welfare spending, then the task of finding a paired comparison is more determinate. In this situation, one searches for a country with higher levels of welfare spending, a different status on the variable of interest, and similarities on all other factors that might affect the outcome. Let us say that the researcher's hypothesis concerns the constitutional separation between executive and legislature – the American doctrine of "separation of powers." In this circumstance, Canada might be the most appropriate choice for a most-similar analysis, since that country has a parliamentary executive but shares many other political, cultural, and social features with the United States.[27]

If an offhand survey of available cases is insufficient to identify a most-similar case – either because the number of potential candidates is large and/or because the similarities and differences among them are not well known – the researcher may resort to truth tables (with comprehensive listings of attributes) or matching techniques (see Chapter Five) as a way of identifying appropriate cases.

Thus far, I have discussed the spatial components of most-similar comparison – where variation across cases is essentially static (there is no change, or at least no change of trend, in the variables of interest across the chosen cases). This conforms to a Spatial Comparison, as discussed in Chapter Six. Wherever comparative cases embody longitudinal variation, they offer an additional dimension for causal analysis. Indeed, the best choice for most-similar analysis is a pairing that provides a Dynamic Comparison – replicating the virtues of a classic experiment (but without a manipulated intervention). Here, one can compare the outcome of interest before and after an intervention to see what effect it may have had in that case – a sort of pre- and post-test. Unfortunately, for purposes of exploring the role of the separation of powers in U.S. welfare state development, there are no obvious comparison cases of this nature. That is, no countries that are reasonably well matched with the United States have instituted constitutional changes in their executive (e.g., from presidential to parliamentary, or vice versa).[28] Nor, for that matter, has the United States.

Within-Case Analysis

Regardless of how informative cross-case evidence (either large-N or small-N) might be, one is unlikely to be satisfied that one has satisfactorily explained an outcome until one has explored *within-case* evidence. If there is a specific hypothesis that organizes the research, research designs may be Dynamic, Spatial, Longitudinal, or Counterfactual (see Table 6.1).

---

[27] The United States/Canada comparison is a fairly common one, though not all scholars reach the same conclusions (e.g., Epstein 1964; Lipset 1990).

[28] France adopted a semipresidential system in 1958. However, the primary locus of legislative sovereignty still resides in parliament, so it is not a good test of the theory.

Let us return to the previous hypothesis – the structure of the executive in conditioning a weak welfare state in the United States – to see how these research designs might play out.

Since states within the union also pursue welfare policies, and since their causal relationships may be similar to those that obtain at a national level, one might exploit variation within and across states to illuminate causal factors operative at the national level, where our ultimate theoretical interest lies. Suppose that a state decides to abolish its executive office (the governor), creating what is, effectively, a parliamentary system at the state level. Here is a terrific opportunity for a Dynamic Comparison. That state's welfare levels can be measured before and after the intervention, and that state may also be compared to another state(s) that did not undergo constitutional change.

Suppose that at least one state in the union has always possessed a parliamentary system of government (from 1776 to the present). Under this circumstance there is no intervention that can be studied, and no pre- and post-test may be administered. Still, one might compare levels of spending in that state to those in similar states that have separate-powers constitutions in an attempt to judge the effects of constitutional structure on social policy and political development. This constitutes a Spatial Comparison.

A Longitudinal Comparison might be established at the national level. The American welfare state has been growing for some time, and whatever causal dynamics are at work today have presumably been operative for some time. Granted, there has never been a parliamentary executive in the United States, so there is no change on the variable of theoretical interest. However, there have been changes in the relative strength of the president and Congress, and this may offer some leverage on the question. There are also periods during which both branches have been controlled by the same party, and periods of divided party control. These may be compared according to the level of new legislation that they produce. This provides a picture of what the U.S. welfare state might look like today if *all* periods of American history had been periods of single-party rule.[29] To be sure, it may be doubted whether such brief periods of unified party control approximate the political circumstances of parliamentary systems; this is, at best, a poor substitute for a change in constitutional status, the actual variable of interest.

---

[29] Mayhew (1991).

Evidently, with this particular research question the opportunities for within-case empirical analysis are quite limited. As a consequence, the researcher who wishes to apply a "parliamentary" explanation to the American welfare state is likely to lean heavily upon Counterfactual Comparison. What course would the American welfare state have taken if the United States possessed a parliamentary system? This is a difficult matter to reconstruct. However, intelligent speculation on this point may be highly informative.[30]

The employment of counterfactual reasoning in the analysis of individual outcomes is well established. Yet it also raises dicey questions of causal logic – for, in principle, virtually any event occurring prior to the outcome and having some plausible causal connection to it might be invoked as a necessary antecedent cause. The laggard American welfare state might be attributed to the American Revolution, the Civil War, early democratization, weak and porous (and generally corrupt) bureaucracies, the failure of the Knights of Labor in the 1880s, Progressive-era reforms, World War One, the 1920s, the New Deal, the compromise between representatives of capital and labor after World War Two, the Cold War, and so forth. Each of these prior developments has been considered critical, by at least some historians, to the subsequent development (i.e., nondevelopment) of the American welfare state. And all of these arguments are more or less plausible.

This is not an atypical situation, for most outcomes can be traced back to a wide variety of prior "turning points." The causal regress is, in principle, infinite, as is the number of possible counterfactual scenarios. (What if Gompers had failed to maintain control over the AFL? What if businesses had not been so hostile to the organization of labor unions in the interwar period?) Recall that in a *generalizing* case study, one's consideration of causal factors is limited to those that might plausibly explain variation across a broader population of cases. But no such restriction applies to single-outcome studies. Consequently, this genre of endeavor is rather intractable, for the outcome is radically overdetermined. There are too many possible – and probable – causes. The options are, quite literally, infinite.

Mitigating this problem is a special restriction that applies to the counterfactual analysis of individual outcomes. Philosophers and social scientists have come to agree that the most sensible counterfactual within a field

---

[30] See, e.g., Sundquist (1992).

of possible counterfactuals is that which demands the smallest alteration in the course of actual events, as they really did happen. This principle of causal reconstruction has come to be known as the *minimal-rewrite* rule.[31] The author should play God with history with as light a hand as possible. All other things being equal, when deciding between two explanations of a given outcome the researcher should choose the cause that is most contingent. It is the turning point, the critical juncture, that rightly deserves the label "cause" – not the factors that probably could not have been otherwise. The effect of this criterion is to eliminate absurd conjectures about the course of history. One might suppose, for example, that the American welfare state would have developed differently if Europeans had never discovered America. While perhaps true, this counterfactual is not a very useful reconstruction of history because it envisions a scenario that departs radically from the actual course of events. Of course, the minimal-rewrite rule will not discriminate among all the hypotheses that might be generated through the counterfactual analysis of a single outcome. But, at least it will narrow the field.[32]

Putting Cross-Case and Within-Case Evidence Together

Having reviewed three fundamental methods of single-outcome analysis – nested analysis, most-similar analysis, and within-case analysis – the easy conclusion is that all three of these methods ought to be employed, wherever possible. We gain leverage on a causal question by framing the research design in different ways and evaluating the evidence drawn from those separate and independent analyses. To the extent that a particular explanation of an outcome is confirmed by nested analysis, most-similar analysis, and within-case analysis, one has successfully triangulated.

However, it is not always possible to employ all three methods. Or, to put it more delicately, these three methods are not always equally

---

[31] Bunzl (2004); Cowley (2001); Einhorn and Hogarth (1986); Elster (1978); Fearon (1991); Hart and Honore (1959: 32–3; 1966: 225); Hawthorn (1991); Holland (1986); Mackie (1965/1993: 39); Marini and Singer (1988: 353); Taylor (1970: 53); Tetlock and Belkin (1996: 23–5); Weber (1905/1949). Also known as "cotenability" (Goodman 1947) and "compossibility" (Elster 1978).

[32] Note that the minimal-rewrite rule has the additional effect of nudging single-event analysis away from general, structural causes and toward unique, proximate causes, which are (almost by definition) more contingent. Compare two classic explanations of American exceptionalism: (a) the great frontier (Turner 1893/1972) and (b) the failure of the Knights of Labor in the 1880s (Voss 1993). Evidently, the second event is more likely to have turned out differently than the first.

viable. And even when all three are possible and viable, sometimes the conclusions reached are inconsistent. For example, cross-case evidence may suggest one causal factor and within-case analysis another. The three methods reviewed here might even suggest three different causal factors.

This sort of dissonance is mildly problematic in the generalizing case study, where the purpose of the investigation is to shed light on cross-case causal relationships. Here, one can reasonably dismiss idiosyncratic findings drawn from a single case as "noise" – stochastic variation or variation that for some reason remains unexplained. In single-outcome studies, however, the purpose of the study is to explain *that particular case*. Here, varying results from cross-case and within-case analyses cannot be treated lightly. And here, because the objective is to provide a reasonably complete explanation, it is not permissible to dismiss evidence as part of the error term (noise).

Complicating matters further, certain hypotheses garnered from within-case analysis may be effectively untestable in a cross-case setting. Consider the following arguments that the research team of Acemoglu, Johnson, and Robinson provide to explain Botswana's good policies and institutions and, from thence, its extraordinary economic success in the post-independence era.

1. Botswana possessed precolonial tribal institutions that encouraged broad-based participation and placed constraints on political elites. 2. British colonization had a limited effect on these precolonial institutions because of the peripheral nature of Botswana to the British Empire. 3. Upon independence, the most important rural interests, chiefs and cattle owners, were politically powerful, and it was in their economic interest to enforce property rights. 4. The revenues from diamonds generated enough rents for the main political actors, increasing the opportunity cost of, and discouraging, further rent seeking. 5. Finally, the post-independence political leaders, in particular Seretse Khama and Quett Masire, made a number of sensible decisions.[33]

All these factors are adduced to help explain why Botswana adopted good (market-augmenting) policies and institutions. But few are easily tested across a wide range of country-cases. Does the existence of certain Tswana-like tribal institutions lead to broad-based political participation and constrained elites in other polities? Does "light" imperial control lead to better post-independence politics? Is it advantageous for rural interests to dominate a country politically? Each of these statements, if generalized to include a broad set of country-cases, is questionable. But few are easy to

[33] Acemoglu, Johnson, and Robinson (2003: 113).

test. The final argument, having to do with leadership, is true everywhere almost by definition (good leadership is usually understood as leadership that leads to good policy outcomes), and therefore does not tell us very much. To be sure, the authors present these five arguments as conjoint causes; perhaps all must be present in order for salubrious results to ensue. If so, then the argument is virtually incapable of broader application. This means that we must accept the authors' claims based largely on within-case evidence (plus a smattering of two-case comparisons that address different elements of the story).

It is quite common in single-outcome analysis to rest an inference or a set of inferences upon evidence drawn from that case alone, and there is nothing in principle wrong with this style of argumentation. Nonetheless, Acemoglu, Johnson, and Robinson would be able to make a stronger and more convincing argument if they could show more cross-case evidence for their various propositions. In a few instances, statements made with reference to Botswana seem to fly in the face of other countries' historical experiences. For example, while the authors attribute Botswana's success to its light-handed, noninterventionist colonial history, it seems likely that growth rates in countries around the world are positively correlated with the length and intensity of colonial control – particularly if the colonial power is British, as it was in Botswana.[34] It is possible, of course, that the effect of a rather crude variable like colonialism is not uniform across all countries. Indeed, there is no reason that we should accept uncritically the results of a cross-country regression that tells this particular story. But we have no cause to dismiss it either.

The point of this discussion is not to argue for or against any particular style of evidence but rather to point to a vexing methodological problem that affects virtually all single-outcome analysis. Cross-case and within-case evidence often tell somewhat different stories, and there is usually no easy way to adjudicate between them. About all that one can say is that the strength of each sort of evidence rests upon the particulars of the evidence. Thus, if the cross-case analysis is sketchy – if, for example, the author is suspicious of how key variables have been operationalized, the specification of the model, or the robustness of the results – then she may choose to place less emphasis on these results. Likewise, if the within-case evidence is sketchy – if, for example, the case might be reconstructed in a variety of different ways, each of which provides a plausible fit for

---

[34] Grier (1999); La Porta et al. (1999).

the theory and the evidence – then she may choose to place less emphasis on these results. In short, it all depends.

Conclusion

At this juncture, the reader may have come to the conclusion that single-outcome analysis is singularly difficult, and case study analysis correspondingly easy. This is not the message I wish to convey. Indeed, I indicated at the outset of this chapter that single-outcome arguments are often less uncertain than the corresponding cross-case arguments (for which the case study might be employed as a mode of analysis). A murder may be easier to solve than general problems related to criminal activity.

However, the sort of single-outcome studies that social scientists focus on explaining are also typically the sort that are difficult to parse. And this, in turn, rests upon their singularity. It is the unusualness of the outcome, not the method applied to the single-outcome study, that makes these studies so recalcitrant. The American welfare state will never have a conclusive explanation. The United States is too different from other nations, and there are too few other nations, to allow for this degree of certainty. The same might be said about World War One and the French Revolution. The more unique an outcome the more difficult it is to explain, because we have fewer comparison cases, and the few cases that do present themselves suffer problems of causal comparability. With crimes it is different. This is why judges and juries charged with rendering verdicts generally show greater confidence in their judgments than academics charged with explaining crime (in general).

But academics do not write case studies of individual crimes – unless, of course, those cases are sufficiently unusual to warrant individual treatment (e.g., crimes with immense political repercussions, such as the Watergate burglary). Again, one finds that the single-outcome study is problematic not by reason of any inherent methodological difficulty but rather by virtue of the situations in which it is typically deployed. There is little need for single-outcome studies of typical outcomes. Consequently, single-outcome studies tend to be singular-outcome studies. In sum, it is the choice of topic – not the method – that renders this genre problematic.

Glossary

This glossary was constructed in consultation with other glossaries, including Schwandt (1997), Seawright and Collier (2004), and Vogt (1993). Italicized words are found elsewhere in the glossary. (Very common words such as "case" are typically not italicized.)

Antecedent cause See *causal order*.

Attribute An aspect of a topic or, more specifically, of an *observation*. Synonyms: dimension, property, characteristic. May be measured by a *variable*.

Bias Characterizes a *sample* that is not representative of a *population*, with respect to some inference. Contrast: *representativeness*. (In statistical parlance, bias refers to the properties of *multiple* samples drawn from the same population. This is similar, but not identical, to my usage in the text.)

Binary See *level of measurement*.

Breadth See *population*.

Case A spatially and temporally delimited phenomenon observed at a single point in time or over some period of time – for example, a political or social group, institution, or event. A case lies at the same level of analysis as the principal inference. Thus, if an inference pertains to the behavior of nation-states, cases in that study will be comprised of nation-states. An individual case may also be broken down into one or more *observations*, sometimes referred to as *within-case* observations. Compare: *case study*.

Case-based analysis A variety of analyses that focus on a small number of relatively bounded units. May refer to *case studies*, *single-outcome studies*, or – more tenuously – *Qualitative Comparative Analysis* (QCA).

Case selection The identification of cases chosen for analysis in a study. The first, and perhaps most important, component of case study research design.

Case study The intensive study of a single case for the purpose of understanding a larger class of similar units (a *population* of cases). Synonyms: single-unit study, single-case study, within-case study. Note that while "case study" is singular – focusing on a single unit – a case study *research design* may refer to a work that includes several case studies (e.g., *comparative-historical analysis* or the *comparative method*). Contrast: *single-outcome study* and *cross-case study*.

Causal effect   The impact of an explanatory factor on an outcome. Understood as the change in Y corresponding to a given change in X. Applicable either to a particular case or across a set of cases (averaged).

Causal distance   A *distal* (or structural) cause lies far from the effect it is intended to explain. A *promixal* (or proximate) cause lies close to the effect it is intended to explain. *Causal mechanisms* are generally composed of proximal causes; they are, in any case, more proximal than the structural cause they are enlisted to help explain.

Causal factor   See *independent variable*.

Causal inference   A causal relationship is one where – minimally – a causal factor (X) may be said to raise the probability of an effect occurring (Y). Contrast: *descriptive inference*. See Gerring (2005).

Causal mechanism   That which explains a covariational relationship between X and Y. The causal pathway, or connecting thread, between X and Y, usually embodied in a theory or model. See *causal order*.

Causal order   A causal argument may be conceptualized as consisting of a structural (a.k.a. antecedent, exogenous) cause (X_1), an intermediate cause (X_{1a}), and an outcome (Y). The intermediate cause(s) performs the role of a *causal mechanism*, a pathway from X_1 to Y.

Ceteris paribus   All other things being equal. In the context of research design, this means that whatever variation is being exploited for the purpose of investigating causal relationships is the product of the causal factor of interest (X_1) and not of other confounding factors (X_2). If the researcher is comparing a case before and after an intervention to see what effects the intervention might have had on some outcome (Y), she must assume that the case remains similar, pre- and post-intervention, in all other respects that might affect Y (and cannot be attributed to X_1). If the researcher is comparing two cases that differ in their properties on a causal factor of interest (X_1), she must assume that they are the same on all other dimensions (X_2) that might affect Y.

Comparative method   Causal analysis focused on a small number of regions or states where spatial variation assumes a *most-similar* format. There may, or may not, be temporal variation encompassing the causal factor(s) of interest. See Collier (1993).

Comparative-historical analysis   Causal analysis focused on a small number of regions or states where spatial variation assumes a *most-similar* format and temporal variation includes the causal factor(s) of special interest. A species of the *comparative method* in which spatial and temporal variation are combined in a single study. See Mahoney and Rueschemeyer (2003).

Continuous (scalar) variable   See *level of measurement*.

Correlation   See *covariation*.

Counterfactual comparison   See *experimental template*.

Counterfactual thought experiment   An attempt to replay the events in a particular case history in order to determine what the result might have been under a different set of circumstances. An essential tool of causal analysis when the possibilities of real (observable) variation are meager or where the outcome of interest lies in the past (and cannot be effectively re-created).

Covariation The association of two factors (variables), said to covary. Covariational patterns may be diachronic (a.k.a. temporal, time-series, longitudinal, historical), synchronic (a.k.a. spatial, cross-sectional), or both. Covariation may be located at different *levels of analysis*. Synonyms: correlation, association.

Critical juncture/path dependence A critical juncture refers to the contingent moment in a longer trajectory. It is followed by a period of path dependence in which a given trajectory is maintained, and perhaps reinforced ("increasing returns").

Cross-case study Refers in this text to a large-sample study where the sample consists of multiple cases (representing the same units that comprise the central inference), analyzed statistically. Contrast: *case study*.

Cross-sectional See *covariation*.

Crucial case A case that offers particularly compelling evidence for, or against, a proposition. Synonym: critical case. Assumes two varieties: least-likely and most-likely. A least-likely case is one that is very unlikely to validate the predictions of a model or a hypothesis. If a least-likely case is found to be valid, this may be regarded as strong confirmatory evidence. A most-likely case is one that is very likely to validate the predictions of a model or a hypothesis. If a most-likely case is found to be invalid, this may be regarded as strong disconfirming evidence.

Dependent variable See *variable*.

Descriptive inference Answers questions about who, what, when, and how. May include proximate causes. Contrast: *causal inference*.

Deterministic An invariant causal relationship; there are no random (stochastic) components. Usually, deterministic arguments take the shape of necessary, sufficient, or necessary-and-sufficient causal relationships. Contrast: *probabilistic*.

Deviant case A case exemplifying deviant values according to some general model.

Diachronic See *covariation*.

Dichotomous scale See *level of measurement*.

Distal cause See *causal distance*.

Diverse case A case exemplifying diverse values along relevant dimensions (X_1, Y, or X_1/Y). Uses: to illuminate (a) the full range of variation on X_1 or Y (an open-ended probe), or (b) the various causal pathways or causal types exhibited by X_1/Y (a more determinate hypothesis).

Domain See *population*.

Dynamic comparison See *experimental template*.

Endogenous cause See *causal order*.

Equifinality Multiple causal paths leading to the same outcome.

Ethnography Work conducted "in the field," that is, in some *naturalistic* setting where the researcher observes her topic. Near-synonyms: field research, participant observation.

Exogenous cause See *causal order*.

Experimental research design A design where the causal factor of interest (the treatment) is manipulated by the researcher. May also incorporate a *randomized* control group. Contrast: *observational research design*.

LIBRARY, UNIVERSITY OF CHESTER

Experimental template   Classic experimental research designs achieve variation through time and across space, thus maximizing leverage on the fundamental problem of causal inference. When this template is adopted for use in case study research, the latter may be understood as part of a matrix with four cells (see Figure 6.1). The Dynamic Comparison mirrors the paradigmatic laboratory experiment, since it exploits temporal and spatial variation. The Longitudinal Comparison employs only temporal variation and is similar in design to the experiment without control. The Spatial Comparison employs only spatial variation; it purports to measure the outcome of interventions that occurred at some point in the past (but that are not directly observable). The Counterfactual Comparison relies on variation (temporal and/or spatial) that is imaginary.

External validity   See *validity*.

Extreme case   A case exemplifying unusual values on X_1 or Y relative to some univariate distribution (measured or assumed).

Falsifiability   The possibility that a theory or hypothesis may be proven wrong. A nonfalsifiable hypothesis is one that cannot be disproven by appeal to empirical evidence.

Field research   See *ethnography*.

Hermeneutics   See *interpretivism*.

Hypothesis   A specific, and hence *falsifiable*, supposition. A causal hypothesis suggests a specific X_1/Y relationship across a (more or less) defined population of cases – for example, "Proportional representation electoral systems moderate ethnic conflict (in all democratic polities where substantial ethnic heterogeneity is present)." A hypothesis may be connected to a larger theory or theoretical framework (a.k.a. paradigm), or it may stand alone. Near-synonyms: argument, inference, proposition, thesis.

Independent variable   See *variable*.

Inference   See *hypothesis*.

Influential case   A case with a configuration of scores on various independent variables that strongly influences a general cross-case model of causal relations, and which therefore may merit close attention (i.e., case study analysis).

Intermediate cause   See *causal mechanism* and *causal order*.

Internal validity   See *validity*.

Interpretivism   Broadly, the study of human meanings and intentions. More narrowly, the attempt to interpret human behavior in terms of the meanings assigned to it by the actors themselves. Near-synonyms: hermeneutics, *Verstehen*.

Intervention   Any change in a key causal variable that can be observed through time, whether experimental (a manipulated treatment) or observational (a natural treatment).

K   The total number of *variables* in an analysis.

Large-N   See *observation*.

Least-likely case   See *crucial case*.

Level of analysis   The level of aggregation at which an analysis takes place. If a hypothesis is concerned primarily with the behavior of nation-states, then lower levels of analysis would include individuals, institutions, and other actors at a substate level. Usually, case study work incorporates evidence at a lower level of analysis than the proposition of primary interest, thus providing *within-case* observations.

Level of measurement Measurements (scales) may be dichotomous (a.k.a. binary, e.g., 0/1), nominal (e.g., yellow, red, green), ordinal (e.g., strongly agree, agree, neither agree nor disagree, disagree, strongly disagree), interval (e.g., degrees Fahrenheit), or ratio (an interval scale with a true zero, e.g., degrees Kelvin). Dichotomous, nominal, and ordinal scales are all categorical. Interval and ratio scales are continuous.

Longitudinal comparison See *experimental template.*

Method of difference See *most-similar cases.*

Minimal-rewrite rule In a *single-outcome study,* there are always multiple potential factors that may be invoked as "causes." From among these potential explanations, the most useful counterfactual is that which requires the least alteration in the course of actual events. The researcher should focus on the most contingent cause, not on more or less permanent features of the landscape.

Most-different cases Cases are different in all respects except the variables of theoretical interest (X_1 and Y). Synonym: method of agreement (J. S. Mill).

Most-similar cases Cases are similar in all respects except the variables of theoretical interest (X_1, Y, or X_1/Y). Synonym: Method of difference (J. S. Mill).

N See *observation.*

Naturalistic Research settings that are, or resemble, "real-life" settings. Unobtrusive methods of research. Contrast with laboratory experiments and other artificial settings.

Natural experiment See *quasi-experiment.*

Necessary cause See *deterministic.*

Nested analysis Understood in this text as the employment of a large-N cross-case analysis in order to shed light on a single outcome. Used in the context of a *single-outcome study.* Near-synonym: nested inference.

Nominal scale See *level of measurement.*

Noncomparable observations Observations that are not comparable (non–unit homogenous) to one another.

Observation The most basic element of any empirical endeavor. Any piece of evidence enlisted to support a proposition. Conventionally, the number of observations in an analysis is referred to by the letter N. (Confusingly, N is also used to refer to the number of cases.) If observations are comparable they may be represented as rows in a rectangular dataset.

Observational research design A design where the causal factor of interest is not manipulated by the researcher. Contrast: *experimental research design.*

Operationalization Formulation of a concept in terms of measurable indicators, or of a general theory in terms of testable hypotheses. The issue of operationalization is the issue of measurement – that is, how do I know concept A or theory B when I see it?

Ordinal scale See *level of measurement.*

Participant observation *Ethnographic* work in which the researcher is a participant in the activity under study.

Path dependence See *critical juncture/path dependence.*

Pathway case   A case that embodies a distinct causal path from X_1 to Y such that potential confounders (X_2) are isolated from the analysis and the true relationship between X_1 and Y can be more easily observed. Useful for the identification of causal mechanisms.

Population   The universe of cases and observations to which an inference refers. Usually, much larger than the *sample* under investigation. Synonyms: breadth, domain, scope.

Probabilistic   A model or process – specifically, a causal relationship – with random (stochastic) properties. In a statistical model, these are captured by the error term.

Process tracing   A style of analysis used to reconstruct a causal process that has occurred within a single case. (Because the event of interest has occurred in the past, this sort of analysis generally cannot employ a manipulated treatment.) Its defining features are that (a) multiple types of evidence (noncomparable observations) are employed for the verification of a single causal outcome and (b) the causal process itself is usually quite complex, involving a long causal chain and perhaps multiple switches, feedback loops, and the like.

Proposition   See *hypothesis*.

Proximal (proximate) cause   See *causal distance*.

Qualitative   Having few *observations* (small-N), and hence analyzed with words rather than numbers. (Another, unrelated meaning of *qualitative* refers specifically to *variables*, specifically those that are categorical rather than continuous.) Contrast: *quantitative*.

Qualitative Comparative Analysis (QCA)   A method of analyzing causal relationships associated with the work of its inventor, Charles Ragin, that is sensitive to necessary and sufficient relationships, conjunctural causes, and causal *equifinality*, but which also manages to incorporate a large number of cases. Later versions of QCA, abbreviated "fs/QCA," incorporate elements of probabilism and fuzzy-set theory.

Quantitative   Having many *observations* (large-N). Analyzed with numbers (statistically) rather than words. Contrast: *qualitative*.

Quasi-experiment   An *observational* study that nonetheless has the properties of an *experimental* research design. Synonym: natural experiment.

Randomization   A process by which cases in a sample are chosen randomly (with respect to some subject of interest). An essential element for experiments that use control groups, since the treatment of control groups must be similar (in all respects relevant to the inference), and the easiest way to achieve this is through random selection. Not recommended for case study analysis.

Representativeness   A *sample* is representative when its cases (and observations) are similar (i.e., comparable, unit homogeneous) to a broader *population* in all respects that might affect the causal relationship of interest. Synonym: typical. Antonym: *bias*.

Research design   Generally, the way in which empirical evidence is brought to bear on a hypothesis. Includes *case selection* and case analysis.

Sample   The set of cases (and observations) upon which the researcher is focused. Assumed to be representative of some *population*, which is usually larger than the sample. A case study focused on a single case comprises a sample of one, though the term is rarely used in this context.

Scope   See *population.*

Selection bias   A form of *bias* that is introduced whenever the treatment (the causal factor of interest) is not randomly assigned across cases, thus violating the *ceteris paribus* assumption of causal analysis.

Single-outcome study   Seeks to explain a single outcome occurring within a single case. Near-synonyms: particularizing case study, idiographic case study. Contrast: *case study.*

Small-N   See *observation.*

Spatial Comparison   See *experimental template.*

Stochastic   See *probabilistic.*

Structural cause   See *causal order.*

Sufficient cause   See *deterministic.*

Synchronic   See *covariation.*

Triangulation   The use of multiple methods, often at different *levels of analysis.*

Typical case   A case exemplifying a typical value according to some model. Statistical measure: a low-residual case (on-lier). Uses: to probe causal mechanisms.

Unit   In most situations, equivalent to a case. Pertains to the spatial (not the temporal) components of a case.

Unit of analysis   The species of *observations* that will be analyzed in a particular *research design.* If the design is *synchronic,* then the unit of analysis is spatial (e.g., nations or individuals). If the design is *diachronic,* then the unit of analysis is temporal (e.g., decades, years, minutes). If the design is both synchronic and diachronic, then the unit of analysis has both spatial and temporal components (e.g., country-years). Evidently, the unit of analysis may change in the course of a given study. Even so, within the context of a particular research design it must remain constant.

Unit homogeneity   The comparability of cases or observations in all respects that might affect a particular causal relationship. Near-synonyms: causal homogeneity, equivalence.

Validity   Internal validity refers to the correctness of a *hypothesis* with respect to the *sample* (the cases actually studied by the researcher). External validity refers to the correctness of a *hypothesis* with respect to the *population* of an inference (cases not studied). The key element of external validity thus rests upon the *representativeness* of the *sample.*

Variable   An *attribute* of an observation or a set of observations. Depicted as vertical columns in a rectangular dataset. In the analysis of causal relations, variables are understood either as independent (a.k.a. explanatory or exogenous), denoted X, or as dependent (endogenous), denoted Y. In this text, X_1 refers to the independent variable of theoretical interest (if any), and X_2 refers to the vector of control variables (variables that might affect Y but are not of central theoretical concern). Note that my usage of the term *variable* is quite general and does not presume statistical analysis.

Verstehen   See *interpretivism.*

Within-case study   Analysis of observations within a single case. May be small-N or large-N. Contrast: *cross-case study.*

X   See *variable.*

X-centered analysis   *Exploratory* research where the puzzle or question concerns a particular causal factor (X_1) but no specific outcome (Y).

X₁/Y–centered analysis *Confirmatory* research into a specific, *falsifiable* causal hypothesis – the posited relationship between X_1 (a particular causal factor) and Y (the outcome).

Y See *variable*.

Y-centered analysis *Exploratory* research where the puzzle or question concerns a particular outcome (Y) but (at least initially) no particular causal factor (X_1).

References

Abadie, Alberto, and Javier Gardeazabal. 2003. "The Economic Costs of Conflict: A Case Study of the Basque Country." *American Economic Review* (March): 113–32.

Abadie, Alberto, David Drukker, Jane Leber Herr, and Guido W. Imbens. 2001. "Implementing Matching Estimators for Average Treatment Effects in Stata." *The Stata Journal* 1: 1–18.

Abbott, Andrew. 1990. "Conceptions of Time and Events in Social Science Methods: Causal and Narrative Approaches." *Historical Methods* 23:4 (Fall): 140–50.

Abbott, Andrew. 1992. "From Causes to Events: Notes on Narrative Positivism." *Sociological Methods and Research* 20:4 (May): 428–55.

Abbott, Andrew. 1997. "On the Concept of Turning Point." *Comparative Social Research* 16: 85–105.

Abbott, Andrew. 2001. *Time Matters: On Theory and Method.* Chicago: University of Chicago Press.

Abbott, Andrew, and John Forrest. 1986. "Optimal Matching Methods for Historical Sequences." *Journal of Interdisciplinary History* 16:3 (Winter): 471–94.

Abbott, Andrew, and Angela Tsay. 2000. "Sequence Analysis and Optimal Matching Methods in Sociology." *Sociological Methods and Research* 29: 3–33.

Abell, Peter. 1987. *The Syntax of Social Life: The Theory and Method of Comparative Narratives.* Oxford: Clarendon Press.

Abell, Peter. 2004. "Narrative Explanation: An Alternative to Variable-Centered Explanation?" *Annual Review of Sociology* 30: 287–310.

Abrami, Regina M., and David M. Woodruff. 2004. "Toward a Manifesto: Interpretive Materialist Political Economy." Paper presented at the annual meeting of the American Political Science Association, Chicago.

Acemoglu, Daron, Simon Johnson, and James A. Robinson. 2003. "An African Success Story: Botswana." In Dani Gardeazabal (ed.), *In Search of Prosperity: Analytic Narratives on Economic Growth.* Princeton, NJ: Princeton University Press, 80–122.

Achen, Christopher H. 1986. *The Statistical Analysis of Quasi-Experiments.* Berkeley: University of California Press.

Achen, Christopher H. 2002. "Toward a New Political Methodology: Microfoundations and ART." *Annual Review of Political Science* 5: 423–50.

Achen, Christopher H. 2005. "Let's Put Garbage-Can Regressions and Garbage-Can Probits Where They Belong." *Conflict Management and Peace Science* 22: 1–13.

Achen, Christopher H., and Duncan Snidal. 1989. "Rational Deterrence Theory and Comparative Case Studies." *World Politics* 41 (January): 143–69.

Achen, Christopher H., and W. Philips Shively. 1995. *Cross-Level Inference.* Chicago: University of Chicago Press.

Adcock, Robert. 2002. "Determinism and Comparative-Historical Analysis: Clarifying Concepts and Retrieving Past Insights." Paper presented at the annual meeting of the American Political Science Association, Boston, August 29.

Adcock, Robert. 2005. "What Is a Concept?" Political Concepts: A Working Paper Series of the Committee on Concepts and Methods, Paper No. 1 (April). <http://www.concepts-methods.org/papers.php>

Adcock, Robert, and David Collier. 2001. "Measurement Validity: A Shared Standard for Qualitative and Quantitative Research." *American Political Science Review* 95:3 (September): 529–46.

Alesina, Alberto, Arnaud Devleeschauwer, William Easterly, Sergio Kurlat, and Romain Wacziarg. 2003. "Fractionalization." *Journal of Economic Growth* 8:2: 155–94.

Alesina, Alberto, and Edward Glaeser. 2004. *Fighting Poverty in the US and Europe: A World of Difference.* Oxford: Oxford University Press.

Alesina, Alberto, Edward Glaeser, and Bruce Sacerdote. 2001. "Why Doesn't the US Have a European-Style Welfare State?" *Brookings Papers on Economic Activity* 2: 187–277.

Alesina, Alberto, Sule Ozler, Nouriel Roubini, and Phillip Swagel. 1996. "Political Instability and Economic Growth." *Journal of Economic Growth* 1:2 (June): 189–211.

Alexander, Jeffrey, Bernhard Giesen, Richard Munch, and Neil Smelser, eds. 1987. *The Micro-Macro Link.* Berkeley: University of California Press.

Allen, William Sheridan. 1965. *The Nazi Seizure of Power: The Experience of a Single German Town, 1930–1935.* New York: Watts.

Allison, Graham T. 1971. *Essence of Decision: Explaining the Cuban Missile Crisis.* Boston: Little, Brown.

Almond, Gabriel A. 1956. "Comparative Political Systems." *Journal of Politics* 18 (August): 391–409.

Alperovitz, Gar. 1996. *The Decision to Use the Atomic Bomb.* New York: Vintage.

Alston, Lee J. 2005. "The 'Case' for Case Studies in Political Economy." *The Political Economist* 12:4 (Spring–Summer): 3–19.

Alston, Lee, Gary Libecap, and Bernardo Mueller. 1999. *Titles, Conflict and Land Use: The Development of Property Rights and Land Reform on the Brazilian Amazon Frontier.* Ann Arbor: University of Michigan Press.

Amenta, Edwin. 1991. "Making the Most of a Case Study: Theories of the Welfare State and the American Experience." In Charles C. Ragin (ed.), *Issues and Alternatives in Comparative Social Research.* Leiden: E. J. Brill, 172–94.

Anderson, Christopher J., and Christine A. Guillory. 1997. "Political Institutions and Satisfaction with Democracy: A Cross-National Analysis of Consensus and Majoritarian Systems." *American Political Science Review* 91:1 (March): 66–81.

Angrist, Joshua D., and Alan B. Krueger. 2001. "Instrumental Variables and the Search for Identification: From Supply and Demand to Natural Experiments." *Journal of Economic Perspectives* 15:4 (Fall): 69–85.

Anscombe, G. E. M. 1958. "On Brute Facts." *Analysis* 18: 69–72.

Aronson, Eliot, Phoebe Ellsworth, J. Merrill Carlsmith, and Marti Gonzales. 1990. *Methods of Research in Social Psychology.* New York: McGraw-Hill.

Asch, Solomon. 1956. "Opinions and Social Pressure." *Scientific American* 193: 31–5.

Athens, L. 1997. *Violent Criminal Acts and Actors Revisited.* Urbana: University of Illinois Press.

Back, Hanna, and Patrick Dumont. 2004. "A Combination of Methods: The Way Forward in Coalition Research." Paper presented at the annual meeting of the American Political Science Association, September 2–5.

Bailey, Mary Timney. 1992. "Do Physicists Use Case Studies? Thoughts on Public Administration Research." *Public Administration Review* 52:1 (January/February): 47–54.

Banerjee, Abhijit V., and Lakshmi Iyer. 2002. "History, Institutions, and Economic Performance: The Legacy of Colonial Land Tenure Systems in India." Unpublished paper, Department of Economics, MIT.

Banfield, Edward C. 1958. *The Moral Basis of a Backward Society.* Glencoe, IL: Free Press.

Barrett, Christopher B., and Jeffrey W. Cason. 1997. *Overseas Research: A Practical Guide.* Baltimore: Johns Hopkins University Press.

Barro, Robert J. 1996. "Democracy and Growth." *Journal of Economic Growth* 1 (March): 1–27.

Barro, Robert J. 1999. "Determinants of Democracy." *Journal of Political Economy* 107:6 (December): 158–83.

Bartels, Larry M. 1991. "Instrumental and 'Quasi-Instrumental' Variables." *American Journal of Political Science* 35:3 (August): 777–800.

Barth, Fredrik. 1969. *Ethnic Groups and Boundaries: The Social Organization of Cultural Differences.* Boston: Little, Brown.

Bates, Robert H., Avner Greif, Margaret Levi, Jean-Laurent Rosenthal, and Barry Weingast. 1998. *Analytic Narratives.* Princeton, NJ: Princeton University Press.

Becker, Howard S. 1934. "Culture Case Study and Ideal-Typical Method." *Social Forces* 12:3: 399–405.

Becker, Howard S. 1958. "Problems of Inference and Proof in Participant Observation." *American Sociological Review* 23:6 (December): 652–60.

Becker, Howard S. 1970. "Life History and the Scientific Mosaic." In his *Sociological Work: Method and Substance.* Chicago: Aldine, 63–73.

Belsey, David A., Edwin Kuh, and Roy E. Welsch. 2004. *Regression Diagnostics: Identifying Influential Data and Sources of Collinearity.* New York: Wiley.

Benbasat, Izak, David K. Goldstein, and Melissa Mead. 1987. "The Case Research Strategy in Studies of Information Systems." *MIT Quarterly* 11:3 (September): 369–86.

Bendix, Reinhard. 1963. "Concepts and Generalizations in Comparative Sociological Studies." *American Sociological Review* 28:4 (August): 532–39.

Bendix, Reinhard. 1978. *Kings or People: Power and the Mandate to Rule.* Berkeley: University of California Press.

Bendor, Jonathan, and Thomas H. Hammond. 1992. "Rethinking Allison's Models." *American Political Science Review* 86:2 (June): 301–22.

Bennett, Andrew. 1999. *Condemned to Repetition? The Rise, Fall, and Reprise of Soviet-Russian Military Interventionism, 1973–1996.* Cambridge, MA: MIT Press.

Bennett, Andrew, and Colin Elman. 2006. "Qualitative Research: Recent Developments in Case Study Methods." *Annual Review of Political Science* 9 (forthcoming).

Bennett, Andrew, Joseph Lepgold, and Danny Unger. 1994. "Burden-Sharing in the Persian Gulf War." *International Organization* 48:1 (Winter): 39–75.

Bentley, Arthur. 1908/1967. *The Process of Government.* Cambridge, MA: Harvard University Press.

Berger, Bennett M. 1995. *An Essay on Culture: Symbolic Structure and Social Structure.* Berkeley: University of California Press.

Berg-Schlosser, Dirk, and Gisele De Meur. 1997. "Reduction of Complexity for a Small-N Analysis: A Stepwise Multi-Methodological Approach." *Comparative Social Research* 16: 133–62.

Bernard, L. L. 1928. "The Development of Method in Sociology." *The Monist* 38 (April): 292–320.

Bernhard, H. Russell. 2001. *Research Methods in Anthropology: Qualitative and Quantitative Approaches.* Lanham, MD: Rowman and Littlefield.

Bertrand, Marianne, and Sendhil Mullainathan. 2004. "Are Emily and Greg More Employable than Lakisha and Jamal? A Field Experiment on Labor Market Discrimination." *American Economic Review* 94:4 (September): 991–1013.

Bevan, David, Paul Collier, and Jan Willem Gunning. 1999. *Nigeria and Indonesia.* Oxford: Oxford University Press.

Bhagwati, Jagdish N. 1995. "Trade Liberalisation and Fair Trade Demands: Addressing the Environmental and Labour Standards Issues." *The World Economy* 18:6 (November): 745–59.

Bhaskar, Roy. 1978. *A Realist Theory of Science.* Sussex: Harvester Press.

Bloch, Marc. 1941/1953. *The Historian's Craft.* New York: Vintage Books.

Blumer, Herbert. 1969. *Symbolic Interactionism: Perspective and Method.* Berkeley: University of California Press.

Bock, Edwin A. 1962. *Essays on the Case Study Method.* New York: Inter-University Case Program.

Boix, Carles, and Luis Garicano. 2002. "Democracy, Inequality and Country-Specific Wealth." Unpublished paper, Department of Political Science, University of Chicago.

Boix, Carles, and Susan C. Stokes. 2003. "Endogenous Democratization." *World Politics* 55:4 (July): 517–49.

Bollen, Kenneth A. 1993. "Liberal Democracy: Validity and Method Factors in Cross-National Measures." *American Journal of Political Science* 37: 1207–30.

Bollen, Kenneth A., and Robert W. Jackman. 1985. "Regression Diagnostics: An Expository Treatment of Outliers and Influential Cases." *Sociological Methods and Research* 13: 510–42.

Bonoma, Thomas V. 1985. "Case Research in Marketing: Opportunities, Problems, and a Process." *Journal of Marketing Research* 22:2 (May): 199–208.

Bosk, C. L. 1981. *Forgive and Remember: Managing Medical Failure.* Chicago: University of Chicago Press.

Bound, John, David A. Jaeger, and Rigina M. Baker. 1995. "Problems with Instrumental Variables Estimation When the Correlation between the Instruments and the Endogenous Explanatory Variable Is Weak." *Journal of the American Statistical Association* 90:430 (June): 443–50.

Bowman, Kirk, Fabrice Lehoucq, and James Mahoney. 2005. "Measuring Political Democracy: Case Expertise, Data Adequacy, and Central America." *Comparative Political Studies* 38:8 (October): 939–70.

Brady, Henry E. 2004. "Data-Set Observations versus Causal-Process Observations: The 2000 U.S. Presidential Election." In Henry E. Brady and David Collier (eds.), *Rethinking Social Inquiry: Diverse Tools, Shared Standards.* Lanham, MD: Rowman & Littlefield, 267–72.

Brady, Henry E., and David Collier, eds. 2004. *Rethinking Social Inquiry: Diverse Tools, Shared Standards.* Lanham, MD: Rowman & Littlefield.

Brady, Henry E., Michael C. Herron, Walter R. Mebane, Jr., Jasjeet Singh Sekhon, Kenneth W. Shotts, and Jonathan Wand. 2001. "Law and Data: The Butterfly Ballot Episode." *PS: Political Science and Politics* 34:1 (March): 59–69.

Brady, Henry E., and John E. McNulty. 2004. "The Costs of Voting: Evidence from a Natural Experiment." Paper presented at the annual meeting of the Society for Political Methodology, Stanford University, July 29–31.

Braumoeller, Bear F. 2003. "Causal Complexity and the Study of Politics." *Political Analysis* 11:3: 209–33.

Braumoeller, Bear F., and Gary Goertz. 2000. "The Methodology of Necessary Conditions." *American Journal of Political Science* 44:3 (July): 844–58.

Breman, Anna, and Carolyn Shelton. 2001. "Structural Adjustment and Health: A Literature Review of the Debate, Its Role-Players and Presented Empirical Evidence." CMH Working Paper Series, Paper No. WG6:6. World Health Organization, Commission on Macroeconomics and Health.

Brenner, Robert. 1976. "Agrarian Class Structure and Economic Development in Pre-Industrial Europe." *Past and Present* 70 (February): 30–75.

Brooke, M. 1970. *Le Play: Engineer and Social Scientist.* London: Longman.

Brown, Christine, and Keith Lloyd. 2001. "Qualitative Methods in Psychiatric Research." *Advances in Psychiatric Treatment* 7: 350–6.

Brown, James Robert. 1991. *Laboratory of the Mind: Thought Experiments in the Natural Sciences.* London: Routledge.

Brown, Michael E., Sean M. Lynn-Jones, and Steven E. Miller, eds. 1996. *Debating the Democratic Peace.* Cambridge, MA: MIT Press.

Browne, Angela. 1987. *When Battered Women Kill.* New York: Free Press.

Bryce, James. 1921. *Modern Democracies*, 2 vols. London: Macmillan.

Buchbinder S., and E. Vittinghoff. 1999. "HIV-Infected Long-Term Non-progressors: Epidemiology, Mechanisms of Delayed Progression, and Clinical and Research Implications." *Microbes and Infection* 1:13 (November): 1113–20.

Bueno de Mesquita, Bruce. 2000. "Popes, Kings, and Endogenous Institutions: The Concordat of Worms and the Origins of Sovereignty." *International Studies Review* 2:2: 93–118.

Bulmer, Martin. 1984. *The Chicago School of Sociology: Institutionalization, Diversity and the Rise of Sociological Research*. Chicago: University of Chicago Press.

Bunge, Mario. 1997. "Mechanism and Explanation." *Philosophy of the Social Sciences* 27 (December): 410–65.

Bunzl, Martin. 2004. "Counterfactual History: A User's Guide." *American Historical Review* 109:3 (June): 845–58.

Burawoy, Michael. 1998. "The Extended Case Method." *Sociological Theory* 16:1 (March): 4–33.

Burawoy, Michael, Joshua Gamson, and Alice Burton. 1991. *Ethnography Unbound: Power and Resistance in the Modern Metropolis*. Berkeley: University of California Press.

Burgess, Ernest W. 1927. "Statistics and Case Studies as Methods of Social Research." *Sociology and Social Research* 12: 103–20.

Burgess, Ernest W. 1928. "What Social Case Studies Records Should Contain to Be Useful for Sociological Interpretation." *Social Forces* 6: 524–32.

Burgess, Ernest W. 1941. "An Experiment in the Standardization of the Case Study Method." *Sociometry* 4: 329–48.

Buthe, Tim. 2002. "Taking Temporality Seriously: Modeling History and the Use of Narratives as Evidence." *American Political Science Review* 96:3 (September): 481–93.

Cameron, David. 1978. "The Expansion of the Public Economy: A Comparative Analysis." *American Political Science Review* 72:4 (December): 1243–61.

Campbell, Angus, Philip E. Converse, Warren P. Miller, and Donald E. Stokes. 1960. *The American Voter*. New York: Wiley.

Campbell, Donald T. 1968/1988. "The Connecticut Crackdown on Speeding: Time-Series Data in Quasi-Experimental Analysis." In E. Samuel Overman (ed.), *Methodology and Epistemology for Social Science*. Chicago: University of Chicago Press, 222–38.

Campbell, Donald T. 1975/1988. " 'Degrees of Freedom' and the Case Study." In E. Samuel Overman (ed.), *Methodology and Epistemology for Social Science*. Chicago: University of Chicago Press, 377–88.

Campbell, Donald T. 1988. *Methodology and Epistemology for Social Science*, ed. E. Samuel Overman. Chicago: University of Chicago Press.

Campbell, Donald T., and Julian Stanley. 1963. *Experimental and Quasi-Experimental Designs for Research*. Boston: Houghton Mifflin.

Campoy, Renee. 2004. *Case Study Analysis in the Classroom: Becoming a Reflective Teacher*. Thousand Oaks, CA: Sage.

Canon, David T. 1999. *Race, Redistricting, and Representation: The Unintended Consequences of Black Majority Districts*. Chicago: University of Chicago Press.

Card, David, and Alan B. Krueger. 1994. "Minimum Wages and Employment: A Case Study of the Fast-Food Industry in New Jersey and Pennsylvania." *American Economic Review* 84:4 (September): 772–93.

Carpenter, Daniel P. 2001. *The Forging of Bureaucratic Autonomy: Reputations, Networks, and Policy Innovation in Executive Agencies, 1862–1928*. Princeton, NJ: Princeton University Press.

Chandra, Kanchan. 2004. *Why Ethnic Parties Succeed: Patronage and Ethnic Head Counts in India*. Cambridge: Cambridge University Press.

Chang, Eric C. C., and Miriam A. Golden. In process. "Electoral Systems, District Magnitude and Corruption." *British Journal of Political Science* (forthcoming).

Chatfield, Chris. 1995. "Model Uncertainty, Data Mining and Statistical Inference." *Journal of the Royal Statistical Society, Series A (Statistics in Society)* 158:3: 419–66.

Chernoff, Brian, and Andrew Warner. 2002. "Sources of Fast Growth in Mauritius: 1960–2000." Unpublished paper, Center for International Development, Harvard University.

Chong, Dennis. 1993. "How People Think, Reason, and Feel about Rights and Liberties." *American Journal of Political Science* 37:3 (August): 867–99.

Cioffi-Revilla, Claudio, and Harvey Starr. 1995. "Opportunity, Willingness and Political Uncertainty: Theoretical Foundations of Politics." *Journal of Theoretical Politics* 7: 447–76.

Coase, Ronald H. 1959. "The Federal Communications Commission." *The Journal of Law and Economics* 2 (October): 1–40.

Coase, Ronald H. 2000. "The Acquisition of Fisher Body by General Motors." *The Journal of Law and Economics* 43:1 (April): 15–31.

Cochran, William G. 1977. *Sampling Techniques*. New York: Wiley.

Cohen, Morris R., and Ernest Nagel. 1934. *An Introduction to Logic and Scientific Method*. New York: Harcourt Brace.

Collier, David. 1993. "The Comparative Method." In Ada W. Finifter (ed.), *Political Science: The State of the Discipline II*. Washington, DC: American Political Science Association, 105–19.

Collier, David, and James E. Mahon, Jr. 1993. "Conceptual 'Stretching' Revisited: Adapting Categories in Comparative Analysis." *American Political Science Review* 87:4 (December): 845–55.

Collier, David, and James Mahoney. 1996. "Insights and Pitfalls: Selection Bias in Qualitative Research." *World Politics* 49 (October): 56–91.

Collier, Ruth Berins, and David Collier. 1991/2002. *Shaping the Political Arena: Critical Junctures, the Labor Movement, and Regime Dynamics in Latin America*. Notre Dame, IN: University of Notre Dame Press.

Colomer, Josep M. 1991. "Transitions by Agreement: Modeling the Spanish Way." *American Political Science Review* 85: 1283–1302.

Converse, Philip E., and G. Dupeux. 1962. "Politicization of the Electorate in France and the United States." *Public Opinion Quarterly* 16 (Spring): 1–23.

Cook, Thomas, and Donald Campbell. 1979. *Quasi-Experimentation: Design and Analysis Issues for Field Settings*. Boston: Houghton Mifflin.

Cooley, Charles H. 1927. "Case Study of Small Institutions as a Method of Research." *Publications of the American Sociological Society* 22: 123–33.

Coppedge, Michael J. 2002. "Nested Inference: How to Combine the Benefits of Large-Sample Comparisons and Case Studies." Paper presented at the annual meeting of the American Political Science Association, Boston.

Coppedge, Michael J. 2004. "The Conditional Impact of the Economy on Democracy in Latin America." Paper presented at the conference Democratic Advancements and Setbacks: What Have We Learnt?, Uppsala University, Sweden, June 11–13.

Cornell, Svante E. 2002. "Autonomy as a Source of Conflict: Caucasian Conflicts in Theoretical Perspective." *World Politics* 54 (January): 245–76.

Corsini, Raymond J. 2004. *Case Studies in Psychotherapy*. Stanford, CT: Thomson Learning.

Cottrell, Leonard S., Jr. 1941. "The Case-Study Method in Prediction." *Sociometry* 4 (November): 858–70.

Coulthard, Malcolm, ed. 1992. *Advances in Spoken Discourse Analysis*. London: Routledge.

Cowley, Robert, ed. 2001. *What If? 2: Eminent Historians Imagine What Might Have Been*. New York: Putnam.

Cox, Gary W., Frances McCall Rosenbluth, and Michael Gardeazabal. 2000. "Electoral Rules, Career Ambitions and Party Structure: Comparing Factions in Japan's Upper and Lower House." *American Journal of Political Science* 44:1: 115–22.

Cunningham, J. Barton. 1997. "Case Study Principles for Different Types of Cases." *Quality and Quantity* 31: 401–23.

Dahl, Robert A. 1961. *Who Governs? Democracy and Power in an American City*. New Haven, CT: Yale University Press.

Danto, Arthur C. 1985. *Narration and Knowledge*. New York: Columbia University Press.

Davidson, Donald. 1963. "Actions, Reasons, and Causes." *The Journal of Philosophy* 60:23 (November): 685–700.

Davidson, P. O., and C. G. Costello, eds. 1969. *N = 1: Experimental Studies of Single Cases*. New York: Van Nostrand Reinhold.

Dawid, A. Phillip. 2000. "Causal Inference without Counterfactuals (with Discussion)." *Journal of the American Statistical Association* 95: 407–24, 450.

DeFelice, E. Gene. 1986. "Causal Inference and Comparative Methods." *Comparative Political Studies* 19:3 (October): 415–37.

Denzin, Norman K., and Yvonna S. Lincoln, eds. 2000. *Handbook of Qualitative Research*, 2d ed. Thousand Oaks, CA: Sage.

Desch, Michael C. 2002. "Democracy and Victory: Why Regime Type Hardly Matters." *International Security* 27:2 (Fall): 5–47.

De Soto, Hernando. 1989. *The Other Path: The Invisible Revolution in the Third World*. New York: Harper and Row.

Dessler, David. 1991. "Beyond Correlations: Toward a Causal Theory of War." *International Studies Quarterly* 35: 337–55.

Deyo, Frederic, ed. 1987. *The Political Economy of the New Asian Industrialism.* Ithaca, NY: Cornell University Press.

Dillman, Don A. 1994. *How to Conduct Your Own Survey.* New York: Wiley.

Dion, Douglas. 1998. "Evidence and Inference in the Comparative Case Study." *Comparative Politics* 30 (January): 127–45.

Diprete, Thomas A., and Marcus Gangl. 2004. "Assessing Bias in the Estimation of Causal Effects: Rosenbaum Bounds on Matching Estimators and Instrumental Variables Estimation with Imperfect Instruments." Unpublished manuscript.

Doherty, Daniel, Donald Green, and Alan Gerber. 2006. "Personal Income and Attitudes toward Redistribution: A Study of Lottery Winners." *Political Psychology* 27:3: 441–58.

Doorenspleet, Renske. 2000. "Reassessing the Three Waves of Democratization." *World Politics* 52 (April): 384–406.

Doyle, M. W. 1983. "Kant, Liberal Legacies, and Foreign Affairs." *Philosophy and Public Affairs* 12: 205–35.

Drass, Kriss, and Charles C. Ragin. 1992. *QCA: Qualitative Comparative Analysis.* Evanston IL: Institute for Policy Research, Northwestern University.

Dufour, Stephane, and Dominic Fortin. 1992. "Annotated Bibliography on Case Study Method." *Current Sociology* 40:1: 167–200.

Dunning, Thad. 2005. "Improving Causal Inference: Strengths and Limitations of Natural Experiments." Unpublished manuscript.

Eaton, Kent. 2002. *Politicians and Economic Reform in New Democracies.* University Park: Pennsylvania State University Press.

Eaton, Kent. 2003. "Menem and the Governors: Intergovernmental Relations in the 1990s." Unpublished manuscript.

Ebbinghaus, Bernhard. 2005. "When Less Is More: Selection Problems in Large-N and Small-N Cross-National Comparisons." *International Sociology* 20:2 (June): 133–52.

Eckstein, Harry. 1975. "Case Studies and Theory in Political Science." In Fred I. Greenstein and Nelson W. Polsby (eds.), *Handbook of Political Science, vol. 7. Political Science: Scope and Theory.* Reading, MA: Addison-Wesley 94–137.

Edge, Wayne A., and Mogopodi H. Lekorwe, eds. 1998. *Botswana: Politics and Society.* Pretoria: J. L. van Schaik.

Efron, Bradley. 1982. "Maximum Likelihood and Decision Theory." *The Annals of Statistics* 10:2: 340–56.

Eggan, Fred. 1954. "Social Anthropology and the Method of Controlled Comparison." *American Anthropologist* 56 (October): 743–63.

Eichengreen, Barry. 1992. *Golden Fetters: The Gold Standard and the Great Depression, 1919–1939.* New York: Oxford University Press.

Einhorn, Hillel J., and Robin M. Hogarth. 1986. "Judging Probable Cause." *Psychological Bulletin* 99:3: 3–19.

Elder, G. H. 1985. "Perspectives on the Life Course." In his *Life Course Dynamics.* Ithaca, NY: Cornell University Press, 23–49.

Elman, Colin. 2003. "Lessons from Lakatos." In Colin Elman and Miriam Fendius Elman (eds.), *Progress in International Relations Theory: Appraising the Field.* Cambridge, MA: MIT Press.

Elman, Colin. 2005. "Explanatory Typologies in Qualitative Studies of International Politics." *International Organization* 59:2 (April): 293–326.

Elman, Miriam, ed. 1997. *Paths to Peace: Is Democracy the Answer?* Cambridge: Cambridge University Press.

Elster, Jon. 1978. *Logic and Society: Contradictions and Possible Worlds.* New York: Wiley.

Elster, Jon. 1998. "A Plea for Mechanisms." In Peter Hedstrom and Richard Swedberg (eds.), *Social Mechanisms: An Analytical Approach to Social Theory.* Cambridge: Cambridge University Press, 45–73.

Elton, G. R. 1970. *Political History: Principles and Practice.* New York: Basic Books.

Emerson, Robert M. 1981. "Observational Field Work." *Annual Review of Sociology* 7: 351–78.

Emerson, Robert M., ed. 2001. *Contemporary Field Research: Perspectives and Formulations.* Thousand Oaks, CA: Sage.

Emigh, Rebecca. 1997. "The Power of Negative Thinking: The Use of Negative Case Methodology in the Development of Sociological Theory." *Theory and Society* 26: 649–84.

Epstein, Leon D. 1964. "A Comparative Study of Canadian Parties." *American Political Science Review* 58 (March): 46–59.

Ertman, Thomas. 1997. *Birth of the Leviathan: Building States and Regimes in Medieval and Early Modern Europe.* Cambridge: Cambridge University Press.

Esping-Andersen, Gosta. 1990. *The Three Worlds of Welfare Capitalism.* Princeton, NJ: Princeton University Press.

Estroff, S. E. 1985. *Making It Crazy: An Ethnography of Psychiatric Clients in an American Community.* Berkeley: University of California Press.

Evans, Peter B. 1995. *Embedded Autonomy: States and Industrial Transformation.* Princeton, NJ: Princeton University Press.

Feagin, Joe R., Anthony M. Orum, and Gideon Sjoberg. 1991. *A Case for the Case Study.* Chapel Hill: University of North Carolina Press.

Fearon, James. 1991. "Counter Factuals and Hypothesis Testing in Political Science." *World Politics* 43 (January): 169–95.

Fearon, James D., and David D. Laitin. 1996. "Explaining Interethnic Cooperation." *American Political Science Review* 90:4: 715–35.

Feng, Yi. 2003. *Democracy, Governance, and Economic Performance: Theory and Evidence.* Cambridge, MA: MIT Press.

Fenno, Richard F., Jr. 1978. *Home Style: House Members in Their Districts.* Boston: Little, Brown.

Fenno, Richard F., Jr. 1986. "Observation, Context, and Sequence in the Study of Politics." *American Political Science Review* 80:1 (March): 3–15.

Fenno, Richard F., Jr. 1990. *Watching Politicians: Essays on Participant Observation.* Berkeley, CA: IGS Press.

Ferejohn, John. 2004. "External and Internal Explanation." In Ian Shapiro, Rogers M. Smith, and Tarek E. Masoud (eds.), *Problems and Methods in the Study of Politics.* Cambridge: Cambridge University Press, 144–69.

Fisher, Ronald Aylmer. 1935. *The Design of Experiments.* Edinburgh: Oliver and Boyd.

Fisman, Raymond. 2001. "Estimating the Value of Political Connections." *American Economic Review* 91:4 (September): 1095–1102.

Flyvbjerg, Bent. 2004. "Five Misunderstandings about Case-Study Research." In Clive Gardeazabal, Giampietro Gobo, Jaber F. Gubrium, and David Silverman (eds.), *Qualitative Research Practice*. London: Sage, 420–34.

Fogel, Robert W. 1992. "Problems in Modeling Complex Dynamic Interactions: The Political Realignment of the 1850s." *Economics and Politics* 4:1: 215–54.

Foran, John. 1997. "The Comparative-Historical Sociology of Third World Social Revolutions: Why a Few Succeed, Why Most Fail." In John Foran (ed.), *Theorizing Revolution*. London: Routledge, 227–67.

Foreman, Paul. 1948. "The Theory of Case Studies." *Social Forces* 26: 408–19.

Franklin, Ronald D., David B. Allison, and Bernard S. Gorman, eds. 1997. *Design and Analysis of Single-Case Research*. Mahwah, NJ: Lawrence Erlbaum Associates.

Freedman, David A. 1991. "Statistical Models and Shoe Leather." *Sociological Methodology* 21: 291–313.

Friedman, Milton. 1953. "The Methodology of Positive Economics." In his *Essays in Positive Economics*. Chicago: University of Chicago Press, 3–43.

Friedman, Milton, and Anna Jacobson Schwartz. 1963. *A Monetary History of the United States, 1867–1960*. Princeton, NJ: Princeton University Press.

Gadamer, Hans-Georg. 1975. *Truth and Method*, trans. Garrett Barden and John Cumming. New York: Seabury Press.

Garfinkel, Harold. 1967. *Studies in Ethnomethodology*. Englewood Cliffs, NJ: Prentice Hall.

Geddes, Barbara. 1990. "How the Cases You Choose Affect the Answers You Get: Selection Bias in Comparative Politics." In James A. Stimson (ed.), *Political Analysis, Vol. 2*. Ann Arbor: University of Michigan Press, 131–50.

Geddes, Barbara. 2003. *Paradigms and Sand Castles: Theory Building and Research Design in Comparative Politics*. Ann Arbor: University of Michigan Press.

Geertz, Clifford. 1973. "Thick Description: Toward an Interpretive Theory of Culture." In his *The Interpretation of Cultures*. New York: Basic Books, 3–30.

Geertz, Clifford. 1978. "The Bazaar Economy: Information and Search in Peasant Marketing." *American Economic Review* 68:2: 28–32.

Geertz, Clifford. 1979a. "Deep Play: Notes on the Balinese Cockfight." In Paul Rabinow and William M. Sullivan (eds.), *Interpretive Social Science: A Reader*. Berkeley: University of California Press, 195–240.

Geertz, Clifford. 1979b. "'From the Native's Point of View': On the Nature of Anthropological Understanding." In Paul Rabinow and William M. Sullivan (eds.), *Interpretive Social Science: A Reader*. Berkeley: University of California Press, 225–41.

Geertz, Clifford. 1983. *Local Knowledge*. New York: Basic Books.

George, Alexander L. 1979. "Case Studies and Theory Development: The Method of Structured, Focused Comparison." In Paul Gordon Lauren (ed.), *Diplomacy: New Approaches in History, Theory, and Policy*. New York: The Free Press, 43–68.

George, Alexander L., and Andrew Bennett. 2005. *Case Studies and Theory Development.* Cambridge, MA: MIT Press.

George, Alexander L., and Richard Smoke. 1974. *Deterrence in American Foreign Policy: Theory and Practice.* New York: Columbia University Press.

Gerber, Alan S., and Donald P. Green. 2000. "The Effects of Canvassing, Direct Mail, and Telephone Contact on Voter Turnout: A Field Experiment." *American Political Science Review* 94: 653–63.

Gerber, Alan S., and Donald P. Green. 2001. "Do Phone Calls Increase Voter Turnout? A Field Experiment." *Public Opinion Quarterly* 65: 75–85.

Gerring, John. 2001. *Social Science Methodology: A Criterial Framework.* Cambridge: Cambridge University Press.

Gerring, John. 2003. "Interpretations of Interpretivism." *Qualitative Methods: Newsletter of the American Political Science Association Organized Section on Qualitative Methods* 1:2 (Fall 2003): 2–6.

Gerring, John. 2004. "What Is a Case Study and What Is It Good For?" *American Political Science Review* 98:2 (May): 341–54.

Gerring, John. 2005. "Causation: A Unified Framework for the Social Sciences." *Journal of Theoretical Politics* 17:2 (April): 163–98.

Gerring, John. 2006a. "Single-Outcome Studies: A Methodological Primer." *International Sociology* 21:5 (September): 707–34.

Gerring, John. 2006b. "Global Justice as an Empirical Question." *PS: Political Science and Politics* (forthcoming).

Gerring, John. 2007a. "The Case Study: What It Is and What It Does." In Carles Boix and Susan Stokes (eds.), *Oxford Handbook of Comparative Politics.* Oxford: Oxford University Press, forthcoming.

Gerring, John. 2007b. "Case Selection for Case Study Analysis: Qualitative and Quantitative Techniques." In Janet Box-Steffensmeier, Henry E. Brady, and David Collier (eds.), *Oxford Handbook of Political Methodology.* Oxford: Oxford University Press, forthcoming.

Gerring, John. 2007c. "Is There a (Viable) Crucial-Case Method?" *Comparative Political Studies* (March), forthcoming.

Gerring, John, and Paul A. Barresi. 2003. "Putting Ordinary Language to Work: A Min-Max Strategy of Concept Formation in the Social Sciences." *Journal of Theoretical Politics* 15:2 (April): 201–32.

Gerring, John, Philip Bond, William Barndt, and Carola Moreno. 2005. "Democracy and Growth: A Historical Perspective." *World Politics* 57:3 (April) 323–64.

Gerring, John, Allen Hicken, Rob Salmond, and Michael F. Thies. 2005. "Electoral Reform and the Policy Process: An Iterated Natural Experiment." Research proposal, Department of Political Science, Boston University. <http://www.bu.edu/polisci/JGERRING/electoralreform.pdf>

Gerring, John, and Rose McDermott. 2005. "Experiments and Quasi-Experiments: Toward a Unified Framework for Research Design." Unpublished manuscript.

Gerring, John, and Jason Seawright. 2005. "Selecting Cases in Case Study Research: A Menu of Options." Unpublished manuscript.

Gerring, John, and Strom Thacker. Forthcoming. *Good Government: A Centripetal Theory*. Unpublished manuscript.

Gerring, John, Strom Thacker, and Carola Moreno. 2005a. "Do Neoliberal Policies Save Lives?" Unpublished manuscript.

Gerring, John, Strom Thacker, and Carola Moreno. 2005b. "A Centripetal Theory of Democratic Governance: A Global Inquiry." *American Political Science Review* 99:4 (November): 567–81.

Gerring, John, and Craig Thomas. 2005. "What Is 'Qualitative' Evidence? When Counting Doesn't Add Up." Unpublished manuscript.

Gibbons, Michael T., ed. 1987. *Interpreting Politics*. New York: New York University Press.

Gibson, James L., Gregory A. Caldeira, and Lester Kenyatta Spence. 2002. "The Role of Theory in Experimental Design: Experiments without Randomization." *Political Analysis* 10:4: 362–75.

Giddings, Franklin Henry. 1924. *The Scientific Study of Human Society*. Chapel Hill: University of North Carolina Press.

Gill, Christopher J., Lora Gabin, and Christopher H. Schmid. 2005. "Why Clinicians Are Natural Bayesians." *BMJ* 330 (May 7): 1080–3.

Gill, Jeff. 1999. "The Insignificance of Null Hypothesis Testing." *Political Research Quarterly* 52:3 (September): 647–74.

Glaser, Barney G., and Anselm L. Strauss. 1967. *The Discovery of Grounded Theory: Strategies for Qualitative Research*. New York: Aldine de Gruyter.

Glaser, James. 2003. "Social Context and Inter-Group Political Attitudes: Experiments in Group Conflict Theory." *British Journal of Political Science* 33 (October): 607–20.

Glennan, Stuart S. 1992. "Mechanisms and the Nature of Causation." *Erkenntnis* 44: 49–71.

Goertz, Gary. 2003. "The Substantive Importance of Necessary Condition Hypotheses." In Gary Goertz and Harvey Starr (eds.), *Necessary Conditions: Theory, Methodology and Applications*. New York: Rowman and Littlefield, 65–94.

Goertz, Gary, and Jack Levy, eds. Forthcoming. *Causal Explanations, Necessary Conditions, and Case Studies: World War I and the End of the Cold War*. Unpublished manuscript.

Goertz, Gary, and Harvey Starr, eds. 2003. *Necessary Conditions: Theory, Methodology and Applications*. New York: Rowman and Littlefield.

Goggin, Malcolm L. 1986. "The 'Too Few Cases/Too Many Variables' Problem in Implementation Research." *Western Political Quarterly* 39:2 (June): 328–47.

Goldstone, Jack A. 1991. *Revolution and Rebellion in the Early Modern World*. Berkeley: University of California Press.

Goldstone, Jack A. 1997. "Methodological Issues in Comparative Macrosociology." *Comparative Social Research* 16: 121–32.

Goldstone, Jack A. 2003. "Comparative Historical Analysis and Knowledge Accumulation in the Study of Revolutions." In James Mahoney and Dietrich Rueschemeyer (eds.), *Comparative Historical Analysis in the Social Sciences*. Cambridge: Cambridge University Press, 41–90.

Goldstone, Jack A., et al. 2000. "State Failure Task Force Report: Phase III Findings." Available at <http://www.cidcm.umd.edu/inscr/stfail/SFTF%20Phase%20III%20Report%20Final.pdf>.

Goldthorpe, John H. 1997. "Current Issues in Comparative Macrosociology: A Debate on Methodological Issues." *Comparative Social Research* 16: 121–32.

Goldthorpe, John H. 2000. *On Sociology: Numbers, Narratives, and the Integration of Research and Theory*. Oxford: Oxford University Press.

Gomm, Roger, Martyn Hammersley, and Peter Foster. 2000. *Case Study Method: Key Issues, Key Texts*. Thousand Oaks, CA: Sage.

Goode, William J., and Paul K. Hart. 1952. *Methods in Social Research*. New York: McGraw-Hill.

Goodin, Robert E., and Anneloes Smitsman. 2000. "Placing Welfare States: The Netherlands as a Crucial Test Case." *Journal of Comparative Policy Analysis* 2:1 (April): 39–64.

Goodman, Nelson. 1947. "The Problem of Counterfactual Conditionals." *Journal of Philosophy* 44:5 (February): 113–28.

Gordon, Sanford C., and Alastair Smith. 2004. "Quantitative Leverage through Qualitative Knowledge: Augmenting the Statistical Analysis of Complex Causes." *Political Analysis* 12:3: 233–55.

Gosnell, Harold F. 1926. "An Experiment in the Stimulation of Voting." *American Political Science Review* 20:4 (November): 869–74.

Gourevitch, Peter Alexis. 1978. "The International System and Regime Formation: A Critical Review of Anderson and Wallerstein." *Comparative Politics* 10: 419–38.

Green, Donald P., and Alan S. Gerber. 2001. "Reclaiming the Experimental Tradition in Political Science." In Helen Milner and Ira Katznelson (eds.), *State of the Discipline*, vol. III. New York: Norton, 805–32.

Green, Donald P., and Ian Shapiro. 1994. *Pathologies of Rational Choice Theory: A Critique of Applications in Political Science*. New Haven, CT: Yale University Press.

Greene, William H. 2002. *Econometric Analysis*, 5th ed. Englewood Cliffs, NJ: Prentice Hall.

Greenstein, Fred. 1982. *The Hidden-Hand Presidency: Eisenhower as Leader*. New York: Basic Books.

Greif, Avner. 1998. "Self-Enforcing Political Systems and Economic Growth: Late Medieval Genoa." In Robert H. Bates, Avner Greif, Margaret Levi, Jean-Laurent Rosenthal, and Barry Weingast, *Analytic Narratives*. Princeton, NJ: Princeton University Press, 23–63.

Grier, Robin M. 1999. "Colonial Legacies and Economic Growth." *Public Choice* 98: 317–35.

Griffin, Larry J. 1992. "Temporality, Events, and Explanation in Historical Sociology: An Introduction." *Sociological Methods and Research* 20:4 (May): 403–27.

Griffin, Larry J. 1993. "Narrative, Event-Structure Analysis, and Causal Interpretation in Historical Sociology." *American Journal of Sociology* 98: 1094–1133.

Gubrium, Jaber F., and James A. Holstein, eds. 2002. *Handbook of Interview Research: Context and Method.* Thousand Oaks, CA: Sage.

Gujarati, Damodar N. 2003. *Basic Econometrics*, 4th ed. New York: McGraw-Hill.

Gutting, Gary, ed. 1980. *Paradigms and Revolutions: Appraisals and Applications of Thomas Kuhn's Philosophy of Science.* Notre Dame, IN: University of Notre Dame Press.

Haber, Stephen H., Armando Razo, and Noel Maurer. 2003. *The Politics of Property Rights: Political Instability, Credible Commitments, and Economic Growth in Mexico, 1876–1929.* Cambridge: Cambridge University Press.

Hahn, Jinyong. 1998. "On the Role of the Propensity Score in Efficient Estimation of Average Treatment Effects." *Econometrica* 66:2 (March): 315–31.

Hall, Peter A. 2003. "Aligning Ontology and Methodology in Comparative Politics." In James Mahoney and Dietrich Rueschemeyer (eds.), *Comparative Historical Analysis in the Social Sciences.* Cambridge: Cambridge University Press, 373–404.

Hamel, Jacques. 1993. *Case Study Methods.* Thousand Oaks, CA: Sage.

Hamilton, Gary G. 1977. "Chinese Consumption of Foreign Commodities: A Comparative Perspective." *American Sociological Review* 42:6 (December): 877–91.

Hamilton, James D. 1994. *Time Series Analysis.* Princeton, NJ: Princeton University Press.

Hammersley, Martyn. 1989. *The Dilemma of Qualitative Method: Herbert Blumer and the Chicago Tradition.* London: Routledge and Kegan Paul.

Hammersley, Martyn, and Paul Atkinson. 1983. *Ethnography: Principles in Practice.* New York: Tavistock.

Hammersley, Martyn, and Roger Gomm. 2000. "Introduction." In Roger Gomm, Martyn Hammersley, and Peter Foster (eds.), *Case Study Method: Key Issues, Key Texts.* Thousand Oaks, CA: Sage, 1–32.

Haney, Craig, and Philip Zimbardo. 1977. "The Socialization into Criminality: Becoming a Prisoner and a Guard." In J. Trapp and F. Levine (eds.), *Law, Justice and the Individual in Society: Psychological and Legal Issues.* New York: Holt, Rinehart and Winston, 198–223.

Harre, Rom. 1970. *The Principles of Scientific Thinking.* Chicago: University of Chicago Press.

Hart, H. L. A., and A. M. Honore. 1959. *Causality in the Law.* Oxford: Oxford University Press.

Hart, H. L. A., and A. M. Honore. 1966. "Causal Judgment in History and in the Law." In William H. Dray (ed.), *Philosophical Analysis and History.* New York: Harper and Row, 213–37.

Hart, Paul 't. 1994. *Groupthink in Government: A Study of Small Groups and Policy Failure.* Baltimore: Johns Hopkins University Press.

Hart, Roderick P. 1997. *DICTION 4.0: The Text-Analysis Program.* Thousand Oaks, CA: Sage.

Hartz, Louis. 1955. *The Liberal Tradition in America.* New York: Harcourt, Brace and World.

Hawthorn, Geoffrey. 1991. *Plausible Worlds: Possibility and Understanding in History and the Human Sciences*. Cambridge: Cambridge University Press.

Haynes, B. F., G. Pantaleo, and A. S. Fauci. 1996. "Toward an Understanding of the Correlates of Protective Immunity to HIV Infection." *Science* 271: 324–8.

Healy, William. 1923. "The Contributions of Case Studies to American Sociology." *Publications of the American Sociological Society* 18: 147–55.

Heckman, James J., Hidehiko Ichimura, Jeffrey Smith, and Petra Todd. 1998. "Characterizing Selection Bias Using Experimental Data." *Econometrica* 66: 1017–98.

Heckman, James J., and Jeffrey A. Smith. 1995. "Assessing the Case for Social Experiments." *Journal of Economic Perspectives* 9: 85–110.

Hedstrom, Peter, and Richard Swedberg, eds. 1998. *Social Mechanisms: An Analytical Approach to Social Theory*. Cambridge: Cambridge University Press.

Heidbreder, Edna. 1933. *Seven Psychologies*. New York: Random House.

Helper, Susan. 2000. "Economists and Field Research: 'You Can Observe a Lot Just by Watching.'" *American Economic Review* 90:2: 228–32.

Hempel, Carl G. 1942. "The Function of General Laws in History." *Journal of Philosophy* 39: 35–48.

Herrera, Yoshiko M., and Devesh Kapur. 2005. "Improving Data Quality: Actors, Incentives, and Capabilities." Unpublished manuscript, Department of Government, Harvard University.

Hersen, Michel, and David H. Barlow. 1976. *Single-Case Experimental Designs: Strategies for Studying Behavior Change*. Oxford: Pergamon Press.

Hexter, J. H. 1971. *The History Primer*. New York: Basic Books.

Hicks, Alexander. 1999. *Social Democracy and Welfare Capitalism: A Century of Income Security Politics*. Ithaca, NY: Cornell University Press.

Hicks, Alexander, Toya Misra, and Tang Hah Ng. 1995. "The Programmatic Emergence of the Social Security State." *American Sociological Review* 60 (June): 329–49.

Hirsch, E. D. 1967. *Validity in Interpretation*. New Haven, CT: Yale University Press.

Hirschman, Albert O. 1970. "The Search for Paradigms as a Hindrance to Understanding." *World Politics* 22:3 (March): 329–43.

Ho, Daniel E., Kosuke Imai, Gary King, and Elizabeth A. Stuart. 2004. "Matching as Nonparametric Preprocessing for Reducing Model Dependence in Parametric Causal Inference." Unpublished manuscript.

Hochschild, Jennifer L. 1981. *What's Fair? American Beliefs about Distributive Justice*. Cambridge, MA: Harvard University Press.

Holland, Paul W. 1986. "Statistics and Causal Inference." *Journal of the American Statistical Association* 81: 945–60.

Horowitz, Donald L. 1985. *Ethnic Groups in Conflict*. Berkeley: University of California Press.

Houser, Daniel, and John Freeman. 2001. "Economic Consequences of Political Approval Management in Comparative Perspective." *Journal of Comparative Economics* 29: 692–721.

Houtzager, Peter P. 2003. "Introduction." In Peter P. Houtzager and Mick Moore (eds.), *Changing Paths: International Development and the Politics of Inclusion.* Ann Arbor: University of Michigan Press.

Howard, Marc Morjé. 2003. *The Weakness of Civil Society in Post-Communist Europe.* Cambridge: Cambridge University Press.

Howson, Colin, and Peter Urbach. 1989. *Scientific Reasoning: The Bayesian Approach.* La Salle, IL: Open Court.

Hoy, David Couzens. 1982. *The Critical Circle: Literature, History, and Philosophical Hermeneutics.* Berkeley: University of California Press.

Hsieh, Chang-Tai, and Christina D. Romer. 2001. "Was the Federal Reserve Fettered? Devaluation Expectations in the 1932 Monetary Expansion." NBER Working Paper W8113 (February).

Huber, Evelyne, Charles Ragin, and John D. Stephens. 1993. "Social Democracy, Christian Democracy, Constitutional Structure and the Welfare State." *American Journal of Sociology* 99:3 (November): 711–49.

Huber, Evelyne, and John D. Stephens. 2001. *Development and Crisis of the Welfare State: Parties and Policies in Global Markets.* Chicago: University of Chicago Press.

Huber, John D. 1996. *Rationalizing Parliament: Legislative Institutions and Party Politics in France.* Cambridge: Cambridge University Press.

Hull, Adrian Prentice. 1999. "Comparative Political Science: An Inventory and Assessment since the 1980s." *PS: Political Science and Politics* 32: 117–24.

Humphreys, Macartan. 2005. "Natural Resources, Conflict, and Conflict Resolution: Uncovering the Mechanisms." *Journal of Conflict Resolution* 49:4: 508–37.

Huntington, Samuel P. 1958. "Arms Races: Prerequisites and Results." *Public Policy* 8: 41–83.

Imai, Kosuke. 2005. "Do Get-Out-The-Vote Calls Reduce Turnout? The Importance of Statistical Methods for Field Experiments." *American Political Science Review* 99: 283–300.

Jackman, Robert W. 1985. "Cross-National Statistical Research and the Study of Comparative Politics." *American Journal of Political Science* 29:1 (February): 161–82.

Janoski, Thomas. 1991. "Synthetic Strategies in Comparative Sociological Research: Methods and Problems of Internal and External Analysis." In Charles C. Ragin (ed.), *Issues and Alternatives in Comparative Social Research.* Leiden: E. J. Brill, 59–81.

Janoski, Thomas, and Alexander Hicks, eds. 1993. *Methodological Advances in Comparative Political Economy.* Cambridge: Cambridge University Press.

Jenicek, Milos. 2001. *Clinical Case Reporting in Evidence-Based Medicine,* 2d ed. Oxford: Oxford University Press.

Jensen, Jason L., and Robert Rodgers. 2001. "Cumulating the Intellectual Gold of Case Study Research." *Public Administration Review* 61:2 (March/April): 235–46.

Jervis, Robert. 1989. "Rational Deterrence: Theory and Evidence." *World Politics* 41:2 (January): 183–207.

Jessor, Richard, Anne Colby, and Richard A. Shweder, eds. 1996. *Ethnography and Human Development: Context and Meaning in Social Inquiry*. Chicago: University of Chicago Press.

Jocher, Katharine. 1928. "The Case Study Method in Social Research." *Social Forces* 7: 512–15.

Johnson, Chalmers. 1983. *MITI and the Japanese Miracle: The Growth of Industrial Policy, 1925–1975*. Stanford, CA: Stanford University Press.

Joireman, Sandra Fullerton. 2000. *Property Rights and Political Development in Ethiopia and Eritrea*. Athens, OH: Ohio University Press.

Kaarbo, Juliet, and Ryan K. Beasley. 1999. "A Practical Guide to the Comparative Case Study Method in Political Psychology." *Political Psychology* 20:2: 369–91.

Kagel, John H., and Alvin E. Roth, eds. 1997. *Handbook of Experimental Economics*. Princeton, NJ: Princeton University Press.

Karl, Terry Lynn. 1997. *The Paradox of Plenty: Oil Booms and Petro-States*. Berkeley: University of California Press.

Katz, Jack. 1999. *How Emotions Work*. Chicago: University of Chicago Press.

Katzenstein, Peter, ed. 1996. *The Culture of National Security: Norms and Identity in World Politics*. New York: Columbia University Press.

Katznelson, Ira. 1997. "Structure and Configuration in Comparative Politics." In Mark Irving Lichbach and Alan S. Zuckerman (eds.), *Comparative Politics: Rationality, Culture, and Structure*. Cambridge: Cambridge University Press.

Kaufman, Herbert. 1960. *The Forest Ranger: A Study in Administrative Behavior*. Baltimore: Johns Hopkins University Press.

Kazancigil, Ali. 1994. "The Deviant Case in Comparative Analysis." In Mattei Dogan and Ali Kazancigil (eds.), *Comparing Nations: Concepts, Strategies, Substance*. Cambridge: Blackwell, 213–38.

Kazdin, Alan E. 1976. "Statistical Analyses for Single-Case Experimental Designs." In Michel Hersen and David H. Barlow (eds.), *Single-Case Experimental Designs: Strategies for Studying Behavior Change*. Oxford: Pergamon Press, 265–316.

Kazdin, Alan E. 1982. *Single Case Research Designs*. Oxford: Oxford University Press.

Keen, Justin, and Tim Packwood. 1995. "Qualitative Research: Case Study Evaluation." *BMJ* (August 12): 444–6.

Kemp, Kathleen A. 1986. "Race, Ethnicity, Class and Urban Spatial Conflict: Chicago as a Crucial Case." *Urban Studies* 23:3 (June): 197–208.

Kendall, Patricia L., and Katherine M. Wolf. 1949/1955. "The Analysis of Deviant Cases in Communications Research." In Paul F. Lazarsfeld and Frank N. Stanton (eds.), *Communications Research, 1948–1949* (New York: Harper and Brothers, 1949). Reprinted in Paul F. Lazarsfeld and Morris Rosenberg (eds.), *The Language of Social Research*. New York: Free Press, 1995, 167–70.

Kennedy, Craig H. 2005. *Single-Case Designs for Educational Research*. Boston: Allyn and Bacon.

Kennedy, Peter. 2003. *A Guide to Econometrics*, 5th ed. Cambridge, MA: MIT Press.

Khong, Yuen Foong. 1992. *Analogies at War: Korea, Munich, Dien Bien Phu, and the Vietnam Decisions of 1965*. Princeton, NJ: Princeton University Press.

Kinder, Donald, and Thomas R. Palfrey, eds. 1993. *The Experimental Foundations of Political Science*. Ann Arbor: University of Michigan Press.

Kindleberger, Charles. 1973. *The World in Depression: 1929–1939*. Berkeley: University of California Press.

King, Charles. 2004. "The Micropolitics of Social Violence." *World Politics* 56:3: 431–55.

King, Gary. 1989. *Unifying Political Methodology: The Likelihood Theory of Statistical Inference*. New York: Cambridge University Press.

King, Gary, James Honaker, Anne Joseph, and Kenneth Scheve. 2001. "Analyzing Incomplete Political Science Data: An Alternative Algorithm for Multiple Imputation." *American Political Science Review* 95:1 (March): 49–69.

King, Gary, Robert O. Keohane, and Sidney Verba. 1994. *Designing Social Inquiry: Scientific Inference in Qualitative Research*. Princeton, NJ: Princeton University Press.

King, Gary, and Langche Zeng. 2004a. "The Dangers of Extreme Counterfactuals." Unpublished manuscript.

King, Gary, and Langche Zeng. 2004b. "When Can History Be Our Guide? The Pitfalls of Counterfactual Inference." Unpublished manuscript.

Kirschenman, Kathryn M., and Joleen Neckerman. 1991. "'We'd Love to Hire Them, but . . .': The Meaning of Race for Employers." In Christopher Jencks and Paul E. Peterson (eds.), *The Urban Underclass*. Washington: Brookings, 203–34.

Kittel, Bernhard. 1999. "Sense and Sensitivity in Pooled Analysis of Political Data." *European Journal of Political Research* 35: 225–53.

Kittel, Bernhard. 2005. "A Crazy Methodology? On the Limits of Macroquantitative Social Science Research." Unpublished manuscript, University of Amsterdam.

Kittel, Bernhard, and Hannes Winner. 2005. "How Reliable is Pooled Analysis in Political Economy? The Globalization–Welfare State Nexus Revisited." *European Journal of Political Research* 44:2 (March): 269–93.

Komarovsky, Mirra. 1940. *The Unemployed Man and His Family: The Effect of Unemployment upon the Status of the Man in Fifty-nine Families*. New York: Dryden Press.

Kratochwill, T. R., ed. 1978. *Single Subject Research*. New York: Academic Press.

Krippendorff, Klaus. 2003. *Content Analysis: An Introduction to its Methodology*. Thousand Oaks, CA: Sage.

Kritzer, Herbert M. 1996. "The Data Puzzle: The Nature of Interpretation in Quantitative Research." *American Journal of Political Science* 40:1 (February): 1–32.

Krutz, G. S., R. Flesher, and J. R. Bond. 1998. "From Abe Fortas to Zoe Baird: Why Some Presidential Nominations Fail in the Senate." *American Political Science Review* 92: 871–81.

Kuhn, Thomas S. 1962/1970. *The Structure of Scientific Revolutions*. Chicago: University of Chicago Press.

Laitin, David D. 1998. *Identity in Formation*. Ithaca, NY: Cornell University Press.

Lakatos, Imre. 1978. *The Methodology of Scientific Research Programmes*. Cambridge: Cambridge University Press.

Lamoreaux, Naomi R., and Jean-Laurent Rosenthal. 2004. "Legal Regime and Business's Organizational Choice: A Comparison of France and the United States during the Mid-Nineteenth Century." NBER Working Paper 10288.

Lancaster, Thomas D. 1986. "Electoral Structures and Pork Barrel Politics." *International Political Science Review* 7 (January): 67–81.

Lancaster, Thomas D., and W. David Patterson. 1990. "Comparative Pork Barrel Politics: Perceptions from the West German Bundestag." *Comparative Political Studies* 22 (January): 458–77.

Lane, Robert. 1962. *Political Ideology: Why the American Common Man Believes What He Does*. New York: Free Press.

La Porta, Rafael, Florencio Lopez-de-Silanes, Andrei Shleifer, and Robert W. Vishny. 1998. "Law and Finance." *Journal of Political Economy* 106:6: 1113–55.

La Porta, Rafael, Florencio Lopez-de-Silanes, Andrei Shleifer, and Robert W. Vishny. 1999. "The Quality of Government." *Journal of Economics, Law and Organization* 15:1: 222–79.

Lasswell, Harold. 1931. "The Comparative Method of James Bryce." In Stuart A. Rice (ed.), *Methods in Social Science*. Chicago: University of Chicago Press, 468–79.

Latane, Bibb, and John Darley. 1970. *The Unresponsive Bystander: Why Doesn't He Help?* New York: Appleton-Century-Crofts.

Laver, Michael, Kenneth Gardeazabal, and J. Garry. 2003. "Extracting Policy Positions from Political Text Using Words as Data." *American Political Science Review* 97:2 (May): 311–31.

Lawler, Robert W., and Kathleen M. Carley. 1996. *Case Study and Computing: Advanced Qualitative Methods in the Study of Human Behavior*. Norwood, NJ: Ablex Publishing.

Lawrence, Robert Z., Charan Devereaux, and Michael Watkins. 2005. *Making the Rules: Case Studies on US Trade Negotiation*. Washington, DC: Institute for International Economics.

Lazarsfeld, Paul F., and Allen H. Barton. 1951. "Qualitative Measurement in the Social Sciences: Classification, Typologies, and Indices." In Daniel Lerner and Harold D. Lasswell (eds.), *The Policy Sciences*. Stanford: Stanford University Press, 155–92.

Lazarsfeld, Paul F., Bernard Berelson, and Hazel Gaudet. 1948. *The People's Choice*. New York: Columbia University Press.

Lazarsfeld, Paul F., and W. S. Robinson. 1940. "The Quantification of Case Studies." *Journal of Applied Psychology* 24: 817–25.

Leamer, Edward E. 1983. "Let's Take the Con out of Econometrics." *American Economic Review* 73:1: 31–44.

Lebow, Richard Ned. 2000. "What's So Different about a Counterfactual?" *World Politics* 52 (July): 550–85.

Lebow, Richard Ned. 2000–01. "Contingency, Catalysts, and International System Change." *Political Science Quarterly* 115:4 (September): 591–616.

Lebow, Richard Ned, and Janice Gross Stein. 2004. "The End of the Cold War as a Non-Linear Confluence." In Richard K. Herrmann and Richard Ned Lebow (eds.), *Ending the Cold War*. New York: Palgrave-Macmillan, 189–218.

Lecroy, Craig Winston. 1998. *Case Studies in Social Work Practice*. Stanford, CT: Thomson Learning.

Lee, Allen S. 1989. "Case Studies as Natural Experiments." *Human Relations* 42:2: 117–37.

Leplin, Jarrett, ed. 1984. *Scientific Realism*. Berkeley: University of California Press.

Lerner, Daniel. 1958. *The Passing of Traditional Society: Modernizing the Middle East*. Glencoe, IL: Free Press.

Levi, Margaret. 1997. "A Model, a Method, and a Map: Rational Choice in Comparative and Historical Analysis." In Mark Irving Lichbach and Alan S. Zuckerman (eds.), *Comparative Politics: Rationality, Culture, and Structure*. Cambridge: Cambridge University Press, 18–41.

Levine, Ross, and David Renelt. 1992. "A Sensitivity Analysis of Cross-Country Growth Regressions." *American Economic Review* 82:4 (September): 942–63.

Levy, Jack S. 1983. "Misperception and the Causes of War: Theoretical Linkages and Analytical Problems." *World Politics* 36: 76–99.

Levy, Jack S. 1990–91. "Preferences, Constraints, and Choices in July 1914." *International Security* 15:3: 151–86.

Levy, Jack S. 2001. "Explaining Events and Developing Theories: History, Political Science, and the Analysis of International Relations." In Colin Elman and Miriam Fendius Elman (eds.), *Bridges and Boundaries: Historians, Political Scientists, and the Study of International Relations*. Cambridge: MIT Press, 39–84.

Levy, Jack S. 2002a. "Qualitative Methods in International Relations." In Frank P. Harvey and Michael Brecher (eds.), *Evaluating Methodology in International Studies*. Ann Arbor: University of Michigan Press, 432–54.

Levy, Jack S. 2002b. "War and Peace." In Walter Carlsnaes, Thomas Risse, and Beth A. Simmons (eds.), *Handbook of International Relations*. London: Sage, 350–68.

Libecap, Gary D. 1993. *Contracting for Property Rights*. Cambridge: Cambridge University Press.

Lieberman, Evan S. 2005a. "Nested Analysis as a Mixed-Method Strategy for Comparative Research." *American Political Science Review* 99:3 (August): 435–52.

Lieberman, Evan S. 2005b. "Politics in *Really* Hard Times: Ethnicity, Public Goods, and Government Responses to HIV/AIDS in Africa." Unpublished manuscript.

Lieberman, Evan S., Marc Morje Howard, and Julia Lynch. 2004. "Symposium: Field Research." *Qualitative Methods: Newsletter of the American Political Science Association Organized Section on Qualitative Methods* 2:1 (Spring): 2–14.

Lieberson, Stanley. 1985. *Making It Count: The Improvement of Social Research and Theory*. Berkeley: University of California Press.

Lieberson, Stanley. 1992. "Small N's and Big Conclusions: An Examination of the Reasoning in Comparative Studies Based on a Small Number of Cases." In Charles S. Ragin and Howard S. Becker (eds.), *What Is a Case? Exploring the Foundations of Social Inquiry*. Cambridge: Cambridge University Press, 105–17.

Lieberson, Stanley. 1994. "More on the Uneasy Case for Using Mill-Type Methods in Small-N Comparative Studies." *Social Forces* 72:4 (June): 1225–37.

Lijphart, Arend. 1968. *The Politics of Accommodation: Pluralism and Democracy in the Netherlands*. Berkeley: University of California Press.

Lijphart, Arend. 1969. "Consociational Democracy." *World Politics* 21:2 (January): 207–25.

Lijphart, Arend. 1971. "Comparative Politics and the Comparative Method." *American Political Science Review* 65:3 (September): 682–93.

Lijphart, Arend. 1975. "The Comparable Cases Strategy in Comparative Research." *Comparative Political Studies* 8 (July): 158–77.

Lipset, Seymour Martin. 1959. "Some Social Requisites of Democracy: Economic Development and Political Development." *American Political Science Review* 53 (March): 69–105.

Lipset, Seymour Martin. 1960/1963. *Political Man: The Social Bases of Politics*. Garden City, NY: Anchor Books.

Lipset, Seymour Martin. 1963. *The First New Nation: The United States in Historical and Comparative Perspective*. New York: Basic Books.

Lipset, Seymour Martin. 1968. *Agrarian Socialism: The Cooperative Commonwealth Federation in Saskatchewan. A Study in Political Sociology*. Garden City, NY: Doubleday.

Lipset, Seymour Martin. 1990. *Continental Divide: The Values and Institutions of the United States and Canada*. New York: Routledge.

Lipset, Seymour Martin, Martin A. Trow, and James S. Coleman. 1956. *Union Democracy: The Internal Politics of the International Typographical Union*. New York: The Free Press.

Lipsey, Mark W., and David B. Wilson. 2001. *Practical Meta-Analysis*. Thousand Oaks, CA: Sage.

Little, Daniel. 1995. "Causal Explanation in the Social Sciences." *Southern Journal of Philosophy* 34 (supplement): 31–56.

Little, Daniel. 1998. *Microfoundations, Method, and Causation*. New Brunswick, NJ: Transaction.

Lott, John R., Jr. 2000. "Gore Might Lose a Second Round: Media Suppressed the Bush Vote." *Philadelphia Inquirer*, November 14, p. 23A.

Lucas, W. 1974. *The Case Survey Method: Aggregating Case Experience*. Santa Monica, CA: Rand.

Lundberg, George A. 1941. "Case Studies vs. Statistical Methods: An Issue Based on Misunderstanding." *Sociometry* 4: 379–83.

Lundervold, Duane A., and Marily F. Belwood. 2000. "The Best Kept Secret in Counseling: Single-Case (N = 1) Experimental Designs." *Journal of Counseling and Development* (Winter): 92–103.

Lupia, Arthur, and Kaare Strom. 1995. "Coalition Termination and the Strategic Timing of Parliamentary Elections." *American Political Science Review* 89: 648–65.

Lustick, Ian. 1996. "History, Historiography, and Political Science." *American Political Science Review* 90:3 (September): 605–18.

Lynd, Robert Staughton, and Helen Merrell Lynd. 1929/1956. *Middletown: A Study in American Culture*. New York: Harcourt, Brace.

MacIntyre, Alasdair. 1971. "Is a Science of Comparative Politics Possible?" In his *Against the Self-Images of the Age: Essays on Ideology and Philosophy*. London: Duckworth, 260–79.

MacIntyre, Andrew. 2003. *Power of Institutions: Political Architecture and Governance*. Ithaca, NY: Cornell University Press.

Mackie, John L. 1965/1993. "Causes and Conditions." In Ernest Sosa and Michael Tooley (eds.), *Causation*. Oxford: Oxford University Press, 33–55.

Mahoney, James. 1999. "Nominal, Ordinal, and Narrative Appraisal in Macro-Causal Analysis." *American Journal of Sociology* 104:4 (January): 1154–96.

Mahoney, James. 2000. "Path Dependence in Historical Sociology." *History and Theory* 29:4 (August): 507–48.

Mahoney, James. 2001. "Beyond Correlational Analysis: Recent Innovations in Theory and Method." *Sociological Forum* 16:3 (September): 575–93.

Mahoney, James, and Dietrich Rueschemeyer, eds. 2003. *Comparative Historical Analysis in the Social Sciences*. Cambridge: Cambridge University Press.

Mahoney, James, and Gary Goertz. 2004. "The Possibility Principle: Choosing Negative Cases in Comparative Research." *American Political Science Review* 98:4 (November): 653–69.

Main, Julie, Tharam S. Dillon, and Simon C. K. Shiu. 2000. "A Tutorial on Case Based Reasoning." In Sankar K. Pal, Tharam S. Dillon, and Daniel S. Yeung (eds.), *Soft Computing in Case Based Reasoning*. New York: Springer-Verlag, 1–28.

Maisel, L. Sandy. 1986. *From Obscurity to Oblivion: Running in the Congressional Primary*. Knoxville: University of Tennessee Press.

Malinowski, Bronislaw. 1922/1984. *Argonauts of the Western Pacific*. Prospect Heights, IL: Waveland.

Mandelbaum, Maurice. 1977. *The Anatomy of Historical Knowledge*. Baltimore: Johns Hopkins University Press.

Manski, Charles F. 1993. "Identification Problems in the Social Sciences." *Sociological Methodology* 23: 1–56.

Maoz, Zeev. 2002. "Case Study Methodology in International Studies: From Storytelling to Hypothesis Testing." In Frank P. Harvey and Michael Brecher (eds.), *Evaluating Methodology in International Studies: Millennial Reflections on International Studies*. Ann Arbor: University of Michigan Press, 455–75.

Maoz, Zeev, Alex Mintz, T. Clifton Morgan, Glenn Palmer, and Richard J. Stoll, eds. 2004. *Multiple Paths to Knowledge in International Politics: Methodology in the Study of Conflict Management and Conflict Resolution*. Lexington, MA: Lexington Books.

Maoz, Zeev, and Ben D. Mor. 1999. "The Strategic Dynamics of Enduring Rivalries: A Comparative Analysis of Case Studies and Quantitative Methods." Paper presented at the annual meeting of the Peace Science Society, Ann Arbor, Michigan, October 8–10.

Marini, Margaret, and Burton Singer. 1988. "Causality in the Social Sciences." *Sociological Methodology* 18: 347–409.

Marks, Gary, and Seymour Martin Lipset. 2000. *It Didn't Happen Here: Why Socialism Failed in the United States*. New York: Norton.

Marshall, Monty G., and Keith Jaggers. 2005. "Polity IV Project: Political Regime Characteristics and Transitions, 1800–2003." Web version. <www.cidcm.umd.edu/inscr/polity/>

Martin, Cathie Jo, and Duane Swank. 2004. "Does the Organization of Capital Matter? Employers and Active Labor Market Policy at the National and Firm Levels." *American Political Science Review* 98:4 (November): 593–612.

Martin, Lisa L. 1992. *Coercive Cooperation: Explaining Multilateral Economic Sanctions*. Princeton, NJ: Princeton University Press.

Mayhew, David R. 1991. *Divided We Govern: Party Control, Lawmaking, and Investigations, 1946–1990*. New Haven, CT: Yale University Press.

Mayo, Deborah G. 1996. *Error and the Growth of Experimental Knowledge*. Chicago: University of Chicago Press.

Mays, Nicolas, and Catherine Pope. 1995. "Qualitative Research: Observational Methods in Health Care Settings." *BMJ* (July 15): 182–4.

McAdam, Doug. 1982. *Political Process and the Development of Black Insurgency, 1930–1970*. Chicago: University of Chicago Press.

McAdam, Doug. 1988. *Freedom Summer*. New York: Oxford University Press.

McAdam, Doug, Sidney Tarrow, and Charles Tilly. 2001. *Dynamics of Contention*. Cambridge: Cambridge University Press.

McArdle, J. J. 1982. "Structural Equation Modeling Applied to a Case Study of Alcoholism." National Institute on Alcohol Abuse and Alcoholism, NIAAA No. AA05743.

McCullagh, Peter, and J. A. Nelder. 1989. *Generalized Linear Models*. London: Chapman and Hall/CRC.

McDermott, Rose. 1997. "Voting Cues in Low-Information Elections: Candidate Gender as a Social Information Variable in Contemporary United States Elections." *American Journal of Political Science* 41: 270–83.

McDermott, Rose. 2002. "Experimental Methods in Political Science." *Annual Review of Political Science* 5: 31–61.

McGraw, Kathleen. 1996. "Political Methodology: Research Design and Experimental Methods." In Robert Goodin and Hans-Dieter Klingemann (eds.), *A New Handbook of Political Science*. New York: Oxford University Press, 769–86.

McKeown, Timothy J. 1983. "Hegemonic Stability Theory and Nineteenth-Century Tariff Levels." *International Organization* 37:1 (Winter): 73–91.

McKeown, Timothy J. 1999. "Case Studies and the Statistical World View." *International Organization* 53 (Winter): 161–90.

McKim, Vaughn R., and Stephen P. Turner, eds. 1997. *Causality in Crisis? Statistical Methods and the Search for Causal Knowledge in the Social Sciences*. Notre Dame, IN: Notre Dame Press.

McNeill, William H. 1991. *The Rise of the West: A History of the Human Community*. Chicago: University of Chicago Press.

Meckstroth, Theodore. 1975. "'Most Different Systems' and 'Most Similar Systems': A Study in the Logic of Comparative Inquiry." *Comparative Political Studies* 8:2 (July): 133–77.

Meehl, Paul E. 1954. *Clinical versus Statistical Predictions: A Theoretical Analysis and a Review of the Evidence*. Minneapolis: University of Minnesota Press.

Megill, Allan. 1989. "Recounting the Past: 'Description,' Explanation and Narrative in Historiography." *American Historical Review* 94:3 (June): 627–53.

Mendelberg, Tali. 1997. "Executing Hortons: Racial Crime in the 1988 Presidential Campaign." *Public Opinion Quarterly* 61:1 (Spring): 134–57.

Merriam, Sharan B. 1988. *Case Study Research in Education: A Qualitative Approach*. San Francisco: Jossey-Bass.

Michels, Roberto. 1911. *Political Parties*. New York: Collier Books.

Miguel, Edward. 2004. "Tribe or Nation: Nation-Building and Public Goods in Kenya versus Tanzania." *World Politics* 56:3: 327–62.

Milgram, Stanley. 1974. *Obedience to Authority*. New York: Harper and Row.

Mill, John Stuart. 1843/1872. *The System of Logic*, 8th ed. London: Longmans, Green.

Miron, Jeffrey A. 1994. "Empirical Methodology in Macroeconomics: Explaining the Success of Friedman and Schwartz's 'A Monetary History of the United States, 1867–1960.'" *Journal of Monetary Economics* 34: 17–25.

Mitchell, J. Clyde. 1983. "Case and Situation Analysis." *Sociological Review* 31:2: 187–211.

Mohr, Lawrence B. 1985. "The Reliability of the Case Study as a Source of Information." In R. F. Coulem and R. A. Smith (eds.), *Advances in Information Processing in Organizations*, vol. 2. Greenwich, CT: JAI Press, 65–97.

Mondak, Jeffery J. 1995. "Newspapers and Political Awareness." *American Journal of Political Science* 39:2 (May): 513–27.

Monroe, Kristen Renwick. 1996. *The Heart of Altruism: Perceptions of a Common Humanity*. Princeton, NJ: Princeton University Press.

Moore, Barrington, Jr. 1966. *Social Origins of Dictatorship and Democracy: Lord and Peasant in the Making of the Modern World*. Boston: Beacon Press.

Moravsik, Andrew. 1998. *The Choice for Europe: Social Purpose and State Power from Messina to Maastricht*. Ithaca, NY: Cornell University Press.

Morgan, Kimberly. 2003. "The Politics of Mothers' Employment: France in Comparative Perspective." *World Politics* 55:2 (January): 259–89.

Morgan, Stephen L. 2002a. "Instrumental Variables and Counterfactual Causality: An Explanation, Application, and Assessment for Non-Economists." Unpublished manuscript.

Morgan, Stephen L. 2002b. "Should Sociologists Use Instrumental Variables?" Unpublished manuscript.

Morgan, Stephen L., and David J. Harding. 2005. "Matching Estimators of Causal Effects: From Stratification and Weighting to Practical Data Analysis Routines." Unpublished manuscript.

Morrow, J. D. 1991. "Alliances and Asymmetry: An Alternative to the Capability Aggregation Model of Alliances." *American Journal of Political Science* 35: 904–33.

Most, Benjamin A., and Harvey Starr. 1984. "International Relations Theory, Foreign Policy Substitutability, and 'Nice' Laws." *World Politics* 36: 383–406.

Moulder, Frances V. 1977. *Japan, China and the Modern World Economy: Toward a Reinterpretation of East Asian Development ca. 1600 to ca. 1918.* Cambridge: Cambridge University Press.

Mulligan, Casey, Ricard Gil, and Xavier Sala-i-Martin. 2002. "Social Security and Democracy." Unpublished manuscript, University of Chicago and Columbia University.

Munck, Gerardo L. 2004. "Tools for Qualitative Research." In Henry E. Brady and David Collier (eds.), *Rethinking Social Inquiry: Diverse Tools, Shared Standards.* Lanham, MD: Rowman & Littlefield, 105–21.

Munck, Gerardo L., and Richard Snyder, eds. 2006. *Passion, Craft, and Method in Comparative Politics.* Baltimore: Johns Hopkins University Press.

Munck, Gerardo L., and Jay Verkuilen. 2002. "Measuring Democracy: Evaluating Alternative Indices." *Comparative Political Studies* 35:1: 5–34.

Neta, Ram. 2004. "On the Normative Significance of Brute Facts." *Legal Theory* 10:3 (September): 199–214.

Neuendorf, Kimberly A. 2001. *The Content Analysis Guidebook.* Thousand Oaks, CA: Sage.

Neustadt, Richard E. 1980. *Presidential Power: The Politics of Leadership from FDR to Carter.* New York: Wiley.

Nicholson-Crotty, Sean, and Kenneth J. Meier. 2002. "Size Doesn't Matter: In Defense of Single-State Studies." *State Politics and Policy Quarterly* 2:4 (Winter): 411–422.

Nissen, Sylke. 1998. "The Case of Case Studies: On the Methodological Discussion in Comparative Political Science." *Quality and Quantity* 32: 339–418.

Njolstad, Olav. 1990. "Learning from History? Case Studies and the Limits to Theory-Building." In Olav Njolstad (ed.), *Arms Races: Technological and Political Dynamics.* Thousand Oaks, CA: Sage, 220–46.

North, Douglass C., Terry L. Anderson, and Peter J. Hill. 1983. *Growth and Welfare in the American Past: A New American History,* 3d ed. Englewood Cliffs, NJ: Prentice Hall.

North, Douglass C., and Robert Paul Thomas. 1973. *The Rise of the Western World.* Cambridge: Cambridge University Press.

North, Douglass C., and Barry R. Weingast. 1989. "Constitutions and Commitment: The Evolution of Institutions Governing Public Choice in Seventeenth-Century England." *Journal of Economic History* 49: 803–32.

O'Donnell, Guillermo, and Philippe Schmitter. 1986. *Transitions from Authoritarian Rule: Tentative Conclusions about Uncertain Democracies.* Baltimore: Johns Hopkins University Press.

Odell, John S. 2001. "Case Study Methods in International Political Economy." *International Studies Perspectives* 2: 161–76.

Odell, John S. 2004. "Case Study Methods in International Political Economy." In Detlef F. Sprinz and Yael Wolinsky-Nahmias (eds.), *Models, Numbers and Cases: Methods for Studying International Relations.* Ann Arbor: University of Michigan, 56–80.

Orum, Anthony M., Joe R. Feagin, and Gideon Sjoberg. 1991. "Introduction: The Nature of the Case Study." In Joe R. Feagin, Anthony M. Orum, and Gideon Sjoberg (eds.), *A Case for the Case Study*. Chapel Hill: University of North Carolina Press, 1–21.

Pahre, Robert. 2005. "Formal Theory and Case-Study Methods in EU Studies." *European Union Politics* 6:1: 113–46.

Palmer, Vivien M. 1928. *Field Studies in Sociology: A Student's Manual*. Chicago: University of Chicago Press.

Papyrakis, Elissaios, and Reyer Gerlagh. 2003. "The Resource Curse Hypothesis and Its Transmission Channels." *Journal of Comparative Economics* 32: 181–93.

Park, Robert E. 1930. "Murder and the Case Study Method." *American Journal of Sociology* 36: 447–54.

Patton, Michael Quinn. 2002. *Qualitative Evaluation and Research Methods*. Newbury Park, CA: Sage.

Patzelt, Werner J. 2000. "What Can an Individual MP Do in German Parliamentary Politics?" In Lawrence D. Longley and Reuven Y. Hazan (eds.), *The Uneasy Relationships between Parliamentary Members and Leaders*. London: Frank Cass.

Petersen, Roger D. 2002. *Understanding Ethnic Violence: Fear, Hatred, and Resentment in Twentieth Century Eastern Europe*. Cambridge: Cambridge University Press.

Phillips, N., and C. Hardy. 2002. *Discourse Analysis: Investigating Processes of Social Construction*. Thousand Oaks, CA: Sage.

Pierson, Paul. 2000. "Increasing Returns, Path Dependence, and the Study of Politics." *American Political Science Review* 94:2 (June): 251–67.

Pierson, Paul. 2004. *Politics in Time: History, Institutions, and Social Analysis*. Princeton, NJ: Princeton University Press.

Piore, Michael J. 1979. "Qualitative Research Techniques in Economics." *Administrative Science Quarterly* 24 (December): 560–69.

Pitkin, Hanna Fenichel. 1972. *Wittgenstein and Justice: On the Significance of Ludwig Wittgenstein for Social and Political Thought*. Berkeley: University of California Press.

Platt, Jennifer. 1992. "'Case Study' in American Methodological Thought." *Current Sociology* 40:1: 17–48.

Popkin, Samuel L. 1977. *The Rational Peasant: The Political Economy of Rural Society in Vietnam*. Berkeley: University of California Press.

Popper, Karl. 1934/1968. *The Logic of Scientific Discovery*. New York: Harper and Row.

Popper, Karl. 1963. *Conjectures and Refutations*. London: Routledge and Kegan Paul.

Porter, Michael. 1990. *The Competitive Advantage of Nations*. New York: The Free Press.

Posen, Barry. 1984. *The Sources of Military Doctrine: France, Britain and Germany Between the World Wars*. Ithaca, NY: Cornell University Press.

Posner, Daniel. 2004. "The Political Salience of Cultural Difference: Why Chewas and Tumbukas are Allies in Zambia and Adversaries in Malawi." *American Political Science Review* 98:4 (November): 529–46.

Poteete, Amy R., and Elinor Ostrom. 2005. "Bridging the Qualitative-Quantitative Divide: Strategies for Building Large-N Databases Based on Qualitative Research." Paper presented at the annual meeting of the American Political Science Association, Washington, D.C.

Powell, Robert. 1999. *In the Shadow of Power: States and Strategies in International Politics*. Princeton, NJ: Princeton University Press.

Pressman, Jeffrey L., and Aaron Gardeazabal. 1973. *Implementation*. Berkeley: University of California Press.

Przeworski, Adam, Michael Alvarez, Jose Antonio Cheibub, and Fernando Limongi. 2000. *Democracy and Development: Political Institutions and Material Well-Being in the World, 1950–1990*. Cambridge: Cambridge University Press.

Przeworski, Adam, and Henry Teune. 1970. *The Logic of Comparative Social Inquiry*. New York: Wiley.

Putnam, Robert D., Robert Leonard, and Raffaella Y. Nanetti. 1993. *Making Democracy Work: Civic Traditions in Modern Italy*. Princeton, NJ: Princeton University Press.

Queen, Stuart. 1928. "Round Table on the Case Study in Sociological Research." *Publications of the American Sociological Society, Papers and Proceedings* 22: 225–7.

Rabinow, Paul, and William M. Sullivan, eds. 1979. *Interpretive Social Science: A Reader*. Berkeley: University of California Press.

Ragin, Charles C. 1987. *The Comparative Method: Moving Beyond Qualitative and Quantitative Strategies*. Berkeley: University of California Press.

Ragin, Charles C. 1992a. "Cases of 'What Is a Case?'" In Charles C. Ragin and Howard S. Becker (eds.), *What Is a Case? Exploring the Foundations of Social Inquiry*. Cambridge: Cambridge University Press, 1–18.

Ragin, Charles C. 1992b. " 'Casing' and the Process of Social Inquiry." In Charles C. Ragin and Howard S. Becker (eds.), *What Is a Case? Exploring the Foundations of Social Inquiry*. Cambridge: Cambridge University Press, 217–26.

Ragin, Charles C. 1997. "Turning the Tables: How Case-Oriented Research Challenges Variable-Oriented Research." *Comparative Social Research* 16: 27–42.

Ragin, Charles C. 2000. *Fuzzy-Set Social Science*. Chicago: University of Chicago Press.

Ragin, Charles C. 2004. "Turning the Tables." In Henry E. Brady and David Collier (eds.), *Rethinking Social Inquiry: Diverse Tools, Shared Standards*. Lanham, MD: Rowman and Littlefield, 123–38.

Ragin, Charles C., and Howard S. Becker, eds. 1992. *What Is a Case? Exploring the Foundations of Social Inquiry*. Cambridge: Cambridge University Press.

Ragsdale, Lynn, and J. G. Rusk. 1993. "Who Are Nonvoters? Profiles from the 1990 Senate Elections." *American Journal of Political Science* 37: 721–46.

Reilly, Ben. 2000/2001. "Democracy, Ethnic Fragmentation, and Internal Conflict: Confused Theories, Faulty Data, and the 'Crucial Case' of Papua New Guinea." *International Security* 25:3: 162–85.

Reilly, Ben. 2001. *Democracy in Divided Societies.* Cambridge: Cambridge University Press.

Reilly, Ben, and Robert Phillpot. 2003. "'Making Democracy Work' in Papua New Guinea: Social Capital and Provincial Development in an Ethnically Fragmented Society." *Asian Survey* 42:6 (November–December): 906–27.

Reiss, Julian. 2003. "Practice Ahead of Theory: Instrumental Variables, Natural Experiments and Inductivism in Econometrics." Unpublished manuscript.

Rice, Stuart A. 1928. *Quantitative Methods in Politics.* New York: Knopf.

Rice, Stuart A., ed. 1931. *Methods in Social Science.* Chicago: University of Chicago Press.

Richter, Melvin. 1969. "Comparative Political Analysis in Montesquieu and Tocqueville." *Comparative Politics* 1:2 (January): 129–60.

Roberts, Clayton. 1996. *The Logic of Historical Explanation.* University Park: Pennsylvania State University Press.

Roberts, Michael J. 2002. "Developing a Teaching Case." Cambridge, MA: Harvard Business School.

Robinson, Denise L. 2001. *Clinical Decision Making: A Case Study Approach.* Philadelphia: Lippincott Williams & Wilkins.

Robinson, W. S. 1951. "The Logical Structure of Analytic Induction." *American Sociological Review* 16:6 (December): 812–18.

Rodgers, Daniel T. 1992. "Republicanism: The Career of a Concept." *Journal of American History* 79:1 (June): 11–38.

Rodrik, Dani, ed. 2003. *In Search of Prosperity: Analytic Narratives on Economic Growth.* Princeton, NJ: Princeton University Press.

Rodrik, Dani. 2005. "Why We Learn Nothing from Regressing Economic Growth on Policies." Unpublished manuscript.

Rogowski, Ronald. 1995. "The Role of Theory and Anomaly in Social-Scientific Inference." *American Political Science Review* 89:2 (June): 467–70.

Rohlfing, Ingo. 2004. "Have You Chosen the Right Case? Uncertainty in Case Selection for Single Case Studies." Working paper, International University, Bremen, Germany.

Rosenbaum, Paul R. 2004. "Matching in Observational Studies." In A. Gelman and X-L. Meng (eds.), *Applied Bayesian Modeling and Causal Inference from Incomplete-Data Perspectives.* New York: Wiley, B-24.

Rosenbaum, Paul R., and Donald B. Rubin. 1985. "Constructing a Control Group Using Multivariate Matched Sampling Methods That Incorporate the Propensity Score." *The American Statistician* 39:1 (February): 33–38.

Rosenbaum, Paul R., and Jeffrey H. Silber. 2001. "Matching and Thick Description in an Observational Study of Mortality after Surgery." *Biostatistics* 2: 217–32.

Rosenzweig, Mark R., and Kenneth I. Wolpin. 2000. "Natural 'Natural Experiments' in Economics." *Journal of Economic Literature* 38: 827–74.

Ross, Frank Alexander. 1931. "On Generalisation from Limited Social Data." *Social Forces* 10: 32–7.

Ross, Michael. 2001. "Does Oil Hinder Democracy?" *World Politics* 53 (April): 325–61.

Roth, Paul A. 1994. "Narrative Explanations: The Case of History." In Michael Martin and Lee C. McIntyre (eds.), *Readings in the Philosophy of Social Science*. Cambridge, MA: MIT Press, 701–12.

Rubin, Donald B. 1974. "Estimating Causal Effects of Treatments in Randomized and Nonrandomized Studies." *Journal of Educational Psychology* 66: 688–701.

Rueschemeyer, Dietrich. 2003. "Can One or a Few Cases Yield Theoretical Gains?" In James Mahoney and Dietrich Rueschemeyer (eds.), *Comparative Historical Analysis in the Social Sciences*. Cambridge: Cambridge University Press, 305–36.

Rueschemeyer, Dietrich, and John D. Stephens. 1997. "Comparing Historical Sequences: A Powerful Tool for Causal Analysis." *Comparative Social Research* 16: 55–72.

Rumsfeld, Donald H. 2002. News transcript, United States Department of Defense. On the web: <http://www.defense.gov/transcripts/2002/t05222002_t522sdma.html>.

Runkel, Philip J., and Joseph E. McGrath. 1972. *Research on Human Behavior: A Systematic Guide to Method*. New York: Holt, Rinehart, and Winston.

Russett, Bruce M. 1970. "International Behavior Research: Case Studies and Cumulation." In Michael Haas and Henry S. Kariel (eds.), *Approaches to the Study of Political Science*. San Francisco: Chandler, 1–15.

Sagan, Scott. 1995. *The Limits of Safety: Organizations, Accidents, and Nuclear Weapons*. Princeton, NJ: Princeton University Press.

Sala-I-Martin, Xavier X. 1997. "I Just Ran Two Million Regressions." *American Economic Review* 87:2: 178–83.

Sarbin, Theodore R. 1943. "A Contribution to the Study of Actuarial and Individual Methods of Prediction." *American Journal of Sociology* 48: 593–602.

Sarbin, Theodore R. 1944. "The Logic of Prediction in Psychology." *Psychological Review* 51: 210–28.

Sartori, Giovanni. 1975. "The Tower of Babble." In Giovanni Sartori, Fred W. Riggs, and Henry Teune (eds.), *Tower of Babel: On the Definition and Analysis of Concepts in the Social Sciences*. International Studies, Occasional Paper No. 6, 7–38.

Sartori, Giovanni. 1976. *Parties and Party Systems*. Cambridge: Cambridge University Press.

Sartori, Giovanni. 1984. "Guidelines for Concept Analysis." In Giovanni Sartori (ed.), *Social Science Concepts: A Systematic Analysis*. Beverly Hills, CA: Sage, 15–48.

Sayer, R. Andrew. 1992. *Method in Social Science: A Realist Approach*, 2d ed. London: Routledge.

Schelling, Thomas C. 1966. *Arms and Influence*. New Haven, CT: Yale University Press.

Scheper-Hughes, Nancy. 1992. *Death without Weeping: The Violence of Everyday Life in Brazil.* Berkeley: University of California Press.

Schickler, Eric. 2001. *Disjointed Pluralism: Institutional Innovation and the Development of the U.S. Congress.* Princeton, NJ: Princeton University Press.

Schmeidler, David. 2001. *A Theory of Case-Based Decisions.* Cambridge: Cambridge University Press.

Schmidt, Steffen W., et al., eds. 1977. *Friends, Followers, and Factions: A Reader in Political Clientelism.* Berkeley: University of California Press.

Schuman, Howard, and Lawrence Bobo. 1988. "Survey-Based Experiments on White Racial Attitudes toward Residential Integration." *American Journal of Sociology* 94:2 (September): 273–299.

Schwandt, Thomas A. 1997. *Qualitative Inquiry: A Dictionary of Terms.* Thousand Oaks, CA: Sage.

Scott, James C. 1998. *Seeing Like a State: How Certain Schemes to Improve the Human Condition Have Failed.* New Haven, CT: Yale University Press.

Scriven, Michael. 1976. "Maximizing the Power of Causal Investigations: The Modus Operandi Method." In G. V. Glass (ed.), *Evaluation Studies Review Annual.* Beverly Hills, CA: Sage, 101–18.

Seawright, Jason, and David Collier. 2004. "Glossary." In Henry E. Brady and David Collier (eds.), *Rethinking Social Inquiry: Diverse Tools, Shared Standards.* Lanham, MD: Rowman and Littlefield, 273–313.

Seawright, Jason, and John Gerring. 2005. "Case Selection: Quantitative Techniques Reviewed." Unpublished manuscript.

Sekhon, Jasjeet S. 2004. "Quality Meets Quantity: Case Studies, Conditional Probability and Counterfactuals." *Perspectives in Politics* 2:2 (June): 281–93.

Sengupta, Somini. 2005. "Where Maoists Still Matter." *New York Times Magazine,* web version, October 30, pp. 1–7. Accessed: 10/30/2005.

Shadish, William R., Thomas D. Cook, and Donald T. Campbell. 2002. *Experimental and Quasi-experimental Designs for Generalized Causal Inference.* Boston: Houghton Mifflin.

Shafer, Michael D. 1988. *Deadly Paradigms: The Failure of U.S. Counterinsurgency Policy.* Princeton, NJ: Princeton University Press.

Shalev, Michael. 1998. "Limits of and Alternatives to Multiple Regression in Macro-Comparative Research." Paper presented at the second conference on The Welfare State at the Crossroads, Stockholm, June 12–14.

Shaw, Clifford R. 1927. "Case Study Method." *Publications of the American Sociological Society* 21: 149–57.

Shugart, Matthew Soberg, and Martin P. Wattenberg, eds. 2001. *Mixed-Member Electoral Systems: The Best of Both Worlds?* Oxford: Oxford University Press.

Silverman, D. 2001. *Interpreting Qualitative Data: Methods for Analysing Talk, Text and Interaction,* 2d ed. Thousand Oaks, CA: Sage.

Simmons, Beth A. 1994. *Who Adjusts? Domestic Sources of Foreign Economic Policy during the Interwar Years.* Princeton, NJ: Princeton University Press.

Simon, J. L. 1969. *Basic Research Methods in Social Science.* New York: Random House.

Skocpol, Theda. 1979. *States and Social Revolutions: A Comparative Analysis of France, Russia, and China*. Cambridge: Cambridge University Press.

Skocpol, Theda. 1994. *Social Revolutions in the Modern World*. Cambridge: Cambridge University Press.

Skocpol, Theda, and Margaret Somers. 1980. "The Uses of Comparative History in Macrosocial Inquiry." *Comparative Studies in Society and History* 22:2 (April): 147–97.

Skowronek, Stephen. 1982. *Building a New American State: The Expansion of National Administrative Capacities 1877–1920*. Cambridge: Cambridge University Press.

Smelser, Neil J. 1973. "The Methodology of Comparative Analysis." In D. P. Warwick and S. Osherson (eds.), *Comparative Research Methods*. Englewood Cliffs, NJ: Prentice Hall, 42–86.

Smelser, Neil J. 1976. *Comparative Methods in the Social Sciences*. Englewood Cliffs, NJ: Prentice Hall.

Smith, C. D., and W. Kornblum, eds. 1989. *In the Field: Research on the Field Research Experience*. New York: Praeger.

Smith, Rogers M. 1997. *Civic Ideals: Conflicting Visions of Citizenship in U.S. History*. New Haven, CT: Yale University Press.

Smith, T. V., and L. D. White, eds. 1921. *Chicago: An Experiment in Social Science Research*. Chicago: University of Chicago Press.

Snow, John. 1855. *On the Mode of Communication of Cholera*. London: Churchill.

Snyder, Jack. 1993. *Myths of Empire: Domestic Politics and International Ambition*. Ithaca, NY: Cornell University Press.

Snyder, Richard. 2001. "Scaling Down: The Subnational Comparative Method." *Studies in Comparative International Development* 36:1 (Spring): 93–110.

Sperle, Diane H. 1933. *Case Method Technique in Professional Training: A Survey of the Use of Case Studies as a Method of Instruction in Selected Fields, and a Study of It*. New York: Bureau of Publications, Teachers College, Columbia University.

Sprinz, Detlef F., and Yael Wolinsky-Nahmias, eds. 2004. *Models, Numbers and Cases: Methods for Studying International Relations*. Ann Arbor: University of Michigan Press.

Spruyt, Hendrik. 1994. *The Sovereign State and Its Competitors*. Princeton, NJ: Princeton University Press.

Srinivasan, T. N., and Jagdish Bhagwati. 1999. "Outward-Orientation and Development: Are Revisionists Right?" Discussion Paper No. 806, Economic Growth Center, Yale University.

Staiger, Douglas, and James H. Stock. 1997. "Instrumental Variables Regression with Weak Instruments." *Econometrica* 65: 557–86.

Stake, Robert E. 1995. *The Art of Case Study Research*. Thousand Oaks, CA: Sage.

Steadman, Dawnie Wolfe. 2002. *Hard Evidence: Case Studies in Forensic Anthropology*. Englewood Cliffs, NJ: Prentice-Hall.

Steinmo, Sven. 1994. "American Exceptionalism Reconsidered: Culture or Institutions?" In Lawrence C. Dodd and Calvin Jillson (eds.), *The Dynamics of American Politics: Approaches and Interpretations*. Boulder, CO: Westview Press, 106–31.

Steinmo, Sven. 1995. "Why Is Government So Small in America?" *Governance* 8: 303–34.

Stiglitz, Joseph E. 2002. *Globalization and Its Discontents*. New York: Norton.

Stiglitz, Joseph E. 2005. "The Overselling of Globalization." In Michael M. Weinstein (ed.), *Globalization: What's New?* New York: Columbia University Press, 228–61.

Stinchcombe, Arthur L. 1968. *Constructing Social Theories*. New York: Harcourt, Brace.

Stoecker, Randy. 1991. "Evaluating and Rethinking the Case Study." *The Sociological Review* 39 (February): 88–112.

Stoker, Laura. 2003. "Is It Possible to Do Quantitative Survey Research in an Interpretive Way?" *Qualitative Methods: Newsletter of the American Political Science Association Organized Section on Qualitative Methods* 1:2 (Fall): 13–16.

Stouffer, Samuel A. 1931. "Experimental Comparison of a Statistical and a Case History Technique of Attitude Research." *Publications of the American Sociological Society* 25: 154–6.

Stouffer, Samuel A. 1941. "Notes on the Case-Study and the Unique Case." *Sociometry* 4: 349–57.

Stouffer, Samuel A. 1950. "Some Observations on Study Design." *American Journal of Sociology* 55:4 (January): 355–61.

Stratmann, Thomas, and Martin Baur. 2002. "Plurality Rule, Proportional Representation, and the German *Bundestag*: How Incentives to Pork-Barrel Differ across Electoral Systems." *American Journal of Political Science* 46:3 (July): 506–14.

Stryker, Robin. 1996. "Beyond History versus Theory: Strategic Narrative and Sociological Explanation." *Sociological Methods and Research* 24:3: 304–52.

Sundquist, James L. 1992. *Constitutional Reform and Effective Government*. Washington, DC: Brookings.

Swank, Duane H. 2002. *Global Capital, Political Institutions, and Policy Change in Developed Welfare States*. Cambridge: Cambridge University Press.

"Symposium: Discourse and Content Analysis." 2004. *Qualitative Methods: Newsletter of the American Political Science Association Organized Section on Qualitative Methods* 2:1 (Spring): 15–39.

"Symposium: Qualitative Comparative Analysis (QCA)." 2004. *Qualitative Methods: Newsletter of the American Political Science Association Organized Section on Qualitative Methods* 2:2 (Fall): 2–25.

Tarrow, Sidney G. 1995. "Bridging the Quantitative-Qualitative Divide in Political Science." *American Political Science Review* 89:2 (June): 471–4.

Tarrow, Sidney G. 1998. *Power in Movement: Social Movements and Contentious Politics*. Cambridge: Cambridge University Press.

Tarrow, Sidney. 2004. "Bridging the Quantitative-Qualitative Divide." In Henry E. Brady and David Collier (eds.), *Rethinking Social Inquiry: Diverse Tools, Shared Standards*. Lanham, MD: Rowman and Littlefield, 171–9.

Taylor, Charles. 1970. "The Explanation of Purposive Behavior." In Robert Borger and Frank Cioffi (eds.), *Explanation in the Behavioral Sciences*. Cambridge: Cambridge University Press.

Taylor, Charles. 1971. "Interpretation and the Sciences of Man." *Review of Metaphysics* 25: 3–51.

Taylor, John R. 1995. *Linguistic Categorization: Prototypes in Linguistic Theory*, 2d ed. Oxford: Clarendon Press.

Teggart, Frederick J. 1939/1967. *Rome and China: A Study of Correlations in Historical Events*. Berkeley: University of California Press.

Temple, Jonathan. 1999. "The New Growth Evidence." *Journal of Economic Literature* (March): 112–56.

Tendler, Judith. 1997. *Good Government in the Tropics*. Baltimore: Johns Hopkins University Press.

Tetlock, Philip E., and Aaron Belkin, eds. 1996. *Counterfactual Thought Experiments in World Politics*. Princeton, NJ: Princeton University Press.

The 9/11 Commission Report: Final Report of the National Commission on Terrorist Attacks upon the United States. 2003. New York: Norton.

Theiss-Morse, Elizabeth, Amy Fried, John L. Sullivan, and Mary Dietz. 1991. "Mixing Methods: A Multistage Strategy for Studying Patriotism and Citizen Participation." *Political Analysis* 3: 89–121.

Thies, Cameron G. 2002. "A Pragmatic Guide to Qualitative Historical Analysis in the Study of International Relations." *International Studies Perspectives* 3: 351–72.

Thies, Michael F. 2001. "Keeping Tabs on Partners: The Logic of Delegation in Coalition Governments." *American Journal of Political Science* 45:3 (July): 580–98.

Thompson, Edward P. 1963. *The Making of the English Working Class*. New York: Vintage Books.

Thompson, Edward P. 1978. *The Poverty of Theory and Other Essays*. New York: Monthly Review Press.

Tilly, Charles. 2001. "Mechanisms in Political Processes." *Annual Review of Political Science* 4: 21–41.

Tocqueville, Alexis de. 1997. *Recollections: The French Revolution of 1848*, ed. J. P. Mayer and A. P. Kerr. New Brunswick, NJ: Transaction.

Tooley, Michael. 1988. *Causation: A Realist Approach*. Oxford: Clarendon Press.

Trachtenberg, Marc. 2005. *Historical Method in the Study of International Relations*. Unpublished manuscript.

Treier, Shawn, and Simon Jackman. 2005. "Democracy as a Latent Variable." Unpublished manuscript, Department of Political Science, Stanford University.

Truman, David B. 1951. *The Governmental Process*. New York: Knopf.

Tsai, Lily. 2007. *Accountability without Democracy: How Solidary Groups Provide Public Goods in Rural China*. Cambridge: Cambridge University Press.

Turner, Frederick Jackson. 1893/1972. *The Turner Thesis Concerning the Role of the Frontier in American History*. Lexington, MA: Heath.

Udry, Christopher. 2003. "Fieldwork, Economic Theory, and Research on Institutions in Developing Countries." *American Economic Association, Papers and Proceedings* 93:2 (May): 107–11.

Vandenbroucke, Jan P. 2001. "In Defense of Case Reports and Case Series." *Annals of Internal Medicine* 134:4: 330–4.

Van Evera, Stephen. 1997. *Guide to Methods for Students of Political Science*. Ithaca, NY: Cornell University Press.

Van Maanen, J. 1988. *Tales of the Field: On Writing Ethnography*. Chicago: University of Chicago Press.

Varshney, Ashutosh. 2002. *Ethnic Conflict and Civic Life: Hindus and Muslims in India*. New Haven, CT: Yale University Press.

Verba, Sidney. 1967. "Some Dilemmas in Comparative Research." *World Politics* 20:1 (October): 111–27.

Verbeek, Bertjan. 1994. "Do Individual and Group Beliefs Matter? British Decision-Making during the 1956 Suez Crisis." *Cooperation and Conflict* 29:4: 307–32.

Verschuren, Piet J. M. 2001. "Case Study as a Research Strategy: Some Ambiguities and Opportunities." *Social Research Methodology* 6:2: 121–39.

Vogt, W. Paul. 1993. *Dictionary of Statistics and Methodology*. Newbury Park, CA: Sage.

von Wright, Georg Henrik. 1971. *Explanation and Understanding*. Ithaca, NY: Cornell University Press.

Voss, Kim. 1993. *The Making of American Exceptionalism: The Knights of Labor and Class Formation in the Nineteenth Century*. Ithaca, NY: Cornell University Press.

Vreeland, James Raymond. 2003. *The IMF and Economic Development*. Cambridge: Cambridge University Press.

Wahlke, John C. 1979. "Pre-Behavioralism in Political Science." *American Political Science Review* 73:1 (March): 9–31.

Waldner, David. 2002. "Anti Anti-Determinism: Or What Happens When Schrodinger's Cat and Lorenz's Butterfly Meet Laplace's Demon in the Study of Political and Economic Development." Paper presented at the annual meeting of the American Political Science Association, Boston.

Waller, Willard. 1934. "Insight and Scientific Method." *American Journal of Sociology* 40:3 (November): 285–97.

Wantchekon, Leonard. 2003. "Clientelism and Voting Behavior: Evidence from a Field Experiment in Benin." *World Politics* (April): 399–422.

Ward, Michael D., and Kristin Bakke. 2005. "Predicting Civil Conflicts: On the Utility of Empirical Research." Paper presented at the Conference on Disaggregating the Study of Civil War and Transnational Violence, University of California Institute of Global Conflict and Cooperation, San Diego, March 7–8.

Warner, W. Lloyd, and Paul S. Lunt. 1941. *Yankee City*, 4 vols. New Haven, CT: Yale University Press.

Weaver, R. Kent, and Bert A. Rockman, eds. 1993. *Do Institutions Matter? Government Capabilities in the United States and Abroad*. Washington, DC: Brookings Institution.

254

References

Weber, Max. 1905/1949. *The Methodology of the Social Sciences*. New York: The Free Press.

Weingast, Barry R. 1998. "Political Stability and Civil War: Institutions, Commitment, and American Democracy." In Robert H. Bates, Avner Greif, Margaret Levi, Jean-Laurent Rosenthal, and Barry Weingast (eds.), *Analytic Narratives*. Princeton, NJ: Princeton University Press, 148–93.

Wendt, Alexander. 1998. "On Constitution and Causation in International Relations." *Review of International Studies* 24: 101–17.

Western, Bruce, and Simon Jackman. 1994. "Bayesian Inference for Comparative Research." *American Political Science Review* 88:2: 412–23.

Whyte, William Foote. 1943/1955. *Street Corner Society: The Social Structure of an Italian Slum*. Chicago: University of Chicago Press.

Wilson, James Q. 1992. *Political Organizations*. Princeton, NJ: Princeton University Press.

Winch, Peter. 1958. *The Idea of a Social Science, and its Relation to Philosophy*. London: Routledge and Kegan Paul.

Winks, Robin W., ed. 1969. *The Historian as Detective: Essays on Evidence*. New York: Harper and Row.

Winship, Christopher, and David J. Harding. 2004. "A General Strategy for the Identification of Age, Period, Cohort Models: A Mechanism Based Approach." Unpublished manuscript.

Winship, Christopher, and Stephen L. Morgan. 1999. "The Estimation of Causal Effects of Observational Data." *Annual Review of Sociology* 25: 659–707.

Winship, Christopher, and Michael Sobel. 2004. "Causal Inference in Sociological Studies." In Melissa Hardy and Alan Bryman (eds.), *Handbook of Data Analysis*. London: Sage, 481–503.

Winters, L. Alan, Neil McCulloch, and Andrew McKay. 2004. "Trade Liberalization and Poverty: The Evidence So Far." *Journal of Economic Literature* 42 (March): 72–115.

Wolin, Sheldon S. 1968. "Paradigms and Political Theories." In Preston King and B. C. Parekh (eds.), *Politics and Experience*. Cambridge: Cambridge University Press, 148–49.

Wong, Wilson. 2002. "Did How We Learn Affect What We Learn? Methodological Bias, Multimethod Research and the Case of Economic Development." *Social Science Journal* 39:2: 247–64.

World Bank. 2003. *World Development Indicators 2003*. Washington, DC: World Bank.

Yanow, Dvora, and Peregrine Schwartz-Shea, eds. 2006. *Interpretation and Method: Empirical Research Methods and the Interpretive Turn*. Armonk, NY: M. E. Sharpe.

Yashar, Deborah J. 2005. *Contesting Citizenship in Latin America: The Rise of Indigenous Movements and the Postliberal Challenge*. Cambridge: Cambridge University Press.

Yin, Robert K. 1994. *Case Study Research: Design and Methods*. Newbury Park, CA: Sage.

Yin, Robert K. 2003. *Case Study Research: Design and Methods*, 3d ed. Thousand Oaks, CA: Sage.

Yin, Robert K. 2004. *Case Study Anthology*. Thousand Oaks, CA: Sage.

Young, Oran R., ed. 1999. *The Effectiveness of International Environmental Regimes: Causal Connections and Behavioral Mechanisms*. Cambridge, MA: MIT Press.

Young, Pauline. 1939. *Scientific Social Surveys and Research*. New York: Prentice Hall.

Znaniecki, Florian. 1934. *The Method of Sociology*. New York: Rinehart.

Name Index

Subject Index